The making of men

The making of men

Masculinities, sexualities and schooling

Máirtín Mac an Ghaill

Open University Press
Buckingham · Philadelphia

Open University Press
Celtic Court
22 Ballmoor
Buckingham
MK18 1XW

and

1900 Frost Road, Suite 101
Bristol, PA 19007, USA

First published 1994

A catalogue record of this book is available from the British Library

ISBN 0 335 15781 5 (pbk)   0 335 15782 3 (hbk)

Library of Congress Cataloging-in-Publication Data

Mac an Ghaill, Máirtín.
    The making of men: masculinities, sexualities and schooling /
Máirtín Mac an Ghaill.
        p.   cm.
    Includes bibliographical references (p.   ) and index.
    ISBN 0-335-15782-3. — ISBN 0-335-15781-5 (pbk.)
    1. Education—Social aspects—England.   2. Masculinity
(Psychology)—England.   3. Sex differences in education—England.
4. Sexism in education—England.   I. Title.
LC191.8.G72E536   1994
370.19′345—dc20   93-37338
                                                                              CIP

Typeset by Vision Typesetting, Manchester
Printed in Great Britain by Biddles Ltd, Guildford and King's Lynn

To Anne and Iestyn. In support of gay and lesbian students.

Contents

Acknowledgements

I am indebted to many people for their help, support and encouragement: Clyde Chitty, Mairead Dunne, Dave Gillborn, Chris Griffin, Bev Skeggs, and Tracey Whitmore for reading early drafts of different chapters; John Skelton and Pat Lee at the Open University Press; the support and teaching staff at Parnell School for their cooperation. Thanks also to the students who participated in this collaborative work for their time and comradeship and a special thanks to their parents and friends for their hospitality. The gay male students were major contributors to the design of this study, and I am indebted to them for developing my understanding of current sexual and racial politics in England. Special thanks and love to Rajinder.

Introduction: Schooling as a masculinizing agency[1]

> it is the task of sociology and the other social sciences to "decon-struct" naturalism, and to determine how actions are given their meaning and significance via social action.
>
> (Hamilton 1986: 7)

I begin with a paradox. In English secondary schools, as elsewhere in the social world, masculine perspectives are pervasively dominant. However, until recently, masculinity has tended to be absent from mainstream educational research. It has been assumed to be unproblematic, with gender issues focusing on femininity and girls' schooling.

Unexpectedly, I have found the study of masculinity, sexuality and schooling theoretically very difficult to explore and emotionally highly challenging.[2] In one secondary school that I taught in, a male student, after hearing that he had passed his exams, gave me a bunch of flowers in the school playground. Within a short period of time, the incident was common knowledge in the staffroom and the male teachers responded with heterosexist jokes. At the same time, the student got into a fight in defending himself against homophobic abuse. The headteacher asked me to report to his office, where he informed me that I had gone too far this time. I began to defend myself, claiming that I could not be held responsible for the fight. The headteacher interrupted me to ask what I was talking about. Suddenly, I realized the symbolic significance of our playground perform-ance: the exchange of flowers between two males was institutionally more threatening than the physical violence of the male fight. The incident also had a racial dimension. In this school, the white dominant teacher perception of Muslim male students was that they were intrinsically more sexist than white males. These teachers were undoubtedly confused by the fact that the student who gave me the flowers was a Muslim.

In ethnographic studies, such events become key moments in which you begin to reconceptualize 'what's going on' in the research arena. I came to read this incident as illustrative of the highly problematic formation of modern modes of masculinity within the context of school life. This was not the framework with which I began the research. My initial focus over-emphasized gender reproduction, with particular reference to male students' future social, occupational and domestic destinies. Young gay students were of critical importance in developing my revised research design. Most significantly, they pointed to the need for me to explore male heterosexuality as a dominant but unstable sexual category. I shifted my focus, so that alongside my concern with examining how external social relations helped to shape masculine identities, I began to explore more systematically internal psychological issues. In short, I began to view schools as sites for the production of sex/gender subjectivities, 'where people conform, deviate, challenge, participate and engage with state apparatuses' (Carlen *et al.* 1992: 30).

In this introduction, I shall explore some of the key issues which emerged from early attempts to examine the interplay of schooling, masculinity and sexuality. During the 1980s, particularly as a result of feminist and gay writings, the changing nature of men's lives and their experiences were hotly debated within the psychological and sociological literature, including sex-role, psychoanalysis and gender and power theories (Weeks 1989; Morgan 1990; Segal 1990; Canaan 1991).[3] By the late 1980s, a number of writers (e.g. Askew and Ross 1988; Heward 1988; Connell 1989; Skeggs 1991) had published texts that offered fresh insights into the relationship between schooling and masculinity. By the 1990s, we have been provided with theoretical frameworks that enable us to begin to analyse systematically and document coherently how masculinity circumscribes English schooling and, in turn, how modern systems of schooling contribute to the formation of contemporary modes of masculinities (see Haywood 1993 and Lee 1993).

In this book, I have attempted to follow Ferguson's (1988: 4) advice, that we need to:

> focus on establishing a language by which pedagogy can be described and then analysed – a vocabulary in the shape of an agreed terminology and a grammar which allows us to reach behind the surface of the events to see their deeper structure and significance . . .
> In short, it represents a deliberate attempt to make the familiar seem strange without being obscure, and thus to enable us to see old things . . . with new eyes.

Throughout the writing of this book, the issue of obscurity has been difficult to resolve. Like Wood (1984), I have found sexuality to be an unclear field of study in which highly complex theories are being developed that fail to connect with individuals' experience. He claims that:

Michel Foucault (1979) is a case in point. His is a complex argument, but he seems to be saying that sexuality has progressively become identified with the whole truth about a person and that, therefore, it occupies a strategic site for the regulation of populations. Sexuality is "deployed" – that is used – by operations of power that survey citizens via their bodies: its sensations, functions and pleasures ... Admittedly, this way of writing about sexuality is only just beginning to be elaborated but, I think, the objection to its overly-abstract nature is not inconsiderable. We are jumping the gun, and perhaps distracting ourselves, if we are looking for one water-tight theory of sexuality, or one (abstract) connection between sexuality, power and the modern social order. This does not mean we collapse the theoretical project, there are parameters to be explored: crucially for me, the area of masculinity.

(Wood 1984: 81)

Another aspect of the complexity of researching and writing in this area is the question of the elusiveness, fluidity and complex interconnectedness of sexualities in modern societies. This has resulted in discussions of key issues being rather wide-ranging. However, I have held on to a broad framework so as to illustrate the institutional complexity of sex/gender regimes that pervasively circumscribe school lives. Also of importance here is the question of the self-representation of my text. I would agree with Evans (1992), who has written of the need to rethink how we represent and describe research participants and how we conceptualize their thinking and subjectivity. He suggests that:

This would involve some experimental writing; searching for different ways of describing the complexity, the multidimensionality, the organization and disorder, the uncertainty and incongruities of the social worlds that we and others inhabit. It would also mean resisting the temptation to produce texts which contain "flat" rather than "rounded" characters.

(Evans 1992: 245)

What is this book about?

I have carried out research in Parnell School for over five years. This book presents the findings of a three-year ethnographic study between 1990 and 1992, which investigated the social construction and regulation of masculinities in a state secondary school. Most of the material in Chapters 1–4 comes from a cohort who were year eleven students during the 1990–91 school year. Chapter 5 is an earlier study of gay students' educational experiences, some of whom attended Parnell School. My primary concern is to explore the processes involved in the interplay between schooling, masculinities and sexualities. A central argument is that in order to understand this complex inter-relationship, it is necessary to move beyond traditional areas of concern regarding gender issues and to view schools as complex gendered and heterosexual arenas. Within this reconceptualized focus, the school's institutional material, social and discursive practices are all salient features in the making of student subjectivities: including student selection, subject allocation and stratification, disciplinary modes of authority, instruments of surveillance and control, and the web of gendered and sexual student–teacher and student–student social relations (Wolpe 1988; Connell 1989).

This social scaffolding of modern state secondary schooling informs and is informed by differentiated masculinities and femininities and the power relations that are contained within them. Due attention is given to the major organizing principles of modern schooling, namely, age, class, racial/ethnic, sex/gender and disability divisions and 'the more subtle inflections of these positions in young people's lives' (Cohen 1989a: 12). A major concern is the critical examination of the way in which dominant definitions of masculinity are affirmed within schools, where ideologies, discourses, representations and material practices systematically privilege boys and men. In this book, empirical findings and theoretical arguments are integrated to propose a comprehensive model for understanding the schooling of young men. Such an account involves the attempt to work through a multi-level analysis that incorporates explanations at the level of state discourses, the institution, social groups and individuals.

In describing the complex nature of these issues, four case studies are presented from the perspectives of male and female students and teachers. Clarke *et al.*'s (1975) definition of culture is useful in examining management, teacher and student cultures in relation to the question of the interplay between schooling, masculinity and sexuality.[4] They suggest that culture is:

> the peculiar and distinctive way of life of a group or class, the meanings, values and ideas embodied in institutions, in social relations, in systems of belief, in mores and customs, in the uses of objects and material life . . . the "maps of meaning" that make things intelligible to its members.
>
> (Clarke *et al.* 1975: 10)

A main argument in this study is that the school microcultures of management, teachers and students are key infrastructural mechanisms through which masculinities and femininities are mediated and lived out. This study is a search for the specific conditions under which schools as deeply gendered and heterosexual regimes, construct relations of domination and subordination within and across these microcultures.

In the rest of this introduction, I shall examine what emerged as the main substantive concerns. Following a discussion of my methodology, I shall look at the rise of New Moralism, schooling in the marketplace, the theoretical shift from sex-roles to deconstruction of sex/gender identities, and power relations. A short summary of what the chapters are about is followed by an outline of the key aims of the book.

Fieldwork

The study's methodology will be dealt with in more detail in Chapter 6, with particular reference to questions concerning the politics and ethics of researching oppressed groups (see Mac an Ghaill 1989a, 1991b). Much of the material presented here was collected from observation, informal discussions and recorded semi-structured interviews with the students and their teachers. Detailed notes were taken and written up each evening. In order to build up student case-histories, I interviewed them individually and in groups. In addition, they kept diaries and helped me to construct questionnaires that they completed. Also, interviews were carried out with the young people's parents. Sharing our life-histories helped to challenge the power asymmetries between the students and myself (Connell 1989: 291–300). I am greatly indebted to feminist methodology (Stanley and Wise 1983; Bhavnani 1991; Skeggs 1992).[5] I have attempted to operationalize an emancipatory research method, as advocated by such critical theorists as Lather (1986), with its emphasis on collaboration, reciprocity and reflexivity.

A major methodological flaw in much conventional work in this area, albeit unintended, is the construction of minorities as 'social problems' or 'victims'. For example, in relation to sexuality, this manifests itself in terms of the ubiquitous search for the pathological origins of homosexuality. That is, the obsessive quest to establish if gays are born or made. Most recently, this has manifested itself in the media's response to research carried out in America that was reported as claiming a genetic basis for homosexuality (Conner 1993; McKie 1993). There has been little critical discussion of the claim, with liberal perspectives remaining within a biological determinist framework that is at present politically in the ascendancy. In this normative academic approach with its voyeuristic methodology, sexual majorities remain invisible to the researcher's gaze. For example, when I asked teachers how male students become heterosexual, they often assumed, working within a commonsense sexual binary logic, that I meant rather than become gay. My primary concern was with the question of how school processes helped shape male students' cultural investment in different versions of heterosexual masculinity. A major issue that emerged in the study was the question of what constitutes young men's heterosexuality within an English secondary school context. I was particularly interested in the political and cultural elements in this sex/gender construction (Brittan and Maynard 1984; Caplan 1987).

The school as a state institution: The rise of the New Moralism

In recent analysis of current education policy, the focus has been on the internal philosophical divisions within the New Right project, which includes the Neo-Conservative emphasis on direct management and the Neo-Liberal emphasis on market forces. A number of writers have argued that the origins of the National Curriculum were informed by the Neo-Conservatives' hostile response to equal opportunities, which they perceived as threatening traditional British cultural values and 'way of life' (Chitty 1989; see also Hillgate Group 1986). Kelly (1992: 20–21), writing of the need to respond to right-wing agendas on sexuality and education, notes that:

> What the last decade has demonstrated is the skill of small groupings within the Conservative party to exploit local controversies, generate enormous media support and have MPs then respond with speedy legislative fixes – a number of these local controversies have been initially located in education and have focused on sexuality and race. Each of these interventions has fed a specific construction of family and nation that lies at the heart of the New Right philosophy: their creation of a "traditional way of life", which they then become defenders of. This spurious unity requires the exclusion, or at least the de-legitimation, of those who represent an alternative set of values: those outside the white "Persil" family – e.g. single women choosing to have children, lesbians and gays; Black families that seek to maintain some of their own cultural values; those who represent sectional interests . . . The success of this ideological strategy is evidenced in the increasing acceptance of the view that equal opportunities programmes promote "minority" interests, when in fact, if successful, they would benefit the majority of the population who are not white, male, heterosexual and able-bodied.

The New Right campaigns have resulted in the introduction of Section 28 of the Local Government Act (1988), which has attempted to restrict the 'promotion of homosexuality' by local authorities. Equally significant, Circular 11/87 has asked schools to help students 'appreciate the benefits of stable married and family life' (Redman, in press). However, as Skeggs (1992: 2) suggests, we need to examine the contradictions of recent central government policies: 'Circular 11/87 speaks of the "objective and balanced manner" required to discuss sex education, whilst the "Choice and Diversity: A New Framework for Schools" admits the battle for hearts and minds that is in operation by openly declaring that "schools should not be, and generally are not value-free zones".' It is also important to note that the main political and theoretical challenges to these legislative changes, which have been under-reported, have come from radical women's, lesbian and gay movements (Stacey 1991).

The Educational Reform Act (ERA) can be read as a specifically gendered piece of legislation, with the promotion of a sex/gender and 'race' blind curricular approach (Skeggs 1992). As Skeggs suggests, it is part of a wider project, whose aim is to construct an alternative to the post-war settlement, with its underlying values of partnership and social equity. Metcalf (1985), provides the political and ideological background to the current shift from the 'soft' welfare state to the 'harder' new realism of market economics. He writes:

> In the popularization of a monetarist economic policy on both sides of the Atlantic, care has been taken to present these strategies as being proper to the competitive instincts of red-blooded American and British males. The call goes out to kill off lame ducks, to foreswear compassion. It is asserted that in the market-place only the fittest should survive, and that a hard, lean industrial sector is necessary. Appeals to machismo and to disdain soft emotions are quite naked, as politicians of the radical right pour scorn on the need to care for the less fortunate, on the whole idea of the welfare state.
>
> (Metcalf 1985: 11)

It is argued in this book that new occupational identities are emerging within schools. This is informed by a shift in public sector masculinities that are underpinned by processes of commercialization, commodification and rationalization within schools.

Schooling goes to market

Davies (1992) has described the current shift in the official reductionist representations of schools as having no intrinsic value (use-value). Rather they are seen as commodities that realize their value in the marketplace (exchange value). She argues:

> There is an even more urgent need to reconceptualise the culture of our schools. In every advanced capitalist country ... there is a restructuring of education, with similar features throughout. The features are: centralised control; decrease in educational expenditure; accentuation of horizontal and hierarchical divisions in education, reversing some of the progressive settlements of the 1960s and 1970s; greater emphasis on vocationalism and instrumentalism; commodification of education (vouchers, marketing principles); increase in privatisation and links with the corporate sector; increased deskilling of the teaching force; a reorganisation of the patterns of teacher education; and a reconstitution of the "crisis" of schooling.
>
> (Davies 1992: 135)

The restructuring and restratification of English schooling during the last decade has been accompanied by the rise of managerialism. As Carr (1989: 17–18) maintains: 'Technical rationality continues to provide the dominant epistemology of practice, and central government's predilection for technological views of teaching is inevitably creating conditions under which a reflective approach to professional development becomes impossible.' Equal opportunities has been influenced by this shift, working within a managerialist pedagogical framework with its emphasis on technicist explanations and solutions. The over-rationalist pedagogy that accompanies this approach underplays the fact that teaching is basically a human social activity in which what we feel is as important as what we know. Holding onto the cognitive and affective elements involved in teaching and learning is a central concern for the future development of equal opportunities and, more specifically within the context of this book, for the future development of sex/sexuality education (Redman, in press).

From sex-roles to the deconstruction of sex/gender identities

Connell (1982: 173–4) has persuasively presented the case against biologically based sex-role theories, suggesting that they are inadequate to explain the complex social and psychological processes involved in the development of gendered subjectivities that are underpinned by institutional and wider material powers. This book will act as a critique of the dominant theoretical and 'commonsense' explanations of sex/gender differences, which underpin much sex education and equal opportunities work in schools. Such approaches often take for granted definitions of femininity and masculinity, which are implicitly assumed to be ahistorical, unitary, universal and unchanging categories. More recently, Arnot (1991) has summarized the main limitations of this earlier work in England, noting that its failure to attain its aims was informed by idealistic intention and a naive approach. She writes:

> Sex-role socialisation, which held together a multitude of projects as diverse as changing school texts, and establishing gender fair teaching styles, non-traditional role models, unbiased careers advice and girl-friendly schools was seen to have a lot to answer . . . The simplicity of the portrayal of the processes of learning and gender identity formation, its assumptions about the nature of stereotyping, its somewhat negative view of girls as victims had all contributed to the creation of particular school based strategies.
>
> (Arnot 1991: 453)

It is argued here that schools are sites of historically varying contradictions, ambiguities and tensions.[6] This is most evident in relation to sex/gender social relations. Schools function to prepare students for the sexual division of labour in the home and the workplace. Furthermore, schools do not merely reflect the dominant sexual ideology of the wider society, but actively produce gender and heterosexual divisions. At the same time, schooling may be a potential significant public site that enables individual young people to achieve a degree of social mobility in the labour market and the development of non-traditional gender identities. Sex-role theory, in denying the contradictory functions of modern schooling, has emphasized a static, ahistorical and over-socialized polarization of gender differences. In so doing, it has failed to incorporate a more dynamic perspective that sees schools as active makers of a range of femininities and masculinities (Henriques *et al.* 1984; Hollway 1989).

As Arnot suggests, one of the major weaknesses of theoretical work in this area has been inadequate conceptions of sex/gender identity formation. More recently, theorists drawing on post-structuralism, psychoanalysis and semiology have provided new ways of thinking about subjective identities (Henriques *et al.* 1984; Hollway 1989; Jones and Moore 1992). For example, Hall (1990) has argued that identities are not historically fixed entities, but rather that they are subjected to the continuous interplay of history, culture and power. He suggests that:

> Identity is not as transparent or unproblematic as we think. Perhaps instead of thinking of identity as an already accomplished fact, which the new cultural practices then represent, we should think, instead, of identity as a "production", which is never complete, always in process, and always constituted within, not outside representation. This view problematises the very authority and authenticity to which the term, "cultural identity", lays claim.
>
> (Hall 1990: 222)

As suggested above, a key issue that emerged during the research was the question of what constitutes male students' heterosexual identity. More specifically, I became interested in the constitutive cultural elements of dominant modes of heterosexual subjectivity that informed male students' learning to act like men within a school arena. These elements consisted of contradictory forms of compulsory heterosexuality, misogyny and homophobia, and were marked by contextual contingency and ambivalence. It is argued in this book that male heterosexual identity is a highly fragile socially constructed phenomenon. The question that emerges here is: How does this fragile construction become represented as an apparently stable, unitary category with fixed meanings? It is suggested that schools alongside other institutions attempt to administer, regulate and reify unstable sex/gender categories. Most particularly, this administration, regulation and reification of sex/gender boundaries is institutionalized through the interrelated material, social and discursive practices of staffroom, classroom and playground microcultures. In turn, male academics have reinforced this institutionalization with their own representations.

In shifting from sex-roles to the deconstruction of sex/gender identities, we need to examine the concept of power in relation to social structure and subjectivity (see Hollway 1984a, b).

Power relations, social structures and subjectivity: From social reproduction to reconstruction

As Smart (1985: 122) has pointed out: 'Within the social sciences the exercise of power has been conceptualized in terms of either the actions of individual or institutional agents, or the effects of structures of systems.' This has been reflected in theoretical debates about social oppressions, which have tended to adopt a dichotomized approach, emphasizing either psychological-based processes of personal prejudice or institutional social structures. Henriques *et al.* (1984) have shown the limitations of this individual–society dualism, with its implicit assumption that individuals can live outside of society or that society is not composed of individuals. This split has manifested itself in the area of schooling and gender differentiation in terms of arguments between liberal and radical feminist positions (Arnot and Weiner 1987).[7] The latter has emphasized the explanatory power of patriarchy as a single overarching structure of domination between men and women. Historically, this radical perspective has provided an important political challenge to mainstream liberal and conservative theory that fails to make power relations problematic. However, in this approach, sex/gender oppression is often understood in terms of what the dominant group 'does' to the subordinate group. It has tended to stress external social structures and the accompanying one-dimensional view of power as repressive. Furthermore, there has been a failure to theorize the interconnectedness between different forms of oppression. In a decompartmentalized policy approach, there has been a tendency to conceptualize gender as something to do with women, sexuality as something to do with lesbians and gays, and 'race' as having something to do with black people (Watney 1987: 56). It is suggested here that we need to go beyond such additive models with their hierarchies of oppression. Rather, we need to think of complex sets of oppression in terms of how they operate, within specific institutional arenas, in terms of the 'politics of difference' located within relations of dominance and subordination (Fanon 1967; Parmar 1989; Mercer 1990).

There is a continuing debate concerning the universal status of the concept of patriarchy as the single primary cause of women's domination (Bhavnani and Coulson 1986; Gilbert and Taylor 1991).[8] For example, Brah (1992: 136) has suggested that: 'As a result of our location within diasporas formed by the history of slavery, colonialism and imperialism, black feminists have consistently argued against parochialism and stressed the need for a feminism sensitive to the international social relations of power.' Connell (1987) also critiques the notion of patriarchy, claiming that it oversimplifies the structures of gender. He talks of a gender order and presents three major structures, focusing on the division of labour, power relations between men and women and sexuality (see also Roman and Christian-Smith 1988; Griffin 1993).

During the last decade, in examining sex/gender power relations within schools and other sites, feminist, gay, lesbian and black researchers have drawn on the work of Foucault (Barrett 1991). Kelly (1992: 26) has summarized Foucault's framework in relation to power, discourse and sexuality:

> [Foucault] takes power as a central theme and suggests that sexuality is best understood as a potential that develops in relation to varying combinations of social definition, regulation, organization and categorization. In his view beings make sense of their behaviour and that of others through discourses: socially produced forms of knowledge which define and organize experience and which always embody power.

There are theoretical advantages in adopting Foucault's de-reification of simple models of coercive state and institutional power, that assumes it is uniformly held by a single dominant group. For Foucault, power is not just repressive, it also has a productive capacity. Of particular importance here is his work on discourses and discursive practices. As Epstein (1993: 10) makes clear in her recent study on changing classroom cultures:

> We are positioned in various discourses as well as taking up positions ourselves. For example, we identify ourselves as heterosexual, lesbian or gay and could not do so if categorising discourses of sexuality did not exist. In this limited sense, we can be said to be "produced" by discourses and discursive practices.

Feminist deconstructionist theory has been important in moving beyond social reproduction models that assume that teachers and subjects are unitary subjects occupying predictable power positions. Walkerdine (1990a: 3) has developed Foucault's work within a school context and describes how (female) teachers and students 'are not unitary subjects uniquely positioned, but are produced as a nexus of subjectivities in relations of power which are constantly shifting, rendering them at one moment powerful and at another powerless' (see Henriques *et al.* 1984: 225). This suggestion that there are a range of positions that may be occupied within different contradictory discourses is useful in understanding the contextual specificity of young heterosexual males learning to be men within a school arena.

However, as Wolpe (1988: 12) points out, Foucault's complex body of work 'raises several controversies including what constitutes power relations'. Epstein (1993) argues that a key omission in Foucault's work is an adequate account of the origins of discourses or how they change. In short, within this framework, we are not clear how institutional structures operate to maintain power relations. As Hall (1988: 53) argues: 'The problem with Foucault . . . is a conception of difference without a conception of articulation, that is a conception of power without a conception of hegemony.'

Connell (1987: 183) provides a concept of hegemonic masculinity, which he argues is constructed in relation to and against femininity and subordinated forms of masculinity. The dominant masculine form is characterized by heterosexuality, power, authority, aggression and technical competence. This is a very useful concept in exploring the construction of contemporary school masculinities. Adopting the original Gramscian (1971) insight that was used in the context of class relations, Connell examines the asymmetrical nature of gender relations, arguing that dominance is never secure but must always be won. Furthermore, this is not achieved simply by coercion but by the winning and shaping of consent for the dominant gender view, which involves the building of strategic alliances. I shall explore the internal struggle over the establishment of a dominant gender view within the framework of teacher ideologies at Parnell School. This is historically located within the Neo-Conservative New Moralism that is discussed below (Weeks 1989).

As Kessler *et al.* (1985) argue in placing power at the centre of an analysis of schooling and masculinity, it is important to comprehend fully the complexity of its dynamic within the school's culture. In this book, the tensions involved in moving beyond mono-causal explanations that employ 'simple' models of power were highlighted for me in relation to two main issues.

First, in looking at male heterosexual teacher discourses in relation to the construction and regulation of heterosexual femininities and masculinities, I have emphasized the need to locate these practices in their specific contexts, in which shifting, contradictory typifications operate. A continuing tension throughout the study was placing this contextual specificity within the broader institutional pattern of a patriarchal social order with the accompanying dominant gender divisions and heterosexual arrangements. It is important to emphasize that it is this broader arena of relations of dominance and subordination, that young heterosexual women and gay young men encountered in developing their sex/gender identities at Parnell School.

Second, it is important to emphasize that working-class male peer-group cultural practices are located within a conceptual framework that is seeking to explore the complex interplay of school organization, masculinity and sexuality. As Carlen *et al.* (1992: 159) suggest, there is a large amount of pain, hurt and suffering around current school arrangements for such young people and their families. This is particularly salient in relation to my concern with the deconstruction of earlier male academic representations of working-class masculinities. It forms the background to this enquiry into the complexities and contradictions of the accounts of black and white working-class young men, positioned within a class and racially dominated state institution.[9] The research focuses upon the confusions and contradictions that are constitutive of the students' construction of gendered and sexual identities in relation to major influences, including increasing central and local state regulation, changing family networks, restructured local labour markets, changing sexual patterns of consumption, peer and leisure group practices and media representations.

What are the chapters about?

Chapter 1 covers two main aspects. First, I examine the range of male teacher masculinities at Parnell School. There is a specific focus upon the impact of wider political changes and recent internal school restructuring in helping to shape male teacher occupational identities. Second, I examine how the school helps to produce different student masculinities. Chapters 2 and 3 critique earlier male academics' representations of young men's schooling. In Chapter 2, young white and black heterosexual male students discuss their experiences of masculinity within a secondary school context. There is a substantive focus on a number of working-class heterosexual peer groups: the 'Macho Lads', the 'Academic Achievers', the 'New Entrepreneurs' and the middle-class 'Real Englishmen' in the relation to the range of subject positions they come to occupy. Chapter 3 explores what constitutes male heterosexuality, and more specifically I examine how young men 'become' heterosexual in a school context. Here, we see the public and private dichotomy of boys learning to be men, while policing sex/gender boundaries. Chapter 4 explores young heterosexual women's experiences of teacher and student school masculinities. Most importantly, the young women identify an important omission in the male accounts, that of power relations. The particular focus of Chapter 5 is a group of young gay male students' educational experiences. They provide a critical account of schooling in a relatively under-researched area at a time when the Neo-Conservative offensive is attempting to reshape 'commonsense' explanations of sexual morality.

Key aims of the book

- To examine the making of masculinities within the local site of the school.
- To explore the social positioning of heterosexual young women and gay male students in relation to the promotion of dominant forms of male heterosexual power.
- To go beyond essentialist sex/gender categories to look at the way masculinities are made and remade in schools.
- To explore how socially and politically constructed unstable sex/

gender categories come to be perceived as 'commonsense' biologically 'fixed' entities.

- To go beyond additive models of oppression and look at complex matrices of power relations, bringing together critical sociological and psychological frameworks.
- To go beyond unitary concepts of the subject and trace through the contextual contingency of identity formation.
- To explore the desexualization and deracialization of school abuse.
- To explore the remasculinization of the curriculum and the emergence of new ways of being a male teacher and male student.
- To explore local sexual cultures of heterosexual male students.
- To examine 'local site of schooling' as a key cultural arena in the processes of normalization, surveillance and control of sex/gender identities.
- To present a critique of the Neo-Conservative New Moralism and its accompanying media campaign of demonization of feminists and the gay and lesbian communities.
- To explore the material, ideological and discursive resources that male teachers and male students draw upon in policing sex/gender boundaries.
- To link up schools to different sites of identity formation, such as the family and local labour markets.
- To deconstruct earlier male academic representations of the schooling of young males.
- To develop an emancipatory methodological framework that gives high status to research participants' knowledges, understandings and feelings.
- To develop a framework that is of value to educational workers in schools and other sites.
- To begin to construct a language in which to explore sexual and ethnic majority identities and more specifically to make visible the complex phenomenon of male heterosexual subjectivity as dominant sexual category.

1

Teacher ideologies, representations and practices

Youth/adolescence remains a powerful cultural and ideological category through which adult society constructs a specific age stage as simultaneously strange and familiar. Youth/adolescence remains the focus of adult fears and pity, of voyeurism and longing.

(Griffin 1993)

Over the years we've seen a lot of different kids go through the place and they've had a lot in common. But during the last few years a lot of the boys seem to be lost. They're paying the price for the Thatcher experiment. They see their fathers and older brothers on the dole. So, a lot of them just give up. You have to feel sorry for this generation. Of course, as they get older, tougher and more bitter, we'll feel sorry for ourselves. They won't forgive us for what we have done to them!

(Allan Watts, teacher)

Introduction

This chapter consists of two main aspects. First, it explores male teacher subjectivities with a specific focus on how broader sociopolitical changes and the internal restructuring of contemporary schooling is helping to shape specific middle-class masculine occupational identities. Second, I intend to explore critically how the social structure of an English secondary school helps to produce a range of student masculinities. The historical specificity of this cultural production will be illustrated by mapping out the range of masculine subject positions that a post-ERA 'entrepreneurial curriculum' has made available to teachers and students. There is an examination of the transmission of official sex/gender codes, through systems of management, instruments of discipline, and institutional values and rituals. Key aspects of the chapter that are explored include: the sexual division of labour, the promotion and legitimation of forms of masculinity and femininity, and the social formation/regulation of male teachers' and male students' sexual subjectivities. Before examining the main areas of concern, I shall describe briefly the structure and location of Parnell School.

The school and its community

Parnell School is an 11–18 co-educational comprehensive, located within a Midlands inner-city industrial area. Like all such cities, the toll of decline in the UK's national industrial base has weighed heavy upon its economy, resources and population. The national and international recession has further contributed to the city's demise, with its declining population. At the time of the research, regional male unemployment was double the national average. Over a third of the city's population was living on or below the poverty line (Loftman and Nevin 1992).

At the time of the research, Parnell School had a majority working-class student population with about 10 per cent having a new middle-class background (see Aggleton 1987a). Approximately 30 per cent of the students were of Asian parentage, 10 per cent African Caribbean and 10 per cent Irish. Most of the students were born in England and there were roughly equal numbers of females and males. There were nine female teachers and three were black. A further description of the school's structure and personnel will be examined later in the chapter in relation to teacher ideologies. First, there is a need to contextualize the study at Parnell School in terms of wider current schooling policy changes.

Schooling in the marketplace: A transitional 'modern' educational settlement

The history of education is littered with the discarded public representations of state schooling. The move beyond the 1944–88 educational interregnum has taken place within a rapidly shifting and highly fractured cultural terrain (Johnson R. 1989). Comprehensive secondary schooling, which during the 1960s and early 1970s acted as a metaphor for social change, has been displaced by the grand metaphor of the market lottery of 'winners' and 'losers'. Following the Labour government's claim in the late 1970s that schools were failing to meet industrial needs, the Conservatives have systematically developed and exploited this discourse of 'blaming the public sector' in terms of the displacement and projection of economic failure on to state schools. By the early 1990s, central elements of the social democratic settlement are being dismantled, including the LEA–school partnership, comprehensive reorganization, anti-racist and anti-sexist education (CCCS 1981; Cultural Studies 1991). A new cultural landscape has developed within a deregulated schooling 'market' constituted by variable forms of privatization, commercialization and commodification (Chitty 1987; Jones 1989; Simon 1992). Hutton (1991) offers a critique of what he calls the 1980s experiment in the futilities of *laissez-faire* economics, that informs current education policy. He writes that:

> Education where the doctrine of opting out and choice has been established to make the operation of markets in schools mimic that in the Stock Exchange, is set to reproduce conditions of quasi-social Apartheid. Good schools will "over shoot" upwards and weaker schools downwards – just as prices do in the market.
>
> (Hutton 1991: 11)

This study of Parnell School has taken place at a time when new schooling hierarchies have emerged within and between the expanding range of schools in the restratified league-tabled social world of: comprehensives, grammars, independents, grant-maintained and city technology colleges (CTCs). Most importantly, this restructuring is based upon the accompanying discriminatory financial awards, including differential funding to 'opt-out' schools and the assisted places scheme. As Walford and Miller (1991) point out in their study of CTCs, this restructuring has been accompanied by the public re-legitimation of inequality of provision for different groups of students, ideologically justified in terms of market diversity and parental choice.

While carrying out this research, what might be called the construction of an entrepreneurial curriculum was in the ascendancy at Parnell School. A number of factors were in play that helped to explain the shift of the school's culture into the 'marketplace'. As part of central government's Parent's Charter, annual school performance tables are to published. Under local management, schools in the area were competing to attract increased numbers of students. In the last decade we have witnessed unprecedented, rapid and substantial policy changes in state schools. The structural changes were experienced most specifically at Parnell School in terms of the plethora of curricular initiatives, including the National Curriculum and testing, the General Certificate of Secondary Education (GCSE), Records of Achievement (ROA)/student profiling, the Technical and Vocational Education Initiative (TVEI) and Personal and Social Education (PSE). Most significantly, the implementation of these initiatives involved changes in management strategies and modes of surveillance, monitoring, evaluation and control of teachers and students (DES 1985; HMI 1985, 1989; Ball 1990; Hugill 1991). Implementation of these initiatives was publicly acted out, re-presented and evaluated as quantitative indices of success in the local schooling market (Rudduck 1990).

It is against this background that I now want to examine the specific mediation of current education policy changes at Parnell School.

Teacher microculture: Educational ideologies

In recent work on the politics of education, I have explored the changing nature of teacher occupational cultures in response to the restructuring of state schooling. In examining their everyday work lives, I have found it heuristically useful to place teachers within an ideological typology that focuses on their different educational and social world views, while exploring questions of professional self-representation. Three main educational ideologies are outlined at Parnell School: that of the 'Professionals', the 'Old Collectivists' and the 'New Entrepreneurs'.[1] These constituted the teachers' microculture, which served to mediate the production of a range of contradictory and fractured masculine identities that the teachers inhabited. Connell (1985: 138) reminds us that: 'To understand the gender regime of a school one must understand the way gender relations impinge on different groups of teachers, the responses they make and the strategies they try to follow.' Teachers operating within the above ideologies with their accompanying professional discourses conceived of sex/gender relations in diverse ways. It is important to note that the complex interrelationship between the teacher ideologies, self-representations and masculine subjectivities is currently taking place, as described above, within an arena of rapid state change and negotiation.

The teacher categories were constructed on the basis of interviews, observation and questionnaires that I gave to all the teaching staff. Most of them accepted the categories that I placed them in. However, there are real dangers in adopting an ideal type approach. It is important to emphasize that these ideologies are not always found in pure form; nor is it possible simplistically to allocate teachers to one or other of the categories. Social reality is more complex. So, for example, I was unable to place several teachers (about 12 per cent) who straddled the categories, and during the research period teachers adopted shifting discourses. Fullan (1982: 127) adds an important qualification to the labelling of teachers, that it may: '. . . run the risk of reifying what is a loose classification system and implying that teachers may not change from one orientation to another'. This warning is of particular salience at a time of rapid educational reform, when teachers may be more likely to shift ideological positions. Hence, they may be read as unstable occupational identities with transitional fusions and alliances emerging (Riseborough and Poppleton 1991).[2] At the time of this research, the Old Collectivists and the Professionals made a strategic alliance to contest the New Entrepreneurs' political new realism. Furthermore, no one ideology held exclusive control; rather, competing ideologies and discourses interacted with a dominant position emerging, which at this time was that of the New Entrepreneurs. An ideal type of each group is given below.

The Professionals

Member of professional association; strong sense of professional loyalty to one's male peers; supported the return to a traditional hierarchical structure of the school administration and organization of the curriculum in terms of streaming, subject-based, commonsense approach to learning; in favour of norm-referenced assessment; opposed to progressive educational theories and methods, including opposition to school anti-sexist initiatives; appealing to the dominant discourse with its binary logic of gender difference between males and females; adopted an authoritarian approach to students and an assimilationist perspective to black students; overtly hostile to recent curricular initiatives; conservative approach to sex education, with tendency to reduce it to presentation of biological facts.

Roughly 25 per cent of the teachers were termed 'Professionals'. They tended to be older members of staff and former grammar school teachers. Their authority and main influence stemmed from their position as senior management and as departmental heads of science, mathematics and languages. This institutional location helped shape a specific mode of masculinity, with a vocabulary that emphasized authority, discipline and control.

The Old Collectivists

Usually a member of a trade union and active in past industrial action; often member of Labour Party; strongly opposed to imposition of the Educational Reform Act and changes in pay and conditions; highly critical of the creation of extra supervisory positions in teaching; strong sense of 'us' and 'them' in relations with headteacher; theoretically based student-centred pedagogy; supported comprehensive education and pastoral care system; in favour of criteria-referenced assessment and course work; strongly supportive of colleagues; promoted values of collectivism, egalitarianism and meritocracy; opposed to new vocationalism; ambivalent to recent curricular innovation but strongly opposed to its philosophical base; articulated liberal/radical position on gender issues in relation to students; primary concern with pastoral care and increasing access for girls and black students; set up anti-sexist and multicultural/anti-racist initiatives that included positive images in careers advice and removing anti-sexist/ anti-racist literature.

Twenty-five per cent of the teachers were classified as 'Old Collectivists'. The term refers not to their age but their fading ideological significance within the school. Their power within the school was based on their positions as heads of special needs, careers and English and senior positions in pastoral care and community links. A specific occupational version of masculinity was developed in this conventional 'feminine' sector of secondary schools, that was informed by an engagement with feminist ideas.

The New Entrepreneurs

Member of teacher association emphasizing professional status of career; opposed to trade unions and industrial action; in favour of no-strike contract agreement; supportive of increased management responsibilities and classroom teachers' accountability and appraisal; adopted a pragmatic pedagogical approach with eclectic selection of ideas and practices from the Professionals and the Old Collectivists; strong commitment to expanding own departments/faculties and promotion of new courses; supporter of enterprise culture; emphasized the importance of public relations in presentation and marketing of schooling as a commodity; implemented modern education technology; overtly ambitious with a strong commit-ment to career advancement; projected high self-profile within school; saw students as clients; adopted an assimilationist approach to black students but used language of multiculturalism, and equal opportunities for girls; highly visible supporter of curricular initiatives, including vocationalism.

Forty per cent of the teachers were classified as 'New Entrepreneurs'. They included five teachers who qualified during the last decade and who were highly influential within this group. Their power was based on their positions as faculty heads and as departmental heads of vocationally orientated subjects, including business studies, computer studies and vocational courses.

Raymond Williams (1961) provides an early classification of three teacher ideologies: the public educators, who believed that education was a natural human right, the old humanists and the industrial trainers, who evolved in the nineteenth century, with the latter group emerging as predominant. His work, with its cogent analysis of the group's internal contradictions, compromises and fragile alliances, remains highly salient to an understanding of the increased confusions and complexities of state school teacher cultures in the early 1990s. Stephen Ball (1990: 4–5) has developed Williams' basic typology, suggesting that, presently, '. . . the public educators are in disarray and that the field of policy-making is overshadowed by the influence of the old humanists and industrial trainers'. Ball's work is particularly sensitive to the disarray experienced by the public educators, represented at Parnell School by the Old Collectivists, accompanying their fading ideological influence in the struggle over curriculum reform. He also identifies the emergence of the 'new progres-sives', who combine elements of the old public educators' position with that of new progressive vocationalism. They were represented at Parnell School by the New Entrepreneurs.

A defining element of the changing teacher occupational cultures was the construction of a new gender regime. As Kessler *et al.* (1985: 42) have suggested:

> . . . the school as an institution is characterised at any given time by a particular gender regime. This may be defined as the pattern of practices that constructs various kinds of masculinity and femininity among staff and students, orders them in terms of prestige and power, and constructs a sexual division of labour within the institution. The gender regime is a state of play rather than a permanent condition. It can be changed deliberately or otherwise, but it is no less powerful in its effects on pupils for that. It confronts them as a social fact, which they have to come to terms with somehow.

A key aspect of the current internal restructuring of the curriculum at Parnell School was the repositioning of the Professional, Old Collectivist and, more recently developed, New Entrepreneur masculinities. I now wish to examine in more detail the specific dynamics of the gender reordering of these occupational cultures.

Headteacher–teacher social relations

Duncan Trimble, the headteacher, as the leading New Entrepreneur, was a highly visible agent in the development and promotion of the new entrepreneurial curriculum project. Headteachers, as institutional 'moral gatekeepers', perform a major organizational role in structuring the self-experience of those who work in schools. More recently, their managerial function as institutional critical reality definers within the school marketplace has made them highly visible (Gillborn 1989). During the last decade their power has increased, with the introduction of local management of schools, legislative changes, the development of educational technologies, new management information systems and prescriptive rule-based systems of control. At the same time, the moral ascendancy of managerialism has been accompanied by the emergence of senior management teams, as a new axis of power relations and as a locus of social orderings (Inglis 1989). This reorganized division of labour can be seen to be creating increased internal divisions and individual hyper-competition within new occupational hierarchies that are differentially valued and rewarded. Within an increasing fractured relationship between heads and teachers, conceptions of management, teaching and professionalism are currently being redefined and at the same time regendered. At Parnell School, the experience of the current management restructuring served to 'reconstitute the teachers' professional identities giving a distinctive orientation to work and educational ideology' (Riseborough 1981: 364). In a public sector profession in transition, new teacher identities are developing in the 1990s, as represented at Parnell School by the recently emerged New Entrepreneurs, that are differentially structured and experienced by male and female teachers.

Duncan Trimble's restructuring of the school organization and curriculum involved him in sponsoring and elevating a hybrid form of 'new masculinity', whose main contradictory themes included bureaucratic centralization of control, rationality, overt forms of career ambition, collegiality and delegation. He could be located within the projected post-Fordist era with its emphasis on small-scale, flat hierarchies and flexible team work, within a differentiated marketplace, in which new school systems are helping to shape new teaching cultures. He is representative of a new 'masculine' authoritarianism, in which overt forms of technologies of power are being displaced by 'modern' forms of technical bureaucratic knowledge. These are developed in the high-tech offices of modern administration, with their dominant discursive themes of managerial efficiency and economic rationality (Furlong 1991). Duncan Trimble spoke of the formation of this new masculine leadership in terms of a fusion of public and private sector 'man':

> I would say in the past, managers in the private sector have been cast as much tougher than those in the public sector. We've been seen as rather soft. It's partly teachers being associated with children. But I think that things have recently changed and some critics would say that school managers have taken on the tough image of the private sector. I think that is a defensive over-reaction to the new climate schools have to operate in. What is happening is that we now have the autonomy to bring together the best from both worlds. And if we're honest it's what was badly needed.

This was contested by the Old Collectivists, who embodied an older form of public sector masculinity. They claimed that the over-rationalistic prescriptions and proscriptions in the planning, implementation and evaluation of curriculum change was illustrative of a significant shift away from the liberal humanist tradition. For them, this manifested itself in terms of the technical rationalist logic that underpinned the shift in conceiving headship in terms of 'chief executive' rather than the 'leading professional', thus underplaying the essentially qualitative human relations that constitute the everyday life of public institutions. From the Old Collectivists' perspective, Duncan Trimble's leadership was a key element in the utilitarian reductionism of schooling to meet economic needs (Smetherham 1988; Gillborn 1989). In the following account, Emma, a history teacher, makes explicit the masculinizing processes involved in the current management changes:

It's probably more clear in the primary sector which is thought of as more feminine. But similar things are occurring here. You get the feeling that the old talk about professionalism, kids' needs and building a supportive place is being thrown out because it's seen as the soft option. In the brave new world of management, we're back to emphasizing that the men are in charge or at least the things that are traditionally associated with them, with masculinity. It's all the talk of systems, strategic planning and turning senior teachers into resource managers.

Davies (1992), adopting a theoretical approach that emphasizes gender *relations* rather than gender *differences*, warns against the reductionism of conflating dominant forms of secondary school management with masculinity *per se*. She writes:

> My thesis is that it is this version of masculinity – competitive, point-scoring, over-confident, sporting, career and status conscious – which has come to dominate school management. It articulates well with the overall themes of schooling, of hierarchy and individuation. It lends itself to divide and rule, and is the breeding ground for the fragmentation of teaching staff which is necessary if teachers are not to become a political force. It is not the only version of masculinity, not the only male typescript in schools, and many men in our research were equally hesitant or realistic about their capabilities as were women. But the competitive manager typescript is by definition the most powerful in terms of defining reality for others.
>
> (Davies 1992: 128)

As indicated in the following account, feminist teachers at Parnell School shared this anti-essentialist linking of masculinity and new management style. However, there were differences between them concerning the building of strategies to contest the current forms of institutional masculine dominance.

Nancy: I think that the new type of school management, moving away from the idea of the head as the leading professional comes easier to a lot of men. It is part of a new style of male management in the 1980s. But not all men are into it and there are women here and elsewhere who have adopted this masculine style; sometimes in an extra exaggerated way, trying to outdo the men.

M.M.:   What do you think of that?

Nancy: It's the argument that women have to be more competitive, tougher than men if they are to get into management positions. It is more evident in the States than here. I understand the argument but I disagree with this strategy. Authoritarians are authoritarians even when they are pretending not to be, like the new male management tries to do. But I accept it's difficult to know the way forward without selling out.

For Nancy, the social relations between Duncan Trimble and the staff were part of the broader arena of sexual politics in operation within the school. This was not recognized by most of the male teachers including Duncan Trimble. As is indicated below, the resulting masculine degendering of staff social relations served to increase the male teachers' confusions concerning the changes taking place.

Cultural interregnum: Teacher ideologies, professional self-representations and masculine subjectivities

The three teacher ideologies help to provide a historical perspective in which to locate the present staff's modes of masculinity. The range of male teacher gender narratives recorded here illustrates the changing masculine hierarchies within a specific state institution. At the time of the research, the Professionals had experienced an earlier gender disruption, when the former boys' grammar school was reorganized as a co-education comprehensive, in which they, as the patriarchal *ancien régime*, were challenged and displaced by the more liberal Old Collectivists. In turn, the Old Collectivists were experiencing the more recent delegitimation of their position with the emergence of a New Entrepreneurial masculinity.

Kessler *et al.* (1985) have described the complex gendering processes operating within school sites. They argue that:

> What school is mainly doing . . . is arbitrating among different kinds of masculinity and femininity. Perhaps we should say that since much of this occurs outside the scope of any conscious policy, the school provides a setting in which one kind or another becomes hegemonic . . . [The school] produces other masculinities but marginalises them, while giving most honor and admiration to a tough and dominant virility.
>
> (Kessler *et al.* 1985: 42)

As pointed out in the Introduction, Connell (1987: 183) develops this concept of hegemonic masculinity, which is constructed in relation to and against femininity and subordinated forms of masculinity. Most importantly, he suggests that the construction of modern school masculinities is achieved not simply by coercion but by the winning and shaping of consent for the dominant gender view, which involves the building of strategic alliances. For Connell, hegemonic masculinity appears to be associated with the high-status academic curriculum. At Parnell School, within a rapidly changing cultural terrain, the construction of hierarchically ordered masculinities, as part of a transitional gender regime, appeared to be more complex and fractured. This is illustrated in this study by exploring the specific dynamics of the interplay between the descending

Old Collectivists' masculinity and the emerging New Entrepreneurial mode, which was currently in the ascendancy.

Biographical details, including memories of significant others and events, were important in shaping male teachers' subjectivities. For example, among the Professionals, older male staff frequently recalled and bitterly regretted the passing of uncontested gender identities of the grammar school era, which clearly delineated masculinity and femininity along a commonsense bipolar system of traditional fixed male and female sex roles. Significant elements of their formative experiences included their fathers' occupation, the sexual division of labour in their parents' home, experience of the army and active involvement in competitive sport. A central concern for this group was the question of dominant forms of English nationality. Their masculine narratives of remembering exhibited a strong sense of loss of national identity in a post-imperial society and its recovery and celebration by Margaret Thatcher within the 'strong state' (Gamble 1988). This imagined past was linked to an orderly school world in which 'the boys knew their place'.

William: It was always foreigners who were weak, not the English. That's how we built such a big empire and influenced the world in its development. We were at the centre and that is when we were proud to be Englishmen; being firm but fair, helping the underdog. Its a bit of a stereotype I know but you get the message. Britain was great and Englishmen were respected around the world and in the schools there was respect for the teachers. The boys knew where they were, with high standards expected and you were allowed to use proper discipline and character building. It may have been a bit harsh at times but look at the results. One of the most satisfying parts of my work is meeting the old boys and they thank you for putting them on the right path.

Ray: I know a lot of liberals here won't agree but Mrs Thatcher restored our leadership role in the world. We had become the sick man of Europe but with a strong economy, the sorting out of the unions, the Falklands war success, England on the sea again. Our national pride and strength was restored. For a decade she helped to restore our pride in ourselves as Englishmen. The only thing she didn't do was win us the World Cup!

M.M.: Has this been reflected in schools?

Ray: The National Curriculum may help. But I think that the rot has gone too far. But there were successes in sorting out the "looney left". I mean we were getting to a stage when it was difficult to state biological facts about girls and boys. And of course this legacy is still with us. A lot of the trendies [the Old Collectivists] here and the new management crowd [the New Entrepreneurs] forget the basics of training pupils.

M.M.: What are those basics?

Ray: Pupils clearly need to know where they stand. Adults have a moral duty to set standards and discipline that help them develop into healthy adults. And the trendies and management crowd know this when it comes to their own children. They're all sent to grammars.

Like the teachers in Chris Heward's (1988) study, the Professionals saw their primary task to be that of making real men of the male students (Beynon 1989). They tended to be more interested in the male than female students' schooling. They believed in coercive discipline, and there was much talk among them of order, discipline and academic and moral standards. The Professionals, many of whom were former grammar school teachers, missed the 'common culture of maleness' that is found in all-male secondary schools (Davidson 1985) and attempted to recreate a fantasized past within specific school spaces, including traditional 'masculine' subject areas, such as the natural sciences, mathematics and competitive team sports.

With each of the teacher groups there tended to be a gap between their private talk and public stance. In practice, the Professionals were more pragmatic than they appeared in interview situations. While spending much time together around the school, they also worked cooperatively with others, particularly with members of the Old Collectivists, within the liberal pedagogical framework of a co-educational comprehensive.

The Old Collectivists, who were more recently displaced as the dominant ideological school force, frequently reminisced about their immediate past, when they represented progressive curriculum modern-izers. They now found themselves in a defensive curricular position, opposed to the New Entrepreneurial curriculum innovations but also conscious of the strategic limitations of their own educational position. They were aware of the significance of their inability to accommodate the new vocationalism within their existing liberal teaching practices. Part of the Old Collectivists' confusion in countering the New Right attack on them as the educational establishment, was that the New Right had reworked earlier critiques developed by progressive educationalists (Johnson R. 1989).

Stephen: In the 70s we led the debates on education, like the Schools Council was very influential. Now, in fact over the last decade we have lost that. I think TVE [Technical and Vocational Education] was significant in turning us from being seen as liberal progressives into liberal reactionaries.
M.M.:   How has that come about?
Stephen: I think what we were talking about the other day. The Left teachers were opposed to narrow vocationalism but at the same time this became associated with opposition to modernizing the curriculum and realistically accepting the only money being put into education that TVE offered. The management crowd [New Entrepreneurs] understood that trend better than us. I guess that history is on their side in terms of their reading of the situation and their emerging as the current power holders. Now we're seen as old educational hippies!

The Old Collectivist male teachers appeared to be experiencing a crisis of masculinity, as part of their wider ideological displacement with the emergence of the New Entrepreneurs. Significant internal factors were in play, associated with the construction of the twin elements of managerialism and the entrepreneurial curriculum. They perceived their own loss of status and responsibility from that of classroom teachers to facilitators and the accompanying new hierarchy of supervisors, over-represented by the New Entrepreneurs, who were seen as acting as agents of quality control. The Old Collectivists linked this internal restructuring to broader external changes in social democratic politics. This has been described by Gamble (1988: 11) in the following terms:

> The crisis in the regime of accumulation and the shifts in the political organisation of the world system which took place in the 1970s were the fundamental changes which made a new politics possible and necessary. But the content of this new politics was often provided by local concerns, specific to institutions and circumstances of particular countries. Nevertheless here too certain common themes can be seen. The institutions and policies of social democracy came under attack almost everywhere. The challenges were made through ideological debate as well as by new political programmes and movements. Many of these challenges began before the appearance of the global crisis of accumulation and hegemony. But they became much stronger once the political and economic foundations of the postwar order had been undermined.

The Old Collectivist male teachers' emotional investments in the social democratic project was severely damaged by this political crisis. They represented a legacy of the 1960s class-based politics. Their collective masculine identity was developed within a political framework that took for granted the rational and progressive unfolding of history as premised in the Enlightenment project. More specifically, their commitments to socialism, the trade union movement and comprehensive schooling represented the major vehicles of attaining social justice and equality in the modernist era (see Giddens 1990; Westwood 1992b: 244–5). Many of them expressed their disillusionment with the failure of this project in terms of anger, resentment, regret and cynicism. Rutherford (1990) captures the Old Collectivists' mood. Writing of the current cultural interregnum, he proposes that:

> We are caught between the decline of the old political identifications and the new identities that are in the process of becoming or yet to be born. Like Laurie Anderson's "urbanscape" in her song "Big Science" the imagery traces of the future are present, but as yet have no representation or substance.

> (Rutherford 1990: 23)

A younger group of male and female teachers, who were involved in 'modern' political movements, including feminism, black politics and environmental issues, criticized the Old Collectivist male teachers for failing to develop a more comprehensive perspective of school oppression. More specifically, they argued for the need to develop anti-oppressive policies and strategies that would acknowledge the specific complex political dynamics of cultural difference.[3] As Johnson (1992: 273) claims:

> The growing consciousness of gender and nationality, race or "ethnicity" necessarily challenges earlier evaluations of past episodes. They undermine the moral framing of class-based accounts; they point up their masculinity or Anglo-ethnicity. This produces painful feelings and difficult dilemmas, as attachments to old heroes . . . are qualified.

The Old Collectivist male teachers appeared to be unable to make this transition in relation to their political attachments. The following accounts indicate the political generational gap between the male Old Collectivists and their younger critics. Henry, a gay teacher, describes the political de-centring of the Old Collectivists, and suggests how the 'new' identity politics challenges 'not only the power of heterosexual men but also the worth of their masculinity . . . with the realization that they are "no longer where the action is" ' (Connell 1987: 234).

Lucy: The liberal men here really don't understand sexual politics. When they talk about anti-sexist education, they're mainly talking in terms of changing the boys, the male pupils. Like they were active in stopping the boys playing football in the playground and taking up all the space. They see sexism as mainly a working-class problem. The liberals are much less aware of how they, as middle-class men, take up space in more hidden ways.

Henry: I think sexual politics has had a much greater effect on schools like this than is realized. You can't always see this but it's there . . . And I think a lot of the straight guys, the liberals, know this deep inside them. They see themselves as victims. As a gay man, who cannot come out at school, it makes me smile. All the sexual discrimination against women and gays, and straight men want us to feel sorry for them.

M.M.:   How do you feel about that?

Henry: Well, I think they are saying something important. A lot of them have been politically active in the past. But the main social movements that are impacting on schools are women, blacks and gays and lesbians. And that is the point, the white straight men cannot take a central role anymore. At present they are confused, guilty, hurt, cynical, you name it and mostly they feel excluded. And they don't know how to rationalize this away.

Stuart Hall (1992) records the difficulty for men in meeting the feminist challenge to transform institutional gender relations. He notes:

> Now that's where I really discovered the gendered nature of power. Long, long after I was able to pronounce the words, I encountered the reality of Foucault's profound insight into the individual reciprocity of knowledge and power. Talking about giving up power is a radically different experience from being silenced.
>
> (Hall 1992: 283)

At Parnell School, a number of the Old Collectivist male teachers engaged with feminist theory. However, they were unable to see the limits of personal consciousness-raising in relation to their own position in the institutional sexual structuring of the school. As with many politically progressive activists, in trying to understand their own contradictory position in a system of oppression, they tended to take for granted the privileges of white straight middle-class masculinity that were ascribed to them. Furthermore, there was little acknowledgement of their own individual and collective cultural investment in the present heterosexual arrangements (Skeggs 1992). They would often begin interviews arguing against structural discrimination against women embedded in dominant masculinizing school processes. However, inevitably, this frequently gave way, like the participants in American Men's studies, to talk of themselves as the 'new oppressed' with the demands of hegemonic masculinity on liberal men (Canaan and Griffin 1990). Invariably, most of them represented themselves as the 'good guys' operating within a sexist society.

Peter: I understand what it must be like to be always discriminated against because you are a woman. But I see myself as on their side. The idea that all men are sexist because they are men is destructive in gender terms. I don't know where you go with that argument. I think that sexism is an evil but women must differentiate politically between those who are against them and those of us who are genuinely trying to change things.

There was little awareness among the Old Collectivist male teachers of the gender structuring of public arenas, such as the staffroom, that highlighted the power of masculinity as an institutional force, operating to marginalize and exclude women, while privileging the masculine perspective. Furthermore, there was little acknowledgement of the predatory heterosexual environment of staffroom, classroom and playground, that female teachers and students frequently recounted to me.

Lucy: In the two schools I have worked in there has been a lot of sexual harassment from the male staff towards female teachers and pupils. Whether it's telling dirty jokes, sexual innuendoes, the leering looks or inappropriate touching. It's deeply ingrained in staffrooms in ways that men just take for granted.

Jane: There are important differences between the male teachers here but there are key threads that they share, that most men take for granted. You might say the male bonding, the staffroom masculine codes, reflect the playground and vice versa. The men do have different styles and some of them are okay, but the aggression, the intense competition, the male networks are all there.

M.M.:   Would you recognize a specific public masculinity in teaching?

Jane: In my view, and the women here differ on this, but I find middle-class masculinity more invidious than the tough working-class boys. Male teachers consistently try to dominate the agenda of any meetings;

management and teaching is about male definitions of what is important. You see the crude ways in which male teachers will take up women's views at staff meetings and present them as their own and congratulate each other for insightful contributions that in fact women said earlier on.

There were different responses from Old Collectivist female teachers – who tended to be more ambivalent – than younger progressive teachers towards the Old Collectivist men. For Nancy, the contradictions of being a heterosexual feminist were difficult to resolve inside an institution in which 'rampant heterosexuality' was a normal part of the culture.

Nancy: Lesbian friends say I have to make compromises in being heterosexual with a male partner, and a son in my case, but I do feel sorry for men of my generation. Some women friends mock that it's the male mid-life crisis, and that if it is, it's lasting a long time for the men we know. White middle-class men feel burnt out, in fact they are.

M.M.:   What's the specifics of these men's experiences?

Nancy: Our generation had a lot of sexual freedom compared to our parents. Of course we can now see that most of the benefits went to the men. But ironically, with the general disillusionment, a lot of unemployment, divorces, etc., women seem to be coping better. Things like we have other areas of our lives, like our emotional commitment to our kids. And the fact that even with the new femininity of the 1960s we had to cope with most of the emotional issues. Men just never seem to grow up, just like the ones you see here. And I agree with my lesbian friends that straight women have partly colluded with this. But it really is difficult to resolve.

As indicated above, at the time of the research the New Entrepreneurs were in the ascendancy as the emerging dominant mode of modern masculinity. They were the 'ideal teachers', whose projected certainties, highlighted in the high-profile public presentation of themselves, contrasted vividly with the Old Collectivists' confusions. The New Entrepreneurs' masculinity was developed within the political nexus of managerialism, vocationalism and commercialization, with its values of rationalism, possessive individualism and instrumentalism (Burton and Weiner 1993).

James: You have to accept that schools are now in competition with each other and there's healthy competition between faculties and departments. A group of us [the New Entrepreneurs] are criticized for our high profile in developing our faculties. Ambition isn't seen as a good thing in education. There's nothing wrong in running the place with efficiency and attracting the interest of local businessmen. LMS [local management of schools] has really helped and GMS [grant-maintained schools] will further develop this.

Stewart: In fact I believe that we are good role models for the pupils to compete to achieve the highest rewards. With the boss we are making this one of the best schools in the area. There's great career opportunities at the present time. But it's not just about promoting yourself all the time. The most successful formula is to combine individual ambition with teamwork.

As Parker (1992: 71–2), argues: '. . . we may regard the school as an intricate masculinizing agency playing host to the production of a range of masculinities within the confines of [particular subjects]'. The New Entrepreneurs mainly taught traditional 'masculine', vocationally orientated subjects, that were the main beneficiaries, both financially and in status terms, from the current new vocationalist curriculum restructuring. However, this was not a passive educational process. Rather, it involved the New Entrepreneurs in actively appropriating and reworking forms of knowledge. Davies (1992: 130), in describing this process, has noted that:

> In terms of hierarchy of knowledge, males have exerted control by designating certain knowledge areas as simultaneously high status and masculine (currently science, maths, technology, but not so long ago, modern languages). It is interesting how particular promising knowledge areas get "captured" by the "dominant", and reworked to show tendencies in their favour. Hence keyboard skills were once dismissed as typing or at best office skills, and designated female; now with computerisation, they are called intermediate technology, and as we all know, are better done by males.

The rise of this dominant curricular and pedagogical perspective is symptomatic of the wider political context of the late 1980s and early 1990s, in which education initiatives are primarily concerned with the quantitative 'masculine' world of the technology of change rather than the qualitative world of values. At Parnell School, senior management were reproducing a positivist-based, technicist approach that was overly preoccupied with the 'how' rather than the 'why' of curriculum change.

This technical rationalist approach involved the reworking of conventional 'masculine' commercial and industrial images, in the process of aligning schools with commerce and industry (Furlong 1991). Johnson (1991a) has captured this modern public sector masculinity. He notes that:

> This is the public (and inner?) narrative of conventional masculinity. It is the story of the classic middle-class career, of the buccaneering entrepreneur, of the hero of the Falklands "task force" (before he is struck down). It is also the story of "man's mastery over nature". Here science and technico-social interventions subordinate a complex natural–social reality ("Nature"), with which women and black people are often aligned.
>
> (Johnson 1991a: 94)

This emerging dominant masculinity contained traces of other masculine forms, pragmatically combining elements of other versions of school masculinity. For example, in appropriating liberal discourses of student entitlement and empowerment, the New Entrepreneurs conflated free-market liberalism with the Old Collectivists' progressive talk of equal opportunities (Avis 1991). In discussions with female teachers, they identified a range of masculine types. Without appealing to a simple male teacher typology, they described the construction of modern school masculinities. They pointed out that there were tendencies for individuals and specific teacher groups ideologically to combine diverse elements in their projection of a version of masculinity.

Lucy: For some teachers, like the more traditional ones, their masculinity is linked to their authority coming from knowledge. They see themselves as experts with notions of scientific objectivity. They're often maths and science teachers. It's probably more natural there in what has been seen as masculine subject areas but you also get others, particularly among the more traditional older teachers. Probably another type gets their masculinity mainly by being authoritarian. You know they'll say men are better at discipline because they can control the kids. They mean the boys. Then you will get others who will flirt a lot with the girls, especially younger men.
M.M.:   Do you think that more recently much has changed?
Lucy: Yes, I think the more recent types we discussed the other day are more complex because they take bits from all the other types and mix them up. In fact that is probably more the norm now for most men teachers than it was ten years ago with a dominant aspect of authoritarianism or flirting or whatever.

This section has illustrated the complexity of the formation of masculine subjectivities within the context of a secondary school. During the last decade, sexual politics has been marked by new public representations, in academic and popular texts, concerning a suggested crisis in contemporary forms of masculinity. Popular discourses, at a time of a political 'backlash' against feminism, have constructed the media-celebrated emergence of the enigmatic 'new man' and 'Essex man' in England, and 'Iron John' in the United States. These popular cultural forms convey a broader concern with current self-representations of masculine identity (Norman 1993). As pointed out above, this found expression at Parnell School in terms of the Old Collectivists' suggestion of a crisis of occupational identity for a group of white middle-class heterosexual men. A major omission in their accounts was an acknowledgement of their position and cultural investments in the existing gendered social relations of domination and subordination. A key element of their institutional power, the sexual division of labour, is now examined.

School as workplace: Redefining a complex sexual division of labour

Ozga (1988) provides the political background to the changing structure of teachers' work. She cites a number of central state initiatives – 'changes in the contractual relationship between teachers and employers; in teachers' negotiation rights (their abolition); in their control over the content of the curriculum and examinations; and changes in the pay and promotion of teaching' (p. ix) – which she contends are fundamentally altering the nature of teaching and leading to increased central control. Furthermore, this is taking place at a time of decreased spending on state education, with Britain spending a lower proportion of its national income on education than other advanced European societies. The teachers at Parnell School were preoccupied with the changing material base of the profession and their own permanent employment in a contracting labour market, in which redundancies, redeployment and short-term contracts have become the norm. This job insecurity has specific implications for male teachers in an occupational sector, whose masculinity is constructed around the middle-class terrain of careerism, individual social mobility and hierarchical status. There was particular concern among experienced staff about the effects of LMS. Ted Wragg (1992) has wryly commented on recent changes in school funding arrangements in an article entitled, 'And for our top scorers a gilt-edged P45'.

> It is one of the paradoxes of education today that we are about to see teachers being made redundant when we are short of teachers. Here we have the ridiculous situation of schools crying out for staff, while at the same time being compelled to lose teachers not because they are incompetent, but because the school faces financial difficulties under local management. The very system that was supposed to liberate schools is now shackled.
>
> (Wragg 1992: 60)

Recently, a sociological concern with teacher deskilling has re-emerged (Ozga 1988). This thesis suggests that the logic of capitalism determines a continual reformulation of jobs, working on the principle of separating conception from execution (Marx 1954). The Old Collectivists suggested that this was taking place at Parnell School, with changes in the pace, content and form of their work, involving increased workloads and management surveillance. In the process of being demoted from professional teacher to facilitator, they were experiencing decreased classroom control in curriculum decision-making.

Liam: It's interesting if you look at the position of the teachers here who came from the working-class via the grammar school. We were escaping from manual work apprenticeships. I was saying to my brother, I may as well have become a chippie [carpenter] like him.

M.M.:   Why do you feel like that?

Liam: Well, now we have apprentice teachers. You see they're taking away our professionalism. At least the old apprenticeship system had a real substance; the teacher apprentice scheme is part of a whole range of government controls to associate us with low-skilled work. And of course this is closely associated with the image that teaching is really women's work. It's as if teaching was becoming too professional, in a male sense.

Brian: There won't be any place for us old timers in the new world they're creating in teaching. Quite simply we'll be too expensive. It's strange watching the older generation being moved out of education. I think that it'll be the school's loss. In many ways we were the chaps who made state teaching a profession by not going off to the private sector when comprehensives came in. We kept a lot of the traditions and standards of the grammar school alive.

Bill: With the unions gone, there's no collective response to the constant deskilling of our work. It really is insidious the way that there's this appeal to our accountability to parents. This is used to push through appraisal and monitoring systems that are eating away at our professionalism. I couldn't advise anyone to come into teaching. The government sees it as low-skilled work. In the two-tier system of teaching that they're creating, the real work of monitoring and controlling goes to the management lot.

It was against this background that different versions of masculinity and femininity were reworked in relation to the diverse and contradictory demands of teachers' work that traditionally has included the curriculum instructor, the 'policeman' and the counsellor. Elsewhere (Mac an Ghaill, in press), I reported that as male teachers in a boys' school experienced failure in their role as academic instructors, the 'soft' role of counsellor was displaced by the 'harder' role of 'policeman'. This had specific curriculum implications, including the reintroduction of intensive forms of curriculum streaming, increased norm-referenced testing, and rigid ability categories replacing motivation as the main explanation of student differential attainment. In short, the restructuring of the curriculum was accompanied by new modes of teacher and student masculinities that were linked to overt forms of surveillance and social control. Later in this chapter, I examine in more detail the differential gendered teacher responses to different class sectors of male students at Parnell School.

At Parnell School, teachers contructed their professional and pedagogical identities within the context of selecting and combining specific responses to the contradictory workplace demands. However, teacher 'choices' did not take place in a socio-historical vacuum. Dominant state and professional discourses circumscribed the 'gendering' of these different work practices. By the late 1980s and early 1990s, with the restructuring of state education, the situation at Parnell School has resulted in increased complexities and contradictions. A highly salient feature within the context of a widening cultural gap between secondary school management and teaching was the promotion of the new gender-specific hierarchies of domination and subordination. At the time of the research, female teachers were involved in a major dispute with the senior management team, which consisted of seven members, only two of whom were women. The female teachers were contesting the masculinization of the administrative functions that had come to predominate school life. High status was being ascribed to the emerging 'hard masculine' functions of: the accountant, the Key Stage tester, the curriculum coordinator, and the information technology (IT) expert. At the same time, female teachers were associated with and directed into the 'soft feminine' functions of profiling and counselling. In short, the remasculinization of teaching was taking place within conventional cultural forms of splitting the rational and the emotional (Cockburn 1983).

Jane: In the past teaching was seen as a relatively good job for women. Especially in primary schools, it was possible to build a good career, even though men have dominated as heads. But now there is something completely different. The recent changes have meant very different things for women and men. It's not just that women haven't done well in the reorganization of the school, though they certainly haven't. It's much deeper than that. New career paths are being institutionalized on gender grounds. All the increase in management and administrative posts and their exaggerated importance. They're seen as "masculine" jobs, aren't they?

There has been much work on the educational division of labour (Lawn and Grace 1987; Ozga 1988; Woods 1990a). One of the major omissions in this area has been an examination of the sexual division of labour in relation to support staff. At Parnell School, with the exception of the male school caretaker and science assistant, all the support staff were working-class women. Many of them spoke of the low esteem that they received from the teachers and students. One of the support staff, an Irish woman, who was actively involved in trade unionism, identified the gender hierarchy and the accompanying class and racial dynamics in operation within the school. The following accounts illustrate the way in which teacher and student masculinities were differentially lived out in relation to the support staff's subordinated femininity.

Bridget: Ever since I've been here little has changed for us. Like teachers would never invite us to meetings. It's like when you asked were we invited to the teachers' women's group. Of course we weren't and that says a lot, doesn't it?
M.M.: Like what?
Bridget: It's all about class. Most of the so-called feminists are like most of the rest of the teachers here. They wouldn't think of you. We're treated like working-class kids' mums. They don't see us unless they want something. It's like you've noticed the dinner women are treated much worse than the women teachers, especially by the older boys. They've just got no respect.
M.M.: There seems to be a lot of Irish women working here.
Bridget: The authorities take on the Irish women, and it's the same with the black women, not to serve the food, that's an important job but to control the kids because they think we can do it better.
M.M.: Why do you think that is?
Bridget: Don't ask me why. It's probably got to do with their racialist stereotypes about immigrant women producing too many kids, so we're supposed to be good at disciplining them. We have the experience, so they think! And they've got the cheek to talk about equal opportunities.
Leonie: The kids here have the most respect for Mr Trimble, then the men teachers. It's harder for the women teachers but we're at the bottom. To tell you the truth, I think the kids pick it up from the teachers, not to have respect for us. You get a few good ones but most of them don't care about us. They're only worried about the pupils when they're in lessons. It's us, us and the secretaries that run the rest of this school, that is the truth.

The female support staff's accounts provide further evidence of the need to contextualize the way in which institutional gender relations are constructed at school level. More specifically, we see the complex articulation of diverse sets of social relations and the resulting experiences of working-class women located at the base of the schooling workplace. Female teachers informed me that a main reason for their failure to identify publicly with the female support staff was their own immediate concerns with their subordinated occupational status in relation to male teachers. I now wish to link this to a discussion of the occupational gender ambiguity of contemporary secondary school teaching, which has differential implications for the positioning of female and male teachers.

Being a male teacher: Constructing middle-class gender-fractured identities

Connell (1985) writes of the apparent incompatibility between the conventional positioning of femininity and the disciplinary role of the teacher. He argues that:

> It is a tension about gender itself. Authority, in our society, is felt to be masculine; to assert it is to undermine one's femininity, in other people's eyes and one's own . . . The contradiction it creates in teaching is registered in the creation of the derogatory comic stereotypes of women teachers: the rigid spinster school-marm, the tweedy hockey mistress, and so on.
>
> (Connell 1985: 153)

At Parnell School, the male teachers and male students colluded in the construction of processes of social closure in relation to female teachers. As illustrated below, the former were particularly derogative in their representation of women in senior administrative positions.

Tony: Women have always found discipline difficult in schools. You're often called in to sort out the mess. And I think that has been accepted because they are not as strong as us and so forth. But now I think that there are new problems. Management teams have to act with intense competition from the local opposition. And this calls for a lot of new management skills women simply don't have.

M.M.: Do you mean women here or women in all schools?

Tony: I know you don't think this kind of thing should be said and I know I'm generalizing, but yes, in my experience, all women. Don't misunderstand me. I'm not blaming women. These are just natural differences.

M.M.: What do mean by natural?

Tony: Well, you know what I mean. Well strong differences that are in men and women and that's just the way it is, whatever you say.

Wayne (student): I would prefer a man in charge and most kids would. Even if you get a woman, she tries to act like a man. But the kids don't take her serious.

M.M.: Why do you think that is?

Wayne: Women teachers are okay in primary schools but not to be in charge in schools like this [secondary].

M.M.: Why should it matter if it's a woman or a man in charge?

Wayne: The bad kids give the school a bad reputation and the women teachers can't control them. It's like your mum and dad. You wouldn't expect your mum to take over your dad's job. It just doesn't look right, does it?

Connell (1985: 155) adds that teaching, which is often seen as a 'soft' job, is not however unambiguously masculine, because it involves emotional engagement and caring for children, which are traditionally defined as women's work. Classroom life is not predisposed to accommodate such emotional ambiguity, which challenges the gender-ascribed 'masculine' function of discipline and 'feminine' function of caring/nurturing, with their attendant juxtaposed connotations of physical strength and emotional vulnerability.

It is difficult for those outside of education to understand how emotionally demanding it is to be in a secondary classroom with over twenty-five young people, many of whom often don't wish to be there. It may be added that after a decade of central government directed media attacks on comprehensive school teachers, many of them are also increasingly ambivalent and resentful about being there. During the research period, I recorded the increasing levels of emotional turmoil and stress emanating from heightened fractured classroom relations. At the same time, the staffroom as the traditional inner-sanctum has given way to increased tensions of individual competitiveness regarding the highly differentiated financial and status rewards associated with the restructuring of teacher careers in the new regime of the schooling marketplace (Woods 1990a).

Kate: In the past, staff knew that teaching was about acting together, supporting each other. A big deal wasn't made of it. It was just taken for granted. And in some ways that's a more feminine approach, even in a place like this with mostly men teachers.

M.M.: What do you mean by it being a feminine approach?

Kate: Well I don't mean all women acted this way and men a different way. It's a cultural thing. Things like we are the ones bringing up the kids and that has to be a supportive thing. Now it's completely different. Everyone seems to be at each other's throats. It's the brave new masculine world of the survival of the strongest. Everyone is supposed to want to be a manager, to be on the SMT [senior management team], getting the big money, kudos, etc.

In order to understand more fully the specific sex/gender dynamics of management–teacher relations at Parnell School, it is necessary to examine the interrelationship between broader themes, such as the dominant

conceptions of power, authority, management and emotional commitment. Seidler (1988) locates the association of authority and masculinity
within the Enlightenment tradition, in which reason is defined in
opposition to nature, that is, our emotions, feelings and desires. He argues
that: 'in traditional masculinity terms we can only strive for independence
through releasing ourselves from all the forms of dependency. This makes
it difficult for men to acknowledge their emotions and needs without
feeling that their masculinity is somehow brought into question' (p. 286).

Within English middle-class culture, the emotional demands that
surround the ambiguity of their control and care functions tend not to get
talked about (Johnson 1991b). The following account was given by Emma,
an English teacher, after taking the lowest set in year ten, who were
regarded as one of the toughest teaching groups. She described the
individual and collective male strategies developed to distance themselves
from feelings of openness and vulnerability. Female teachers compared
male teachers' emotional illiteracy to that of their male partners.

Emma: I used to do a bit of drama at college. But the acting that you have
to do in the classroom is something else. It's realism, fantasy and nightmare
all in one. I'm absolutely shattered. You look around the staffroom and you
see the incredible stress, the burn-out of staff and you wonder how the
older teachers keep going.

M.M.:   Do you think that this is happening in other schools?

Emma: Definitely, it's the main thing that we talk about when you get
together with teachers from other schools. I think that there's a lot of
desperation in the classroom where you're really stuck on your own. It's
funny thinking about it, even when we talk about the really tough kids, we
always think of the troublemakers, we think of them, never of how we feel
unable to cope. I suppose that's where women are luckier. They're expected
or allowed to talk about how they feel.

M.M.:   What do teachers feel?

Emma: I think that people outside would be surprised at some of the bitter
humour and sarcasm used against the kids but it's part of school folklore
that enables teachers to survive in there. And then of course the tough
boys develop their own macho script of cynicism to hide their feelings and
so you end up with another generation of emotionally disabled men.

Following initial resistance from the male teachers to discuss emotional
issues, unexpectedly, from the middle period of the research, some of them
used the interview situation in a confessional mode. The ethical dilemmas
involved in research subject disclosure have been widely discussed in
feminist methodology (Oakley 1991; Skeggs 1992). At a personal level, I
found these teachers' accounts of their inner-dramas difficult to record –
listening to the private emotional turmoil that was translated into defensive
public performances of masculine affirmation and control. There is much
work to be done in this area of dichotomized private–public masculine
personae, a site that may be open to progressive interventions in sex/gender
relations (Jung 1936).

At Parnell School, there was a range of responses to the masculine construction and representation of teacher identities that were not conventionally gender-prescribed, including narratives of personal gender transformation. For example, Bill Stanton explained why he returned to an earlier professional concern with pastoral care and its relationship to his past career and present domestic arrangements.

Bill: Right now there's a lot of cynicism around about teaching and all the changes. That really all the changes are just stepping stones on the career ladder. I was into it until a few years ago when I split up with my partner. Not having the kids at home really shattered me. But like my partner said, when they were there, I never was. We're probably closer now than we were for a long time.

M.M.: How do you feel that you have changed at school?

Bill: That's a good question. I think that one of the ways, one of the main ways I'm trying to change, is to take on more of a pastoral than an administrative role at school, which is what I started out with. You wouldn't believe I came into teaching to help other working-class kids get some of the opportunities I got from the grammar [school]. I wanted to combine good teaching with a more caring approach. I think now that the pastoral can help you in your own emotional life at home. I suppose that makes it dangerous, so few men get involved. I just leave the management and administration of the place to the *real men*!

Peter Sheridan was a senior teacher in the humanities faculty. He explored the complex emotional interrelationship between what are frequently dichotomized in terms of the feminine 'private'/masculine 'public' worlds of professionals. In the interviews, there was a tendency for the male teachers to concentrate on the public arenas of work, career and politics. In contrast, many of the female teachers included talk about their domestic situations. For many of them, the domestic division of labour continued to be a major personal issue to which few of the male teachers appeared to be sympathetic.

Peter: You get to a certain age and you wonder what's it all about. I've just gone forty which has been a turning point for me. I always say I came from a mixed marriage, my mother was a teacher and my father a businessman. He couldn't believe that I chose teaching over the business. To him it was women's work. I've always been closer to my mother emotionally but looking back I felt I needed my father's respect.

M.M.: Was this very important for you?

Peter: Thinking about it, that's where all my basic needs for male approval have stemmed from. So, I was into all this career stuff, head of department at this age, deputy head and then a headship. But I never believed in it, not really, and I was very unhappy and of course my relationships suffered. And in all that time I had no-one to talk to, to really talk to about how I felt. You see underneath I felt it would have been disloyal to my father, as though I was blaming him. I inherited from him a deep fear of failure.

M.M.: So, how have you coped?

Peter: I still have problems with it but now I model myself more on my mother. Of course she's a much better person than my father or I will ever be. I joined a men's support group. And now I think, yes teaching is seen as women's work in our society, but that's fine for me because it allows me to bring together and develop my emotional side at work and home. I am much happier now.

What is emphasized here is the need to bring together the social and psychic dimensions of modern workplaces, that is, the external constraints and internal pressures, feelings and fears, in order to understand more fully the implications of gendered practices. Interestingly, one of the unintended effects of the restructuring of the teaching labour process is that the intensification of work is increasing the tensions between the demands of home and work for men as well as women.

The occupational ambiguity of secondary school teaching provides a critical case-study of the internal fragility and relational dynamics of contemporary sex/gender boundaries. Bill Stanton and Peter Sheridan illustrate that gender categories that often appear as biologically fixed are historically and culturally constructed and are open to deconstruction. Having examined the impact of the restructuring of schooling on male teachers' identity formation, I will now describe how these changes have helped to shape male teachers' responses to male students. My particular focus is the interconnections between the school's social structure and the development of male student identities, which are examined in the next two chapters.

The ascendancy of an entrepreneurial curriculum: The production of student masculinities

Connell (1989: 191) has argued that the institutionalized structure of schooling is central to the production of masculine subjectivities: 'Broadly, the strongest effects of schooling on the construction of masculinity are the indirect effects of streaming and failure, authority pattern, the academic curriculum, and definitions of knowledge – rather than the direct effects of equity programmes or courses dealing with gender.' As indicated above, while the research was being carried out at Parnell School, the construction of an entrepreneurial curriculum project was in the ascendancy. The cumulative effect of the new vocationalist restratification, the restructured authority system with its accompanying disciplinary codes, the curriculum and testing stratification technologies, subject allocation and knowledge selection served to demarcate a range of hierarchically ordered masculinities and femininities.

In an earlier study (Mac an Ghaill 1992) at Parnell School, I reported from a students' perspective the contradictory effects of recent curriculum reforms. The official intention of creating student-centred innovation unintendedly had resulted in their exclusion, disorientation and deskilling.

Initially, I was confused by the teachers' assertion that the curriculum changes had been successful in developing student-centred strategies, while there was little evidence in the students' accounts of this taking place. Reading through the interview data, a possible solution emerged to the differing interpretations, which was based on the conventional masculine splitting of rationality and emotions. The curriculum coordinating team, most of whom were New Entrepreneurs, tended to use *quantitative* indices as evidence of the school's pedagogical shift. This included the *production* of departmental and pastoral policies which they claimed prioritized student needs, the development of courses that emphasized positively what the students could achieve, the introduction of new forms of assessment, including a Record of Achievement that enabled students to be involved actively in negotiating their learning, and training days to plan and prepare for the implementation of these changes. In contrast, the students' evaluation of these changes tended to be expressed in *qualitative* terms. They spoke of how they *felt* teacher–student interpersonal relations had deteriorated, with teachers having less direct classroom contact with them.

I suggested in this earlier study that the ascendancy of the grand metaphor of market forces may be seen to overshadow the essentially human social activity of teacher–student interaction. There appeared to be emerging a new bureaucratic schooling hierarchy of managerial techno-crats, an ideologically divided teaching force, whose interests were being directed to the 'new realism' of the competitive schooling marketplace, and an 'underclass' of excluded, confused students with whom teachers had little time to interact.

Cohen (1990: ix), writing of the reshaping of working-class identities, in relation to the youth labour market demands of 'post-industrial' capitalism notes that: 'the ideology of the enterprise culture has been institutionalised into particular pedagogic and disciplinary forms, and a new generation of working class children find themselves being schooled, or trained, for their subordinate roles in the political economy of Thatcherism'. At Parnell School, specific versions of student masculinities were structured by and acted out in response to specific pedagogic and disciplinary forms of the entrepreneurial curriculum. These are explored more fully in the next chapter, where I examine from male students' perspectives the interplay between changing institutionalized conceptions of academic 'success' and 'failure' and masculine identities. Here I wish to explore the curricular conditions that contributed to the production of dominant and subor-dinated student masculine subjectivities.

Most significantly, the curriculum stratification system was of primary importance in structuring student masculine and feminine identities. As Rattansi (1992: 22) has argued: 'Schools are predominantly institutional sites for the selection and deselection, for the allocation of students to different levels in status hierarchies of subjects in the curriculum and public examinations.' Until recently, these selective processes were embedded in the high-status academic/low-status vocational subject divide. At Parnell

School, TVE funding and private sponsorship of the school's information technology provided the material conditions that challenged the old academic/vocationalism dichotomy. The vocationalization of the curriculum at Parnell School, with its shift from a liberal–humanist schooling paradigm to a technical training paradigm, led to student restratification (Moore 1984). This involved the development of new internal hierarchies between high- and low-status vocational spheres. In turn, this has produced new processes of student deskilling and upskilling. So, for example, the students in the lowest sets tended to be directed into low-level, practical-based vocational subject areas, whose cultures continued to reflect the masculine world of manual labour, with its 'distinctive complex of chauvinism, toughness and machismo' (Willis 1977: 53). In contrast, a new route of social mobility was created for 'high-achieving' students located in the emerging high-status technological and commercial subject areas, such as business studies, technology and computer studies. The creation of this new high-status route was of particular importance for the male students, who were over-represented in these subjects.

M.M.:   But do you think the school contributes to this choice?
Graham: Well, like I said, we have tried to get girls in. But, yes I suppose you're right. We have gone for the boys, not just any boys. We are looking for highly motivated youngsters in our subject. The kind who would have been doing apprenticeships in my time. And they happen to be boys, so we put a lot of effort into selecting the best of them, now we are in a position to do that.

Heward (1991: 36), writing of the construction of private school masculinities, describes 'the process of psychic hardening, loneliness, the suppression of emotion, and the school's rigorous preparation for the academic competition to enter elite colleges as the means whereby the pupils are prepared for leadership positions in business, the professions and public life'. At Parnell School, elements of this selective pedagogical approach were in place. This found expression in the differential treatment of the top academic set, which helped to shape middle-class versions of masculinity, with an emphasis on academic individualism, intensified peer competition, sporting excellence, personal ambition and overt careerism.

Bernstein (1975, 1990), in his discussion of educational codes, argues that in order to understand schools as agents of cultural transmission, it is necessary to examine them in relation to the existing distribution of power and principles of control. More particularly, educational change must be located in the changing distribution of power and form of social control in the wider society. Bernstein sees educational knowledge as the most important determinant of the structure of school experience and discusses its realization through three message systems: curriculum, pedagogy and evaluation (see Roman and Christian-Smith 1988). As Wolpe (1988: 180) points out:

In comprehensive schools, the same stock of knowledge is not readily available to all pupils equally. The various techniques employed in the course of making "normalizing judgements" involving streaming and the demarcation of pupils on grounds of their "ability", and which largely correspond with class membership, are accompanied by the presentation of different forms of knowledge ... Nor is there any basis for believing that the new examination system will eradicate these differences: different levels will still continue to exist and operate.

Despite central government's political rhetoric that the National Curriculum offers entitlement to all students, increased differentiation and individuation are the organizing principles of the new curriculum and testing systems (DES 1988c). At Parnell School, the hierarchical dissemination of knowledge, mediated through the recently introduced Programmes of Study and Standard Attainment Targets apparatus, functioned as modern discursive resources to position students within fixed school subject identities (Kelly 1985).

Liam: I think what's missing in criticisms of national testing is an understanding of what we are doing to the kids. We've always worked with the idea of bright and less bright kids but now it's being institutionalized, with highly public labelling of the successes and the failures. And we've already seen the effects of this with the increased disillusionment and aggression with the lads and the girls in the lowest sets.

Henry: If you place schooling in the market, there has to be winners and losers. National testing is about quality control. We are going to have a whole generation of "SATed" kids. You end up reinforcing a two-tier system. In schools all the effort is going to go into the successful kids and more coercive controls for the losers, and as a teacher you don't want to be associated with the losers.

M.M.:   Is that happening a lot?

Liam: Yes, it's happening in all schools. The losers, especially the boys, are getting tougher and tougher to handle. They remind me of the secondary mod lads I used to teach, except that the kids now have the extra burden of the scrapheap to look forward to.

Another important change in the production and differential dissemination of gendered knowledges at Parnell School was the over-emphasized use of utilitarian forms of knowledge. Again this had particular significance for the low-set students, for whom new vocationalist courses were being devised in order to provide them with realistic expectations of the post-school situation, appropriate attitudes and 'transferable skills' for their place in the labour market. In contrast, male students in the Arts subjects were encouraged to explore knowledges and understandings from their own cultures, which included intuitions, feelings and desires.

Schools as state agents of social control have at their disposal a wide range of disciplinary instruments that constitute a central element of their

institutional political moral economy. These instruments of moral regulation have been identified by Wolpe (1988: 23) and include 'classroom
registers, school assemblies, different forms of punishment . . . school
uniform . . . and normalising judgements which involve ranking and
grading of pupils'. She adds: 'These judgements assess the pupils and
reduce them to what Foucault terms a coherent "normative order" (see
Foucault 1982)'. The links between the construction of the differentiated
masculinities and the stratification and regulation of the black and white
working-class students' school careers was made most visible by the latter's
over-representation in the 'non-academic' curriculum sets. Here, 'tough'
male teachers helped to create 'tough' student masculinities. At Parnell
School, new forms of authority and disciplinary codes were developed in
response to the linked concerns of competition in the local schooling
marketplace and the skilling regimes of central government employment
schemes. This manifested itself in terms of the introduction of new
educational technologies and new modes of student surveillance and
instruments of control, including increased monitoring and assessment.
This had specific implications for the 'non-academic' male students, who
were positioned by the school management as a major threat to the
projected self-representation of a modern, successful school in the local
market. Equally significant, the vocationalization of the curriculum was
discussed in terms of instilling social discipline, for this sector of
working-class students, that in the past had been provided by employment.

A main argument in this book is that schools actively produce teacher
and student masculine identities. This section has illustrated the historical
specificity of this cultural production, by mapping out the range of
masculinities that a post-ERA 'entrepreneurial curriculum' has made
available. Having delineated this general pattern, I now wish to examine in
more detail the specific institutional dynamics involved in the 'making of
men', with particular reference to the system of teacher sex/gender
typifications in operation at Parnell School.

Administrative systems of teacher sex/gender typifications: The making of men[4]

As suggested in the Introduction, a key issue that emerged during the
research was the question of what constitutes male students' heterosexuality. More specifically, I became interested in the constitutive cultural
elements of dominant modes of heterosexual subjectivity that informed
male students' learning to act like men within a school arena. These
elements consisted of contradictory forms of compulsory heterosexuality,
misogyny and homophobia, that were marked by contextual contingency
and ambivalence. Chapter 3 reports these findings from the male students'
perspective. It is argued in this book that heterosexuality is a highly fragile,

socially constructed phenomenon. The question that emerges here is, how does it become fixed as an apparently stable, unitary category? It is suggested that schools alongside other institutions attempt to administer, regulate and reify unstable sex/gender categories. Most particularly, this administration, regulation and reification of sex/gender boundaries is institutionalized through the interrelated social and discursive practices of staffroom, classroom and playground microcultures. Much work remains to be done on the specific dynamics of these processes at the local level of the school.

For Skeggs (1991: 128–9), the framing of sexuality within education can be characterized by three different regulative methods.

> The first, Foucault (1979) identifies as the internal discourse of the institution. Historically, he argues, the organisation of education was predicated upon the assumption that sexuality existed, that it was precocious, active and ever present. The second method of regulation involves the process of inclusion and deligitimation of certain forms of sexuality alongside inclusion and control of others . . . The third mechanism of regulation involves the prioritising of masculinity as the norm through the organisational structure and pedagogy of education. Taken together the processes of regulation and normalisation provide an interpretative framework of discourses of sexuality around a grid of possibilities which students draw from and are located within.

In this study, there was a major disjuncture between students' and teachers' discussion of the processes of normalization and regulation of heterosexuality. In Chapters 2 and 3, heterosexual male students provide accounts of how teachers actively contributed to the development of their sexual identities. In Chapter 4, heterosexual female students describe the collusion of male teachers and students in the promotion of dominant forms of heterosexuality. In Chapter 5, young gay male students point to the universality and naturalization of heterosexuality as the norm, and identify specific forms of institutional social regulation and boundary maintenance that operate at school level. In contrast, the male and female teachers attempted to make sexuality invisible, frequently subsuming it within a more general discourse of gender. Most of them informed me that they had never discussed with students different forms of sexuality other than heterosexuality. One main exception was in personal and social education lessons, where homosexuals were identified as a high-risk group for HIV/AIDS (I shall discuss the students' experience of sex/sexuality education at Parnell School in Chapter 5).

Much has been written from a sex-role perspective on teachers' gender typifications of female and male students. Historically, this work has been important in placing gender issues on progressive local state policy agendas. However, as argued in the Introduction, such an approach does not offer a sufficiently sophisticated lens with which to view the complexity, contradictions and contextual contingency of how different schools actively help to produce gendered and sexual student subjectivities. In one of the best early studies on gender stratification and teacher typifications, Stanworth (1983) points to the limitations of quantitative work that established that male and female teachers preferred to work with boys. She critiqued this work for failing to address the issue of the quality of the teacher–student interaction. Most significantly, this approach failed to understand that there was no straightforward relationship between prejudiced teachers and differential expectations of female and male students. Drawing on the work of Keddie (1971) and Davies (1975), Stanworth points to the disparities between teacher beliefs and classroom practices. Hence, she concludes that:

> We should not be surprised then when teachers who are strongly committed to equality of the sexes, nevertheless regard boys as more enthusiastic, more logical and more able to grasp new concepts – as was true of the teachers of fifth form pupils in the urban comprehensive studied by Lyn Davies.
>
> (Stanworth 1983: 22)

Sex-role theory is based on an idealist analysis of the curriculum, that reduces the sex/gender structuring of schooling to aberrant teacher prejudice, which is both consistent and systematically translated into practice. At Parnell School, such an explanation was insufficient to explain the complex social interaction of teachers and students in a male-dominated institution. Equally important is the necessity to go beyond the limitations of Walker's (1988) interactionist approach (Skeggs 1989). Rather, school processes of sex/gender typifications are constructed in and through complex matrices of oppression, which include social divisions of class, 'race'/ethnicity, age and disability. This involves concrete diverse social interactions, linked to socio-historical material conditions, belief systems and practices both within the schooling system and the wider society. Historically specific, contradictory sex/gender discourses and typifications are grounded in the social relations of schools (Askew and Ross 1988: 1–17). There is a need for a theoretical framework that focuses upon the complex dynamics of a politics of sex/gender differences within the schooling arena (Brah 1992). This might begin by de-essentializing the figure of the prejudiced male teacher, who is seen as unproblematically reproducing unitary male and female student subjects.

Walkerdine (1984) is particularly helpful in providing an innovative conceptual framework to explore the complexity of male teacher/female student interaction at the microcultural school level. She suggests that:

> What seems to be at issue is not a series of roles or simple identities or images which are fitted on to girls. Nor is it a matter of certain behaviours being "stereotypically feminine" and therefore allowed and others not. Rather, we need to understand the relationship

between those practices which not only define correct femininity and masculinity but which produce positions to occupy.

(Walkerdine 1984: 182)

More recently, a number of studies on the construction of school masculinity have emerged, which focus directly on teacher–student relations (Askew and Ross 1988; Beynon 1989). This work is theoretically important in placing teacher–student interaction within a wider framework of sex/gender power relations, with a particular emphasis on male violence. However, at Parnell School, I found the situation appeared to be more complex. For example, teacher sex/gender discourses and practices were highly contingent on specific contexts, such as staffroom, classrooms, playground or parents' meetings. Hence, the construction and mediation of masculine and feminine student typifications were embedded in a multiple set of power relations, in which a diverse range of material and discursive resources that teachers could draw upon were made available. Avis (1990: 125) captures the institutional dynamics of this more complex schooling arena, when he reminds us that:

The form of pedagogic relations that students experience will be the result of a number of processes, departmental traditions, teachers' subject cultures, and varying constraints under which teachers labour and their solutions to pedagogic problems and subsequent survival strategies.

The institutional contingency of teachers' gender typifications was illustrated by their diverse responses to the male student peer groups' routes through the school. Becker (1952) developed the concept of the 'ideal pupil', to refer to that set of teacher expectations which constitute a taken-for-granted notion of appropriate behaviour. Keddie (1971: 55) has argued that of primary importance to the creation of the 'ideal pupil' are social class judgements of pupils' social, moral and intellectual behaviour. In earlier work (Mac an Ghaill 1988c), I found that teachers tended to identify with middle-class students and saw them as constituting the 'ideal pupil'. Of particular interest at Parnell School was the different teacher reponses to the intra-class school orientations of working-class sub-groups and their accompanying projected masculinities. There was no simple match between teacher perspective and student peer groups but certain tendencies were in operation, resulting in teachers 'sponsoring' individual student routes through the school system. One of the main teacher functions in relation to the New Enterprisers and the Academic Achievers was that of acting as agents of social mobility.

This function has a long tradition in state schools in relation to fractions of the working-class. What has been commented upon less is the gendering of these sponsorships, which at Parnell School were key mechanisms in the formation of a range of student masculinities. This is not to argue that students simply reduplicated or reflected the dominant teacher class and gender ideologies. Nor is it to argue that mutual identification of the teachers and the student sub-groups was consciously created. Rather, there was an internal logic to each group's material practices, ideologies and discourses. However, their logics did intersect at important points. So, for example, there was a convergence between the New Entrepreneur male teachers and the New Enterprise male students, who shared elements of a modern mode of masculinity that was in the ascendancy within the school. Similarly, the Academic Achievers were one of the most popular male student groups with a wide range of male teachers. The Old Professionals praised the Academic Achievers' enthusiasm and intrinsic interest in academic values, contrasting it with the New Enterprisers' utilitarianism and the Macho Lads' disinterest. The Old Liberals, many of whom had working-class origins, strongly identified with the Academic Achievers, praising their diligence and sympathizing with the difficulties of the male student social mobility project.

The teachers spoke of the relational dynamics of their identification with and against different student masculinities. For example, the Old Collectivist female teachers tended to be more positive than their male peers to the white middle-class New Men's modes of contestation, with its emphasis on elaborated verbal self-justification, than the openly threatening Macho Lads' behaviour (see Aggleton 1987a). Many of the male teachers were also critical of the Macho Lads' contestation. However, in relation to the middle-class New Men's behaviour, these male teachers sympathized with the former group.

Lucy: I think that most women teachers would say that Tom's group [new middle-class students] may be frustrating with the way they miss lessons, fail to hand in work on time and generally underachieve. But they're not malicious or aggressive. They are working through a difficult adolescent phase. They will usually argue out their case. They get into a lot of trouble because of such rules on dress and hairstyles that are rather oppressive. A lot of teachers forget what it's like to be young.

Kieron: I'm not trying to condone the irresponsibility of the working-class lads. They're tough and at times quite a handful but at least they're more straight forward than those half hippie middle-class kids. The lads have a tough background and work around here has disappeared. There's not much motivation for them to work hard. And then at fifteen, sixteen the school's basically the worst place for them, treating them like kids. But the middle-class kids have got it all going for them. They'll never apologize or accept that they're wrong. They always have to prove they're right. This happens from the younger years. And the teachers, especially the Heathfield crowd [new middle-class residential area], protect them and excuse them because they've got their sophisticated middle-class talk and rationalizations, their emotional crises and all of that. You can be sure that none of them with all their connections will end up on a training scheme or on the dole.

In the following accounts, female teachers provide some clues to male teachers' ambiguity and contradictory involvement in the construction of the school's hierarchy of student masculinities. At one level, macho male teachers confronted macho male students in their attempt to maintain social control. In this process, the male teachers acted out their responses within an arena, where they took for granted the legitimacy of dominant authority forms. This had serious implications for the female teachers at the school, whom the male teachers criticized for their weak disciplinary control of male students. At another level, authoritarian male teachers colluded with male students' contestation of schooling, which served to confirm and celebrate a normative macho mode of masculinity that many male teachers identified with, highly valued and amplified.

Emma: Adam's crowd have a lot more trouble with male teachers. You know the older men envious of the younger generation. They are at a very attractive age, experimenting and exploring their sexual identities. Some of the more macho teachers have a problem, for example because the group don't believe in competitive sport. These teachers prefer the yobbo footballers, romanticizing their aggressive rebellion. Oh, they'll be tough with the yobs but at the same time you can see them passing on the masculine codes that boys will be boys. All the usual male bonding that cuts across age and status differences.

These teacher sex/gender typifications intersected with racist typifications. However, it is important to stress that these were not linear institutional processes. Parnell School consisted of a highly complex racial map of teacher–student relations, on which there was a wide range of positions from assimilationism to anti-racism. The white teacher/black student social relations were marked by diverse and fragmentary responses from different subject teachers. Furthermore, there were contradictory elements within the teachers' representations of each ethnic group, without which the racist classification could not form a system of knowledge. White teachers selectively drew on contradictory racist constructs in interacting with male and female students. These teachers' differential responses appeared to be particularly influenced by the different sets students were in. As Rattansi (1992: 27–8) argues:

An appreciation of contradiction, ambivalence and context, combined with a sensitivity to the variability of discourses among teachers and their practices also puts into question simplistic models of process whereby [uncontradictory] teacher stereotypes of black pupils are supposedly translated into discriminatory practices that lead to unequal outcomes. Recent research paints a more complex picture of contradictory teacher attitudes varying within and between schools and provoking a range of responses from male and female students.

During the research period, white teachers were in the process of constructing a new hierarchy of ethnic masculinities. Until this time, African Caribbean working-class males were positioned as the most anti-authority of students. They were currently being displaced by Muslim working-class males as the new folk devils, with the accompanying negative categorization, typification and moral evaluation. A racial discourse was in the process of being constructed that was linked to the wider demonization of the Muslim community. Most recently, this has been articulated by the Conservative MP, Winston Churchill.[5] At the same time, this was a gendered discourse with Muslim young men being positioned by teachers at Parnell School as the most sexist of male students.

Stewart: I have been saying it for a long time that with the our ethnic minority children, we have a real problem with the Muslims. I think we have been more aware of the problems with the Muslim girls because of their cultural restrictions. But we haven't faced up to the alienation of some of the Muslim boys and we have some very tough ones here.

Maureen: You end up having to decide between discriminations. If you want to do anything on the gender front, there's a backlash from Muslims about differences in culture. But I don't think it is acceptable. The girls and most especially the Muslim girls are discriminated against in schools and we have to address that, but it's not very easy to know what to do. At times it's like a mine field!

It is argued in this book that in order to understand the sex/gender regime in operation at Parnell School, it is necessary to examine it in relation to other sets of power relations. This was a particularly clear example of the complex intersection between different matrices of institutional power. Furthermore, as indicated above, these interconnections of social oppressions were played out in the racialized terms of white teachers speaking of the difficulties of implementing progressive gender policies as a result of assumed culturally regressive Muslim gender practices.

Summary

In this chapter, I have examined the interplay between current central government education policy, male teacher responses and the shaping of modes of masculinity that are made available to teachers and students. My emphasis has been on the particular dynamics of the institutional cultural production and regulation of sex/gender categories, within a historically specific post-ERA 'entrepreneurial curriculum'. It is against this background of the remasculinization of school structures and processes that I shall locate students' construction of heterosexual masculine identities, which are described in the following two chapters.

2

Local student cultures of masculinity and sexuality

In spite of [the] longstanding recognition of the importance of pupil cultures to the educational process, relatively little work exists on either sexual cultures themselves or their impact on the effectiveness of sexuality education. However, the work that does exist gives a clear sense of the need for sexuality education to take pupils' sexual cultures as its starting place and to recognise the relations of power that are built into these.

(Redman, in press)

Introduction

Chapter 1 suggested that schools were active agents in the making of teacher and student masculinities. Chapters 2 and 3 focus upon heterosexual male students' accounts, which serve to deconstruct earlier male academic representations of young men's schooling. More specifically, in this chapter I wish to examine the way in which heterosexual male students develop a mode of masculinity in relation to the social structure of a secondary school. Of particular importance here is the restratification of state schooling and the development of the new vocationalist curriculum in preparing working-class young men for differentiated labour market destinies. In short, new ways of being a male student are emerging. I also wish to illustrate the limitations of earlier models of student identity formation. Contemporary modes of masculinity are highly complex and contradictory, displaying power, violence, competition, a sense of identity and social support. The substantive focus of this chapter is a number of working-class heterosexual peer groups: the Macho Lads, the Academic Achievers, the New Enterprisers and the new middle-class Real Englishmen. The case-study approach enabled a critical exploration of their values, self-representations and social practices. Alongside the school and local labour markets, students' relations with their families were identified as critical in the cultural production of masculinities. The final section focuses upon white ethnicity, racism and sexuality, which unexpectedly arose as of particular significance in the study.

Differentiated curriculum, differentiated masculinities: The rise of new vocationalism

One of the main developments from the original conception of the study's research design was an increased awareness of the centrality of the official curriculum in making available different versions of masculinity that the students could inhabit. As Askew and Ross (1988: 43) tentatively suggest from their research, there may be 'a direct association between the school organisation, policies on discipline and teaching methods, and the gender behaviour and relations we observed'. More specifically, Connell (1989: 295) has argued that:

> the differentiation of masculinities occurs in relation to a school curriculum which organises knowledge hierarchically and sorts students into an academic hierarchy. By institutionalising academic failure via competitive grading and streaming, the school forces differentiation on the boys. But masculinity is organised on the macro scale – around social power. Social power in terms of access to higher education, entry to professions, command of communication, is being delivered to the boys who are academic "successes". The reaction of the "failed" is likely to be a claim to other sources of power, even other definitions of masculinity. Sporting prowess, physical aggression, sexual conquest may do.

At Parnell School, I found that the institutional categorization of 'academic' and 'non-academic' routes through school and the accompanying teacher–student social relations were crucial elements in the cultural production of different masculinities. Colin Lacey's (1970) work on classroom polarization–differentiation processes helped to orientate my study. Specific masculinities were structured and lived out within the stratified curriculum system at Parnell School. However, the relationship between masculine formation and location within the hierarchically ordered curriculum appeared to be more complex than Connell and Lacey imply. First, at the time of the research, most of the students who were in the lowest sets did not necessarily interpret their school experience in terms of failure. A defining characteristic of their social identity was the projection of a publicly confident heterosexual masculinity. It should be added that Connell's work is based on life-history interviews with adult men recalling their school days. Interestingly, in follow-up interviews with low-stream students, most of whom were on low-status training schemes or unemployed, in retrospect they now considered their secondary schooling in terms of failure. Second, as is suggested in the last chapter, a major effect of the new vocationalist curriculum was the restructuring of the stratification system at Parnell School. This resulted in the redefining of school 'success' and 'failure' and the accompanying masculinities.

Earlier ethnographic representations of white male youth cultures illustrated working-class students' sub-cultural agency and creativity in response to their experiences of stratified school curricula (Willis 1977; Aggleton 1987a). This work has been important in moving beyond state and teacher psychology-based perspectives that are grounded in a dominant English empiricist epistemology. These official social regulatory perspectives, in their explanation of differential schooling outcomes and social destinies, focus upon individual 'problem students', excluding institutional social and discursive practices. Furthermore, politically and theoretically, the early ethnographic work has been important in emphasizing working-class young people's active construction of subordinated masculinities within the interrelated nexus of: schools 'that do nothing but boss them about' (Corrigan 1979), their survivalist peer-group cultures; adolescent psychosexual development; and the anticipation of their future location on low-status training schemes, in low-skilled local labour markets. More recent studies have described how black working-class male students at secondary school level have creatively responded to racially regulated curriculum and pedagogical systems (Gillborn 1990; Mac an Ghaill 1992).[1]

'Modern' male youth peer groups: Local sex/gender cultures[2]

As Connell (1989: 295) suggests, the differentiation of masculinities cannot simply be understood in terms of individual choice. Rather, it is a collective project operating at 'the level of the institution and the organisation of peer group relations'. At Parnell School, male peer-group networks constituted the institutional infrastructure, within which a range of social and sexual identities were negotiated and ritualistically projected. They were a key feature of the student microculture, providing a material and symbolic safe space within which to develop social and discursive practices that served to validate and amplify their masculine reputations. Here, young male students learnt the heterosexual codes that marked their rite of passage into manhood.

Informed by earlier ethnographic work on masculine formations and current work on the impact of recent curriculum policy changes on student cultures, I set out to delineate a range of male peer groups at Parnell School

(Willis 1977; Avis 1990; Woods 1990b; Mac an Ghaill 1992). The exploration of these peer groups may provide a conceptual map, on which to try to make sense of students' masculine formation in terms of their own intercultural meanings within the local conditions of a secondary school (Hollands 1990: 138; Parker 1992). A main criterion in my selection of the student groups was their differing relationships to schooling. The more traditional working-class male peer group of the Macho Lads (academic 'failures') and the upwardly mobile Academic Achievers (academic 'successes') were visible. Alongside these I identified the new middle-class Real Englishmen and the working-class New Enterprisers. With the exception of the Real Englishmen, I have created these categories, that the young men did not use about themselves.[3]

As indicated in the last chapter, there are real limitations in using typologies that often serve to mask the complex meanings that are reductively represented in the selected types. It is adopted here as a heuristic device to highlight the range of masculinities produced in Parnell School. However, it is argued that these are not fixed unitary categories, as earlier representations of peer groups and youth culture have suggested. Connell *et al.* (1982) remain a notable exception. Writing of the different kinds of relationship that students have with school and how these relationships are produced, they warn that:

> No relationship with school exists in isolation, each is conditioned by the presence of others. Second, we are speaking of forms of relationship, not *kinds* of individuals . . . Most kids do find a way of dealing with school . . . [in a more settled way], partly because there is in school life a strong tendency to type-cast kids. Not least along lines of gender.
>
> (Connell *et al.* 1982: 92–3)

Aggleton's (1987a: 120–23) work is also of theoretical importance here. In critiquing the static nature of youth typologies, he calls for a generative grammar of principles that would account for strategies of student responses and their potential transformations. Drawing on Bernstein's (1982) work, Aggleton provides an imaginative framework within which to examine different modes of resistance and contestation: the former being concerned with challenges against 'relations of power structuring relationships between groups'; the latter being concerned with challenges against 'principles of control operating within particular settings'. He illustrates the wide explanatory power of the grammar, which has general application to different cultural groups.[4]

With the exception of the white Real Englishmen's group, the peer groups consisted of white, African Caribbean and Asian students. The groups tended to be more fluid and ill-defined than in much of the writing reported in the 1970s on spectacular working-class youth sub-cultures, 'although there was a number of so called "revivals" as well as continuities in fashion' (Hollands 1990: 152). The students recalled friendship patterns that were initially based on attending a common primary school, but which had given way to a wider peer choice in the upper school. The young men also spoke of having different friendship groups – some influenced by common residence, their parents being friends, or particular shared subject, music or sporting interests. They felt that current youth sub-cultural identity was less fixed than in the past as a result of the fusions of popular musical styles. Sullivan (1993: 4) reports a similar trend in her interview with the band Megadog, in which she suggests that 'the recession has brought about a strange coalition of crusties, ravers and hip-hoppers in a new anti-cult cult'.

William: You wouldn't dress like a band you were into like they did in the past. I mean you couldn't because they have different images themselves. And a lot of different music has come together. It's more mixed up.
Eamonn: For our parents music brought people together more, the clothes and everything. But not now, everything's retro or a bit taken from here and there. Like house music, the raves and all, it's just totally anonymous. It doesn't mean anything.

It is also important to note what might be called the 'ordinary kids' who inhabit non-academic peer groups, which are marked by indifference rather than overt resistance to the official school curriculum. In his discussion of 'ordinary kids', Jenkins (1983: 51) makes the point that there is a certain boundary fluidity between such students and those who adopt a more specific peer-group sub-cultural stance (see also Wolpe 1988; Brown 1989).

One of the main weaknesses of earlier male ethnographic research on young males was the failure to note how intra-class variations, among an internally divided working-class, helps to shape school masculinities (Cohen 1983). I found the interplay of masculinities, intra-class variations and ethnicities highly generative of diverse gender/sexual identities. This is critically important with the recomposition of the working-class in the late 1980s and early 1990s. A crucial element of this recomposition is the current crisis in schooling, and the state response in terms of a new vocationalist curriculum and training regimes that have served to disrupt working-class students' transitions into work (Finn 1987; Hollands 1990).

Feminist scholarship in this area, employing a multidimensional view of power, has not received the attention it deserves. It has addressed itself to major flaws in male ethnographic representations of schooling and masculinity (Griffin 1985a; Skeggs 1988; Bhavnani 1991). One such flaw has been identified by Skeggs (1993) in her critical review of Paul Willis' (1977) *Learning to Labour*. She argues that he failed to theorize how sexuality pervades the power structure of the classroom, and in so doing adopts a reductionist reading of the anti-school 'Lads' behaviour towards women 'as a product of their resistance rather than as a legitimation and articulation of power and domination'. As Skeggs claims, the limitations in such work have now been surpassed by feminist scholars such as McRobbie (1991) and Walkerdine (1990a).

Cockburn (1987: 44) makes clear the complexity of gender resistance, with some young men ridiculed for refusing a macho-style masculinity, while 'others resist the class domination of school precisely by means of masculine codes'. It may be added that for black students the adoption of specific masculine codes of contestation and resistance are also developed in response to schools' racist social and discursive practices. At Parnell School, black students were aware of the historical and current contradictions of black masculinity, with the denial of the patriarchal privileges of power, control and authority that is ascribed to the white male role (Mercer and Julien 1988: 112).

The links between the male students' differing relations to schooling and their developing masculine identities were highlighted in their contrasting narratives. I have summarized these in the following terms: that of the Macho Lads' 'survival against authoritarianism', the Academic Achievers' 'ladders of social mobility', the New Enterprisers' 'making something of your life' and the Real Englishmen's 'looking for real experiences'. These links were further displayed by the students' differential participation in and celebration of formal and informal school rituals, through which masculine subjectivities are constructed and lived out, such as attendance at prize-giving and involvement in the playground smoking gang (Griffin 1993).

The Macho Lads: The three Fs – fighting, fucking and football

At Parnell School, a system of setting was in place. All of the Macho Lads were in the bottom two sets for all subjects. For some, this was a result of demotion, while others were placed there on their arrival at the school. Orientations towards school began to crystallize during year nine. The Macho Lads came together as they found other male students with similar negative responses. Their shared view of the school was of a system of hostile authority and meaningless work demands (see Mac an Ghaill 1988c). They were seen by teachers and students as the most visible anti-school male sub-culture. 'Looking after your mates', 'acting tough', 'having a laugh', 'looking smart' and 'having a good time' were key social practices. As is indicated below, it was 'your [male] mates' who were the significant others in relation to evaluating what school is 'really about' and 'where you are going in the future'. Their vocabulary of masculinity stressed the physical ('sticking up for yourselves'), solidarity ('sticking together') and territorial control ('teachers think they own this place')(see Corrigan 1979; Cockburn 1983; Jenkins 1983).

John: The main way that we protect ourselves is by sticking together [as a gang]. From about the end of the third year a group of us got together and we now have a reputation. A lot of the teachers and the kids won't mess with us and we protect other kids.

Darren: I suppose a lot of kids here are able to defend themselves but it's the teachers that make the rules. It's them that decide that it's either them or us. So you are often put into a situation with teachers where you have to defend yourself. Sometimes it's direct in the classroom. But it's mainly the headcases that would hit a teacher. Most of the time it's all the little things in the place really.

M.M.:   Like what?

Gilroy: Acting tough by truanting, coming late to lessons, not doing homework, acting cool by not answering teachers, pretending you didn't hear them; that gets them mad. Lots of different things.

Peer-group masculine identities were developed in response to the school's differentiated forms of authority. This was highly visible in relation to the Macho Lads' experience of the school's social relations of domination, alienation and infantilism that were mediated through their location in the lowest sets. These social relations were of central importance in the construction of their masculinity through 'conflict with the institutional authority of the school' (Connell 1989: 291; Johnson 1991a).

In the last chapter, I discussed different teacher functions. In relation to the Macho Lads, the primary function was that of policing, which tended to make explicit the construction and moral regulation of teacher and student subjectivities (Walkerdine 1990a). The school disciplinary regime operated in more overt authoritarian modes of interaction with this sector of students. The school's moral imperatives, which included a wide range of disciplinary instruments, were translated into the surveillance of the Macho Lads' symbolic display of working-class masculinity. The senior management, who were becoming experts at decoding the semiotic communication of contestation and resistance, legislated new control and surveillance mechanisms for these 'non-academic' students. At this time there was a vigilant policing, and subsequent banning, of the anti-school male students' clothes, footwear, hairstyles and earrings. This was accompanied by a high-profile surveillance of the students' bodies, with the constant demands of such teacher comments as: 'Look at me when I'm talking to you', 'sit up straight' and 'walk properly down the corridor' (Bourdieu 1986).

As Westwood (1990: 59) notes: 'Discourses as registers of masculinity are worked through a variety of spaces.' Spatially, Parnell School was geared to a set pattern of movement, which systematically discriminated against low-set students, who were viewed with suspicion if during breaks they were found in certain academic locations, such as the science laboratories or computer centre. These students frequently complained about the prefects' arbitrary power as they patrolled corridors and restricted their movement around the school.

Paul: We have different names for the teachers: big ears, big nose, big eyes and that sort of thing.

M.M.:   What does it mean?

Jim: It's obvious. Teachers are always trying to catch you out. They're always trying to rule you. They use different means, some are really nosey, others try to catch you smoking and then others are always trying to get you to tell on your mates.

As Mayes (1986: 29) makes clear, in writing of the culture of school masculinities:

> A masculine ideal which allows competition and aggressive individualism may take its toll. The alternative status sought by the boys who fail in the system may result in an aggressively "macho" stance, dangerous to themselves and others.

The Macho Lads rejected the offical three Rs (reading, writing and arithmetic), and the unofficial three Rs (rules, routines and regulations). They explained why they opted for the three Fs – fighting, fucking and football (Jackson 1968). They interpreted their secondary school biographies as masculine apprenticeships in learning to be 'tough'. Like the 'anti-school' Asian male students, the 'Warriors', in *Young, Gifted and Black* (Mac an Ghaill 1988c), the Macho Lads objected to the *function* not the *style* of teachers, which they saw as primarily causal of school conflict. They refused to affirm the teachers' authority, claiming that it was illegitimate authoritarianism. Spending more time 'on the streets' than other students increased their visibility to the police. Hence, they linked teacher and police authoritarianism, seeing themselves as vulnerable to both state agencies of social control. In response to institutionalized surveillance and interrogation, they developed a specific version of masculinity, around collective strategies of counter-interrogation, contestation and survival (Mac an Ghaill 1988c: 136). Their accounts reminded me of the under-reported experiences of young people in Northern Ireland, who have a longer history of dealing with the 'harder face' of the state, in the context of the British military occupation.

Kevin: I'll tell you something, when we came to this dump we believed in the three Rs, we were right little piss artists, real plonkers. Well we learnt what schools were for, for keeping you down and bossing you about. Over the last couple of years we've been doing the three Fs.
Arshad: When kids come here in the first year, you can see that they're not tough. It's the main thing that you have to learn.
M.M.: Is it very important?
Arshad: In some ways, real ways, you know what I mean, you won't survive. You see the whole place is planned to boss you around. That's the main difference between here and posher schools. Somehow the kids in the posh schools accept it more.
Leon: The teachers think, I'm going to put this little sod down because he thinks he can rule the place. The kid isn't thinking that but the teachers think that he is.
M.M.: Why do the teachers think that?
Leon: I don't know. Teachers have to win all the time, don't they? So, I

don't know, maybe they think, I'll get him before he gets me, you know what I mean?

Noel: Teachers are always suspicious of us [the Macho Lads]. Just like the cops, trying to set you up.

Like Willis's Lads, the Macho Lads at Parnell School made a similar association of academic work with an inferior effeminacy, referring to those who conformed as 'dickhead achievers'. Consequently, they overtly rejected much school work as inappropriate for them as men. They were also a pivotal group within the school in creating a general ethos in which the academic/non-academic couplet was associated with a feminine/ masculine division for a wider group of 'ordinary' male students, who were not overtly anti-school (Jenkins 1983).

Leon: The work you do here is girls' work. It's not real work. It's just for kids. They [the teachers] try to make you write down things about how you feel. It's none of their fucking business.

Kevin: We live in the real world. The world where we are going to end up in – no work, no money with the stupid, slave training schemes. We've gotta sort this out for ourselves, not teachers. They live in their little soft world. They wouldn't survive in our world for five minutes. Now I'm leaving I feel sorry for them. Well, for some of them, some were wicked bastards to the kids.

Arshad: They [the teachers] just look down on us. They think we're nothing because they say, "you're like your brothers, they never got on to good training" [youth training schemes]. Some of them will do the caring bit. "I come from Yorkshire lad, my dad was down the pit and I know what the real world is like." Do they fuck. I wouldn't even ask them, what do you know about being a black man looking for work, when even the white kids round here haven't got work.

The Academic Achievers

The Academic Achievers consisted of a small group of male friends who had a positive orientation to the academic curriculum. In contrast to the recent emergence of the New Enterprisers (discussed below), the Academic Achievers were reminiscent of grammar school 'scholarship boys', adopting the more traditional upwardly social mobile route via academic subject credentialism. There was a high proportion of Asian and white young men from a skilled working-class background represented in this group. However, they did not fit into a homogeneous pattern of being unambiguously pro-school. Rather, their appropriation of the curriculum involved complex social practices, informed by varied cultural invest-ments. There was a range of shifting responses within a broadly positive relationship to the academic curriculum, that included criticism of the teacher practices of infantilism and disciplinary inconsistency (Hollands 1990: 69–73).

As was reported at Kilby School (Mac an Ghaill 1988c), the stages of the students' career at Parnell School were structured so that the teachers' main concern was the needs of the top stream. The Academic Achievers were among those students who had a number of material and social advantages, including: permanent teaching locations, although there was a shortage of classrooms; access to specialist classrooms; provision of the most experienced teachers; the first choice of option subject choices in year nine; and preferential treatment in terms of timetabling, equipment and books. The hidden curriculum was of equal importance in terms of the teachers' high esteem and positive expectations of them. These cumulative material and social conditions helped to shape an institutionally confident student masculinity that was highly valued by the teachers.

I was particularly interested in how working-class male students developed a masculine identity within the context of the contradictions of their participation in the conventional 'feminine' curriculum sector of the arts. During year ten, the Academic Achievers, who spent much of their leisure time in the drama department, became publicly associated with 'feminine' arts subjects. This was made manifest on one occasion, when students severely ridiculed them for their involvement in a play, in which three of them took female roles. For them, this was a continuation of the bullying that they had experienced in their earlier years at the school (Gillborn 1993).

Ashwin: We were in the school band and they would really take the piss, saying we were girls because we carried round violins and that. And then we got into drama, the macho mob were really bad, everyday threatening and punishing us. But now, they still say things but we feel safer and most of the time we just ignore them and don't come in contact with them.

Tony: Me and Ashwin got the worst, picked on every day by the yobs and then the others would start. They'd be in their gangs. It sounds funny but I think it was little things like looking small, I was tiny then, and both of us wore glasses, things like that.

M.M.:   So those things would be picked up then?

Tony: Some kids got much worse. There was a kid who had a limp and they persecuted him for years.

It is important to note here Tony's comments that make clear how bullying is linked to perceptions of a wide range of disabilities (Morris 1991). As Carlen *et al.* (1992: 102) have pointed out:

Gender discipline is not imposed only on young women: normalization programmes for young men are also steeped in gender assumptions about masculinity. Thus although women defined as lacking femininity are likely to be seen as a greater threat because of the way in which the patriarchal construction of the family is a necessary constituent of present capital–labour relations, young men constructed as being less than "masculine" are also likely to come under suspicion and surveillance.

A number of the teachers and the students positioned the Academic Achievers as 'effeminate'. The latter's self-representation and their stance on gender stereotyping was complex. On the one hand, by year eleven, as a result of being physically stronger, having a safe space in the drama department and one of the English teacher's protection, they responded creatively and innovatively to student and teacher heterosexist discursive resources that were employed against them. Their creativity involved parodying and subverting dominant institutional sex/gender meanings. At the same time, they strongly differentiated between masculine and feminine sensibilities within 'feminine' school subjects.

Tony: I think we're more confident now. You have to be in this school. It wasn't just the low-set kids but the men teachers would always be getting at you in little ways.

M.M.:   Like what?

Tony: Oh, stupid things, like put away your handbags or stuff about marrying us off because we stuck around together. I think it helped being in drama. We got more confident with language and how to respond with humour. Like in a school like this, a lot of the male teachers are very defensive, very macho and they've got a lot of power to put you down in front of everyone. So, we just started talking together about taking on the sexual jokes and camping it up. And they just couldn't cope with it. It was great.

M.M.:   Remember in class when Darren said that English literature and drama were girls' subjects? What would you say to that?

Edward: It's just typical. It's different for girls and blokes even if they are doing the same subjects. Girls like feminine writers and all the emotional stuff like they get in their magazines. It's completely different for a bloke. He's more into how to become more like expert, you know what I mean? Like if you look at a lot of the people who write about English Lit, they're nearly all men, like Andy's father lectures at the uni [university].

M.M.:   Why do you think that is the case?

Parminder: Because even if you're doing the same subjects, men and women have completely different things that they're interested in. I think that men would be more intellectual and women more emotional. They just feel different things.

The Academic Achievers illustrate the complexity of students' cultural investment in a specific masculinity. Despite successfully challenging heterosexist jibes, nevertheless they continued to operate within conventional gender essentialist categories.

A main argument of this book is that we need to consider not only gender *differences* but also *relations between* young men and women and *within* young men's peer groups. It is important to see masculinity not simply as complementary to femininity, which tends to reinforce perceived unitary conceptions and 'natural' binary differences. Masculinities are also developed in specific institutional contexts in relation to and against each other. As Heward (1991: 38) reported in her study of public school masculinities, early male identities 'were forged in peer groups with the immediate end of surviving in the competition . . . for friendship, influence and power'. Later in the chapter, this is explored in more detail with reference to the interrelationship of the peer group identities. Equally important to the Academic Achievers' masculine formation were the specific dynamics of the class continuities and discontinuities in relation to the Real Englishmen (discussed below) and the Macho Lads, both of whom ridiculed the Academic Achievers for their school work ethic. The Academic Achievers appeared to be developing a masculine identity in which they would not 'feel at home' either among the middle-class or sectors of the working-class (Walkerdine 1991).

Parminder: Sometimes you wonder if all the learning and study is worth it, you just get down in yourself. You lose mates and you can't really get on with the snobs. I mean you wouldn't want to, would you?
M.M.:   So what keeps you going?
Parminder: I don't know. I like the work a lot of the time and I want to get on and that's what my family wants. I wouldn't like to be like the dossers here. My brother's like them. He's just wasting his life.

Corrigan and Frith (1976: 236) have argued that 'working-class experience, even of bourgeois institutions, is not bourgeois experience'. Similarly, Jenkins (1983: 42) reminds us that working-class academic success is not the same as middle-class success. The Academic Achievers may be in the process of equipping themselves for social mobility and a middle-class post-school destination, but 'it is largely on indigenous working-class principles and practices that they draw'. This was clearly illustrated in relation to the way in which the Academic Achievers were developing an academic identity that was informed by a strong working-class work ethic in contrast to the new middle-class Real Englishmen's 'effortless achievement' (this is explained below) (Aggleton 1987a). For the Academic Achievers, their positive response to school was not reducible to a material utilitarian concern with the gaining of qualifications. Equally important was the symbolic significance of the latter, acting as a public sign of their own high cultural position. There was evidence of their ambiguous relationship to middle-class cultural capital that combined desire and fear. They spent long hours on homework assignments and revising for internal tests and examinations. However, in contrast to the Real Englishmen, they were reticent in class, lacking confidence to articulate what they knew, or question what they didn't. Their fear manifested itself in relation to the Real Englishmen, who embodied what the Academic Achievers desired. Whereas they could easily dismiss the Macho Lads' derisory comments, they were openly intimidated by the Real Englishmen's contempt, feeling unable publicly to match what appeared as sophisticated verbal exchanges.

Mark: You know the Heathfield crowd [new middle-class residential area] are full of bullshit. They're just wankers. But they still make you feel low. They know how to talk to teachers. They share more things, going to the theatre and art galleries and they all go round reading books. And with their background, it's easy for them to be clever. If I have kids, I'll give them the best education because that's what really matters. So they won't feel out of it. So no-one can look down on them.

Andy: A lot of the kids take the piss out of us. But it's different with different groups. With the low-set boys, they're more physical and say bad things you get used to. They're dickheads really. But with the middle-class ones, it's more difficult. They're real snides. When they're all together, they can put you down bad and what can you do? They've got all this alternative humour. I don't even understand it, using big words and all that business.

A central element of the Academic Achievers' masculine identity was their projected future of a professional career. They frequently spoke of their career aspirations as defining them as different from their working-class male peers. Listening to them I was reminded of earlier work I had carried out on teachers' work (Mac an Ghaill 1980). Finn *et al.* (1977) have described the ideology of professionalism as a 'petit-bourgeois strategy for advancing and defending a relatively privileged position'. Like the socially mobile teachers before them, the Academic Achievers appeared to be destined for an ambiguous class position. In understanding this ambiguity, it is necessary to examine what Poulantzas (1975) calls the determinations of the political and ideological levels as well as the economic. As with the teachers, an important aspect of the Academic Achievers' self-representation was the acceptance of the 'mental–manual' division of labour, and their identification with 'mental' production. This explicitly manifested itself in terms of distancing themselves from the Macho Lads, the embodiment of manual labour and 'low-life futures'.

Andy: I think the ones in the top sets can think for themselves more. We're more into the subjects, like history and English. But the nutters [Macho Lads], what are they interested in? They can't think for themselves, so they go round being hard and causing trouble all the time. They'll just end up on the dole.

New Enterprisers

As was pointed out in Chapter 1, the vocationalization of the curriculum at Parnell School led to student restratification, with the development of new internal hierarchies between high- and low-status vocational spheres. In the resulting processes of student deskilling and upskilling, a new route of social mobility was created for the New Enterprisers. Working within the new vocationalist skilling regimes of high-status technological and commercial subject areas, the New Enterprise students were negotiating a new mode of school student masculinity with its values of rationality, instrumentalism, forward planning and careerism (see Hollands 1990). This was illustrated by their utilitarian involvement in mini-enterprise schemes, which were rejected by other sub-groups. They explained their enthusiasm for the schemes in pragmatic terms of their future value in the high-skilled sector of the labour market, which they were planning to enter.

Charles: I picked my subjects carefully, knowing what I want from my future. Most of the academic stuff's a waste of time. I don't think that the teachers know that the real world has changed. One or two, like in business studies, Mr James will talk to you and push you in your ambitions. Like my dad says, you set goals and you work for them.

Wayne: In class you just sit there in most lessons as the teacher just goes on and on, but in business studies and technology you learn a lot, you're really doing something, something that will be useful for your future.

Amerjit: My dad really wished the CTC [City Technology College] was open when I started secondary school. My brother's got in and it's really good . . . They do a lot of technology, so you have a lot of experience when you leave.

In the last chapter, I pointed out that the gender reworking of new vocational subjects was primarily associated with the New Entrepreneurial teachers. At the student level, the New Enterprise students were most active in the gender appropriation of recent curriculum reforms. This included their 'colonizing' the computer club which, as the female students discuss in Chapter 4, had been set up with the official aim of 'changing girls' negative views of technology'.

Among the New Enterprisers and Academic Achievers there were individual complaints against certain teachers for 'treating them like babies', but in principle they affirmed the legitimacy of the teachers' authority. From their different perspectives, they accepted the cultural exchange of student cooperation for qualifications. In developing their masculine identities against the Macho Lads, they were critical of the latter's 'childish' behaviour and the teachers' responses. The Academic Achievers emphasized the Macho Lads' low ability and troublesome behaviour. A major complaint of the New Enterprisers, aware of impression management, was that the teachers were too soft with the Macho Lads and that this would affect the school's reputation with future employers.

Parminder: When you're younger, you mess about. But from about year ten you need to grow up a bit, you know what I mean. The nutters [the Macho Lads] will say they're not treated as grown-ups by the teachers but it's them. They'll always be babies and that's why they won't get anywhere. It's just horrible being here with them.

Stephen: They [the Macho Lads] should just be thrown out. The teachers are trying to make this a good school, but the nutters just give us all a bad name.

The Real Englishmen: 'The arbiters of culture'

A main aim of this research is to deconstruct earlier male academic representations of white and black working-class school masculinities, highlighting the student heterogeneity in terms of the range of masculine identities that are inhabited. It is hoped that a comparative case-study of middle-class young men may make clear the class-specific dynamics of the interplay between schooling and masculinity. In the process, this may make visible a mode of masculinity that tends to be absent from academic and teacher accounts of gender relations. About ten per cent of the student population at Parnell School were from a non-commercial, middle-class background. Their parents' occupations included lecturing, teaching, public relations and work in the media and the arts. As with the working-class students, there was a range of middle-class masculinities, including an emerging group of Politicos, who were involved with environmental and animal rights issues (see Hollands 1990: 119). I chose a small group of male students who displayed an ambivalent response to the academic curriculum and who consequently were the most problematic middle-class peer group for many of the teachers. A similar group has been identified by Peter Aggleton (1987a) in *Rebels Without a Cause*. He was interested in broader issues around patterns of cutural affirmation and 'resistance' and the relationship of these to students' home lives and leisure activities. My findings have much in common with his work, and I am indebted to him in providing a framework within which to explore how a sector of the white English middle-class are negotiating a masculine identity within a school arena.

A central contradiction for the Real Englishmen was that unlike the Macho Lads' overt rejection of formal school knowledge and the potential exchange value it has in the labour market, the Real Englishmen had a more ambiguous relationship to it. They envisaged a future of higher education and a professional career. Like Aggleton's (1987a) 'Spatown Rebels', they defined themselves as a younger generation of the cultural elite, who like modern-day high-priests positioned themselves as the arbiters of culture. From this self-appointed location, they evaluated both teachers and students in terms of their possession of high-status cultural capital (Bourdieu 1986). They were in the process of building a publicly confident school masculinity in which cultural capital was over-valorized.

Thomas: We're different to most of the people here. That's why we don't fit in. They're mostly boring people, no style, very conventional. I mean you couldn't have a real discussion with any of them.

Daniel: The teachers give you all the crap about having the right attitude to work and we shouldn't be going out at night and we shouldn't talk back to them. They have no idea there's some really interesting people out there that they'll never meet. I mean, who needs teachers' advice? What do they know about life?

Like the Macho Lads, the Real Englishmen, albeit on different grounds, refused to affirm the legitimacy of the teachers' authority, though their rebellion tended to take a more individualist and varied form. They brought with them into the school values that emphasized personal autonomy and gave high evaluation to communication strategies. They expected to be able to negotiate with teachers, particularly about compulsory aspects of the curriculum. Teacher–student interaction with this sub-group produced specific conflictual masculine social practices. Many of the teachers found these middle-class students' capacity for elaborated verbal self-justification much more difficult to respond to, than what appeared to them as the Macho Lads' more open contestation of their authority. The teachers were often confused by the Real Englishmen's highly competent communication skills, with their appeal to rationality and fairness, that enabled the latter discursively to invert classroom power relations, with teachers positioned as culturally subordinate.

Edward: Mark's the best when he starts arguing with the teachers. They
   never learn. They start off talking down to him and then realize that he can
   defend himself. They get wickedly mad with him when he quotes some
   European philosopher they've never heard of. Then they're really shown up
   in front of everyone. And they hate that because that's their tactic with the
   kids.

The middle-class young men's name, the Real Englishmen, served as a triple signifier with reference to gender, sexuality and ethnicity, which were highly problematic inter-generational issues for them. The implications of this for their development of a specific mode of masculinity is discussed more fully below. Here I wish to concentrate on the development of their peer-group masculine identity in relation to working-class male peer groups. The Real Englishmen's own masculine values emphasized honesty, being different, individuality and autonomy, which they claimed were absent from middle-class culture. Against this background, the Real Englishmen were more ambivalent than the Academic Achievers towards the Macho Lads. At one level, this involved a fantasy of 'proletarian authenticity'. The Macho Lads were viewed as 'noble savages' for being unpretentious and unconscious of themselves. At another level, the Real Englishmen articulated excessive hostility towards the Macho Lads, who they referred to as 'trash', for their vulgarity and aggression, which was directed towards them. They were particularly resentful as they recalled how in earlier years the working-class lads had bullied them.

Adam: You see it if you go down the arts centre, all the middle-class are
   totally aware of themselves, thinking that people are watching them all the
   time, as if they're always on show. And you see it in the kids, in their
   humour and everything, it's just not real. But the working-class are not so
   aware of their bodies. They are more straightforward, act more
   spontaneous.
Andy: The Macho kids in this place are just wankers. When we first came
   here, they terrorized us. We hadn't mixed with them before. They're just
   very crude and loud. They'd beat you up for looking at them. It's their
   idea of being real men. The girls find them ugly.

The Real Englishmen were also critical of 'hard-working' students, including their middle-class peers and such groups as the working-class

Academic Achievers and the New Enterprisers. The Real Englishmen's dismissive evaluation of these students as 'sloggers' had implications for their relationship to the academic curriculum. From their own self-appointed culturally superior position, they inverted the taken-for-granted relationship between academic success and a positive response to mental labour. Teachers working within discourses of individual under-achievement failed to acknowledge in the young men's response, their collective masculine investment and the links to family social practices. A key element of the students' peer group identity was a highly public display of a contradictory 'effortless achievement' to each other and outsiders (Aggleton 1987a: 73). As members of a cultural elite, they rejected the school's dominant work ethic, assuming that intellectual talent was 'naturally' inscribed within their peer group.

Daniel: Teaching is a low-skill job. They're mostly technicists, not into ideas. They've no idea how patronizing they are to us. They don't like us because we're cleverer than them.

Robert: They're [the teachers] just guardians of mediocrity. They've this idea that you have to work all the time, slog, slog, slog to pass exams.

M.M.:   Why do you think they feel that?

Robert: Because that's how they got through. When Ben asked Williams [science teacher], why do we have to do homework, you could see he had never thought of it. And we joined in. He just couldn't argue his case. So, it came down to the usual crap, because I'm telling you boy. And this is supposed to be funny, teacher humour!

Identifying the differentiated formal curriculum as a major instrument in shaping differentiated peer-group masculine subjectivities was of critical importance. It enabled me to explore the collective nature of their active participation in and contestation of the masculinizing processes involved in the institutional construction and regulation of their gendered and sexual identities. I now wish to examine the relationship between peer-group practices and their orientation to work, as another key feature of the complexity of the young men's identity formation (see Lee 1993).

Regendering waged labour: A white working-class crisis of masculinity[5]

The students at Parnell School are part of a generation whose transition into adulthood is in the process of being reconstituted as a result of high rates of unemployment and punitive legislative changes that have led to the withdrawal of financial state support for young people. The cumulative effects of these social regulatory changes is to increase their dependency on parents or guardians. Harris (1992: 92) has suggested that: 'The end of youth culture ... [is] ... at hand. In real life, the youth of the 1980's in Britain ceased to be a metaphor for change and stylistic innovation and became victims of social and structural change instead.' Such a reading is

not supported by this study. However, the immediate social class experience of students at Parnell School was one of social marginalization,
involving widening regional poverty, diminishing local state services,
increased police surveillance following the urban disturbances, and the
long-term unemployment of family members and friends (Brindle 1993).
Dean (1993) describes the material conditions within which contemporary
inner-city, working-class masculinities are constructed. He notes that:

> It is less than six months since the Policy Studies Institute (PSI) ended
> an exhaustive review of the past fifteen years with the conclusion that
> urban initiatives had achieved "surprisingly little". Like most reports
> it was pessimistic about the future unless there was a dramatic
> increase in resources or more concentrated help on the most deprived
> districts. Across a range of yardsticks the gap between affluent suburb
> and run-down inner city district was widening: pupil–teacher ratios,
> school exam results, training opportunities, unemployment, poverty,
> premature death and infant mortality.
>
> (Dean 1993: 22)

Historically, rites of passage in industrial societies have tended to be
rather ambiguous processes, lacking the collective rituals, structures and
support found in traditional societies. However, more recently, young
people – both collectively and individually – have been constructing
masculine identities in a climate of rapid socio-economic change, which has
led to a major fracturing in the process of coming-of-age in England in the
early 1990s. For example, Willis (1985: 6) speaks of how the young
unemployed now find themselves in a 'new social condition of suspended
animation betweeen school and work. Many of the old transitions into
work, into cultures and organisations of work, into being consumers, into
independent accommodation – have been frozen or broken.' These
transitions are further shaped and differentiated by class, 'race', ethnicity,
gender, sexuality and disability (see Brown 1989; Mac an Ghaill 1992). In
short, we are witnessing highly disorganized and fractured post-compul-
sory school transitions, with large sectors of white and black young people
'learning not to labour' (Stafford 1981).

Brown (1989: 238) argues that the fundamental changes in the relationship between the reward structures of the school and the labour market
may lead to great confusion among large sectors of working-class students
concerning the purpose of school in preparing them for occupational and
social destinies. At Parnell School, there was much evidence of this. But
perhaps more surprising was the range of coping and survival strategies
that were in the process of being established in the young men's transitions
from school. In much of the school-to-work literature, there has been a
concentration on gender differences rather than gender relations (Griffin
1993). In such work, there tends to be a certain unitariness and rigidity in
working-class masculine forms, with little indication of their historical
specificity. In other words, there is theoretical underdevelopment of the

relational status of these sex/gender cultural forms or the possibility that under different conditions they might change. I hope that this study might serve as a necessary critique of this conceptualization of working-class masculinity. One of Hollands' (1990: 102–103) main concerns in his examination of new vocationalist training schemes is to assess their impact in altering traditional working-class patterns of work, with particular reference to the social processes of masculinity and femininity. His research finds a resonance with the new vocationalist-based curriculum and pedagogical changes at secondary school level. Here, students were in the process of constructing new cultural forms of becoming men in relation to waged and domestic labour.

At Parnell School, the emerging diverse intra-class trajectories to employment were acted out in relation to such bridging mechanisms as 'work experience'. The students' responses might be read as a dress-rehearsal for the 'real thing'. Most of the Macho Lads dismissed work experience as an early version of the 'slave training schemes' that their older brothers and friends were on. Similarly, most of the Academic Achievers tended to evaluate their work placements in negative terms. However, their main objection was that it was an unnecessary distraction from examination preparation. Some of them explicitly indicated their aspirations for upward social mobility, distancing themselves from manual labour. This appeared to be particularly significant for those students whose fathers worked or had worked in manual jobs.

Edward: They should just send the low-class kids. It's really for them. Me and my mates hated it. The job I had, it was just dirty and boring all the time. I suppose the only good thing to come out of it was that you would never end up doing that kind of job. But then again we knew that anyway 'coz most our dads are doing it. Could you think of doing that for all your life?

The New Enterprisers made individual complaints about their 'work experience' but overall they thought of it as highly worthwhile. This was in part a consequence of their own preparation, which included active negotiation of specific work placements. When I visited them at work, they tended to show more enthusiasm than the other student sub-groups, emphasizing the opportunities of 'experiencing the real world of proper work'. In contrast to the Macho Lads' defensive masculine stance, the New Enterprisers were in the process of building a positive, confident future work identity.

Bob: A lot of the kids here moaned about going out on work placements, the usual dossers. But it was good for some of us. Like most of our technology class, Mr James got special places for us. I had been in to mine before. My dad says it will be good. It will show that I'm keen to work. A lot of the kids around here are unemployable. So sometimes I think there's not much competition, but you have to keep pushing yourself to get on.

Graham: I really enjoyed getting up and going in. It's more real than a lot of boring school stuff here, with all the writing and it's more grown up. It was good experience. You go for a job and they're going to take the person with the experience. It's just as important as the qualifications, but you need to have them as well.

The Real Englishmen were also active in negotiating work placements. However, in their case, they were not motivated by hoping to enhance future work opportunities. Like Aggleton's (1987a) 'Spatown Rebels', a primary concern of the Real Englishmen – reflecting that of their parents – was the gaining of personal control over the management of space, time and systems of meanings. Hence, they were preoccupied with redefining public and private spheres of experience. So, for example, they sought work places – as they did in their part-time jobs outside school hours – that blurred the boundaries between work and leisure, in which they could socialize with friends while working.

The working-class student responses made an interesting contrast to those of the middle-class Real Englishmen. The Academic Achievers' 'occupational new realism' in relation to the new vocationalist curriculum must be located within the broader terrain. For black and white working-class young men, state schools remain a central ladder of social mobility, albeit for a minority, in a racially and class-stratified society. This was not the case for the Real Englishmen, who as the children of the agents of symbolic control, have alternative employment routes open to them other than those offered by schools and training schemes. As Aggleton (1987a: 135) has demonstrated for this social class, qualifications are relatively insignificant in terms of predicting employment destinies. This is particularly important at the present time, with the expansion of the local service sector, which includes a large network of middle-class parental contacts, who may act as sponsors through higher education and the labour markets.

The Real Englishmen were developing their masculine identity against a background of collective self-confidence which, as a cultural elite, led them to believe they would find employment. It was precisely on these grounds that they were dismissed by the New Enterprisers and the Academic Achievers. These working-class, socially mobile students were severely critical of the privileged middle-class students for their pretentious lifestyle and lack of work effort. They were particularly angry at the Real Englishmen's attempt to appropriate proletarian and black cultural forms, imitating and exaggerating caricatured working-class representations (Jones 1988). Having examined the young men's responses to work experience, I shall now explore their projected future work identities in relation to changing local labour markets.

Willis developed Tolson's (1977) study of masculinity, arguing that work was central to working-class boys' masculine self-representation. By the early 1990s, much appears to have changed in relation to the school–waged labour couplet.[6] The political–economic legacy of the

1980s for large sectors of working-class students, is that of a post-school anticipation of dependency, on low-skilled central government training schemes, as surplus youth labour in late industrial capitalism. Harrison (1993: 10) has described this rapid rise in local unemployment within the West Midlands: 'Last year the jobless figure leapt by more than 1,000 people every week (from 152,700 to 270,500), meaning more than one in ten of working people are on the scrapheap.' Of specific importance here was that following the post-war boom, the last twenty years have seen a major contraction in local manufacturing industries. This was in the order of 46 per cent, thus transforming a relatively prosperous area into one of the poorest in the country (Loftman and Nevin 1992).

At Parnell School, located within the West Midlands, the disruption and accompanying restructuring of the students' transitions from school to waged work, with the collapse of the local economy's manufacturing base, appeared to be creating a crisis in traditional white working-class forms of masculinity. This was of specific significance for the white Macho Lads, whose out-dated mode of masculinity continued to centre around traditional manual waged labour, at a time when their traditional manual work destiny has disappeared.

The current changing material conditions appeared to be less problematic in their effects for African Caribbean and Asian Macho Lads' masculine identity formation. This is not to suggest that mass unemployment, the resulting racialization of poverty and dominant state discourses of black pathology are not a major critical issue for African Caribbean and Asian young men. Nor is it to argue that these social changes go uncontested. However, black communities have a longer history of unemployment in racially structured local labour markets. During a decade of mass structural unemployment, black working-class men within the area have continued to be disproportionately affected by the rapidly contracting regional manufacturing base, as they have been concentrated in the declining metal industries (Brown 1992). A recent local union survey reported that 'black and Asian people are twice as likely to be jobless as white people' (*Evening Mail* 1993). Hence, the Asian and African Caribbean Macho Lads realistically appeared to have less emotional investment in future work in the local area. Further empirical work is required here.

A large number of working-class young men at Parnell School, and most emphatically the Macho Lads, were holding on to conventional views of domestic and waged labour arrangements and responsibilities in terms of a feminine–masculine bipolar split. However, this was against the background that for most of them there was no immediate prospect of finding a job. Hence, the Macho Lads could not appeal to a naturalized gender-divided world of 'breadwinners' and 'homemakers' (Finn 1987).[7]

The Macho Lads constructed their masculinity within a perceived social world divided between the 'hard' and the 'soft'. The white Macho Lads' anti-authoritarianism was accompanied by the valorization of 'masculine' manual labour that informed the group's social practices (Willis 1977;

Jenkins 1983). Inverting the institution's value system, the Macho Lads projected a tough masculine identity against male teachers' and students' involvement in academic feminized work. Like Hollands' (1990: 69–70) 'Manual Labour Lads', the Macho Lads drew on and asserted 'male experiences from the "real world", . . . continuing to mock [teachers] . . . through humour and bravado'. Although their public display of highly ritualized forms of hyper-masculinity often appeared defensive, nevertheless they were deeply rooted in collective investments in wider working-class cultural forms and more concretely linked to their fathers' and older brothers' 'commonsense' gendered world views. They fantasized about an old England of full employment that their fathers occupied. Interestingly, with the exception of Paul, whose mother was active in the trade union movement, the students did not see trade unions as significant in relation to the creation of job opportunities.

Jim: The teachers try and advise us about training. I was telling my dad and he said, what would they know, they've never done a real day's work in their lives. He came up to the school when I was having my options because my mom was working that night. He said to the teachers, do you think you lot can get him a job? And they just kept talking and talking. He said, it made him think, nothing's changed.

The Macho Lads may be seen as inhabiting a descending mode of masculinity within the hierarchy of a working-class school's gender regime. In contrast, the New Enterprise students, like the New Entrepreneurial male teachers, may be viewed as adopting an ascending modernized version of masculinity within an increasingly commercialized school arena. In contrast to the white Macho Lads' nostalgia for an imagined past, the New Enterprisers celebrated an imagined future of flexible work skills in managerial and self-employment positions.

Wayne: A lot of the kids in the low classes [in Parnell School] say that there's no jobs, but my dad has become self-employed. He says there's jobs for people but they have to get out and find them.
M.M.:   And has the school helped you in this?
Wayne: I think it's a lot better now. If you show an interest, then teachers help you. Like the teachers say, you have to learn different skills, so if things change you will look good to the employer because you can do different jobs . . . And if you get a lot of experience, then you can become your own boss. That's what I'm aiming for. You don't want to be working for someone else all your life when you can make more money yourself.

In the local economy, the disappearing 'masculine' manufacturing base was being displaced by an increase in the traditional 'feminine' service sector. As Hutton (1993: 20) has recently pointed out:

A quiet revolution is going on which is transforming the lives of millions of workers in Britain. The world of full-time pensionable employment is retreating before their eyes; and in its stead is emerging an insecure world of contract work, part-time jobs and casualised labour.

A large proportion of this work is being carried out by white and black working-class women (Walby 1990). It was against this background that the regendering of youth waged labour was taking place. This was evident in male students redefining of the sexual division of labour in their part-time work in the service sector. They were in the process of appropriating and redefining conventional female areas of work in supermarkets, video shops and fast food restaurants. Their explanations took different forms. Some of the male students differentiated between male and female spheres by associating the former with a more private world of 'hard physical labour' away from the public gaze of employers and customers. For other male students, the masculine sphere was defined in terms of their own superior gender expertise in relation to recent technological developments.

Graham: Where we work in the supermarket, the boys do all the harder work like filling shelves and dragging things around the warehouse. And you're freer there, away from the boss. And the girls are on the tills talking to the customers and that. Like you would prefer to talk to a girl in a shop wouldn't you?

William: Working in a sweet shop might be more girls' work. But in places like video and hi-fi shops, then it's mainly going to be men because they know about these things don't they?

M.M.: Why do you think that women don't?

William: Well you don't see women in these shops. Like where I work, the girls do the cleaning and making tea and that.

M.M.: Do you think that is because they choose to do that?

William: I don't know. But if you think of it, girls read all the girls' magazines with silly stories and that, but boys are always into video games and making things. So, they must be more interested in it, how things work and all that. Boys are just better at these things. So, they get those jobs that need technical experts more.

Finally, I wish to look at the interrelationship between occupational identity, ethnicity and masculinities. As a result of 'taking' rather than 'making' research problems, social scientists have tended to accept official discourses of ethnicity. Within this shared 'commonsense' framework, Asian and African Caribbean students have become the exclusive focus of 'race-relations' research, resulting in caricatured images of 'under-achiev- ing' African Caribbean males and 'over-achieving' Asians. In this process, England's largest ethnic group – the Irish – are made socially invisible (Conner 1985; Curtis 1985; Hickman 1986; Hazelkorn 1990; Brah 1992; Rattansi 1992).

Brian moved school in year eight and couldn't get into the local Roman Catholic secondary school, so he came to Parnell Comprehensive instead. Born in England, of Irish working-class parents, he indicates the influence of ethnic identity on young masculine formations and the specificity of white English cultural forms in relation to waged labour.

M.M.:   What kind of jobs are you looking for?
Brian: Go on building for a while, get a bit of money and then I'll probably go into nursing.
M.M.:   Why building and nursing?
Brian: I think that they've always been the jobs for immigrants. My dad's a chippy on the buildings and my mum and sister are nurses. So you meet a lot of your own there and that helps, you can feel at home there. And I think that there is a caring side to Irish people.
M.M.:   Men and women?
Brian: Yes, men as well as women. Probably with our big families and all the cousins and that. We've been brought up to think of other people. The English live in their little families with two kids and don't really care about anyone else but themselves. They're more interested in their dogs and things like washing their cars all the time.
M.M.:   Have you English friends?
Brian: I don't think of them as friends. I don't really understand English boys. They're always looking for trouble and they're not very nice to each other. I don't think they're allowed to show any caring for each other. I don't mean Irish lads do all the time, but you could with close friends.
M.M.:   So, how do you cope when you're with them?
Brian: They're separate parts of my life. When I'm with Irish people, I can relax. When I'm with English boys, you just have to act like them, most of the time. Going around taking the piss all the time, trying to get people to look up to you.

For Brian, Irish workers were similarly structurally positioned as black people in relation to racism. However, I do not wish to suggest that there is no difference between black and white immigrants, nor for their children. Racism is contextually contingent and operates in specific ways in and across different institutional sites. 'Colour' as a key signifier of difference is usually identified as locating black people in a highly visible position of racial exclusion. However, 'colour' also has its positive, productive side, enabling black people, who are branded by skin colour, to maintain a continuity of struggle from new arrivals to new natives (*Race Today* 1975: 56).

This section has explored the reconstitution and regendering of young people's waged labour. This needs to be located within the cumulative effects of the shift to the political Right in the wider society, the changing nature of labour processes and local labour market opportunities, new school and work technologies, and a popular media that systematically misrepresents young people as irresponsible urban folk devils, unfit for work. In examining working-class male students' varied responses to these structural changes, it is necessary to emphasize the central position of rapidly changing English family cultural forms in the construction of masculine subjectivities.

Family network–school relations: An 'English' middle-class crisis of masculinity

In concentrating on school structures and teacher discourses in the construction and reproduction of masculine youth forms, there is a danger of unintendedly adopting a mono-causal 'blame the teacher' explanation. It is important to stress that it is the interplay of a number of factors – involving family/kinship relationships, peer networks, media representation, and school and workplace experience – that provides a filter through which masculinities are culturally produced and reproduced. A major issue here was how to conceptualize the interrelationship between students' school experiences and home lives. As Robinson (1988) pointed out, one of the most important characteristics about families in England is their diversity. He notes that there are: 'one-parent' . . . two-parent . . . [and] . . . step-parent families, families with elderly dependents . . . with [and] . . . without married members and so on' (p. 19). Nevertheless, many of the teachers at Parnell School continued to assume the 'moral norm' of a two-parent nuclear family, against which they made judgements about the students' background. They tended to work within a discourse of deficit in relation to white and black working-class parents. Such comments as, 'what can you expect, he's from a "one-parent" family', acted as euphemistic class and racially structured codes that served to position working-class life as pathologically organized. Such comments were not applied to middle-class 'lone-parent' families with whom many teachers found it easier to identify. In Gleeson's (1984) phrase, this is a discourse about 'someone else's children'. In contrast to the dominant teacher representations of working-class families, I found Connell and co-workers' (1982) formulation helpful in exploring complex sets of inter-generational class and gendered relations. In their study of the relationship between home, school and student peer groups, they make the important point that:

> families are not closed universes but places where larger structures meet and interact . . . We do not mean to suggest that families are simply pawns of outside forces anymore than schools are. In both cases, class and gender relations create dilemmas (some insolvable), provide resources (or deny them), and suggest solutions (some of which don't work), to which the family must respond in its collective practice.
>
> (Connell *et al.* 1982: 73)

One of the most surprising findings in this part of the research was how rapid social changes have helped to structure highly differentiated experiences of family life for young people. This included, as discussed above, changing work patterns in the local area, with mass male unemployment in manufacturing and changing patterns of women's work, with an increase in jobs, albeit low paid, in the local service sector. Another significant factor was the large number of lone-parent, mother-headed households and the accompanying feminization of poverty. Third, as made explicit in interviews with the Real Englishmen's mothers, was the influence of modern feminism (see Arnot 1992; David 1993).[8]

Working-class parental affirmation and legitimation of the school's authority was complex and diverse. In interviews with working-class students at Parnell School, parents were frequently mentioned as influencing their orientation to schooling. Nevertheless, there was no predictable mechanistic inter-generational links between parents' and their sons' evaluation of schooling. Parents who were actively supportive of the school sometimes produced Macho Lads, and parents who appeared indifferent or hostile to the school sometimes had as sons Academic Achievers or New Enterprisers (Willis 1977: 73).

Charles: I really admire my dad. He came from nothing, now he's got his own business. He's worked hard and no-one's given him anything. He's pushing me to do well in school, so I can help him or start up my own business. A lot of the kids here are just wasters, just waiting to go on the dole and that.

Working-class male students also spoke of the different advice they received from their mothers and fathers as significant in shaping their response to school and the development of sub-cultural practices.

Mark: If I had listened to my dad, I would have ended up in a factory or on the dole like my brothers and his friends. It is really my mum who has pushed me, encouraged me to stay on at school. She sees education as important and thinks there are opportunities now that she never had. If she hadn't married my dad she could have really gone places and done things herself.

Against the background of recent educational reforms which are making a claim for legitimacy in terms of empowering parents, working-class parents' assessments of schools are informative. A main flaw of such legislation is the failure to acknowledge the differential positioning of parents to schooling and its discourses of social exclusion. Behind this 'apolitical' central government stance is hidden an appeal to 'parents' as a national homogeneous entity. Carby (1980: 2) has attacked the assumed nationalist consensus of official reports and documents, arguing that 'inherent contradictions and conflicting interests . . . within and between. racial, sexual and class groupings are contained by and subsumed under an apparent unity of interests'. Parnell School was regarded by parents as having good relations with them and the wider local community. Nevertheless, some parents voiced a 'working-class suspicion of a formal institution and its mode of working' (Willis 1977: 73). Equally important in shaping their relations with Parnell School were memories of their own schooling. As Connell *et al.* (1982: 166) found: 'working-class people are often injured, insulted and disempowered by their experience with schools'. Such fractured school biographies informed some of the fathers' ambivalent and contradictory support for their sons' education, in 'pushing the kids to get on', while having severe doubts about the value of academic knowlege.

Hollands (1990: 10) suggests that 'the power position within the working-class household is crucial in forming masculine identities'. More specifically, he is critical of earlier academic representations of male youth cultures for failing to explore the significance of the domestic sphere in the transition of young men into adulthood. At Parnell School, male students tended to talk less than female students about their home lives. The domestic division of labour seemed to take more traditional gender forms among the working-class than the middle-class students, but there were significant intra-class variations, with the Academic Achievers and New Enterprisers more home-orientated than the Macho Lads. The latter spoke of spending much of their leisure time out of the house in peer-group activities and showed little awareness of, or concern for, domestic responsibilities. The Real Englishmen claimed that they shared housework jobs. However, as young women point out in Chapter 4, young men did not take responsibility for its organization and had little involvement in looking after younger siblings.

Nava (1984), writing of the different placement of girls and boys to their adulthood, captures the generational specificity of the problematic struc-ture of young masculinities and their ambiguous relation to social power. She suggests that the implications of young men's identification of the temporary nature of their subordination as youth may inform their contentious transition into adulthood. She argues that the accentuated differentiation between manhood and boyhood is a recurring social phenomenon in many cultures. Nava (1984: 15) adds that: 'it echoes . . . the distinctive infantile rupture between boys and their mothers, the common-place absence of fathers from the domestic domain, and may well signal a key aspect of masculinity as a problematic and ambivalent construct' (see also Chodorow 1978).

There was much evidence among the male students in this study to support these arguments. In interviews with the young men, they explained their contestation of the domestic domain and strained relations with par-ents, which were gender-specific in relation to mothers and fathers. How-ever, no one pattern emerged, with some of the young men finding their fathers more problematic and others their mothers. Their explanations also tended to take class-specific cultural forms. I shall begin with the working-class students' views before examining those of the middle-class students.

Parminder: It's the same at home. My dad's really afraid of my mom. She rules our house.
Kevin: My mum used to always show me up when I was younger, especially when I was with my mates. My dad used to stick up for me, told her to leave me alone and stop nagging me. She used to get on my nerves. But

now I think that she accepts me more as a man because I'm bigger than
her.

M.M.:   So what has changed?

Kevin: Well now she wouldn't make me do things around the house. My
sister does it. And she gives me more freedom to come in late. She's just
accepted that I'm grown up now. I'm more of a man.

Stephen: When my dad left I think my mom thought that she could boss me
about more. So we were always fighting. She was trying to control me too
much, treating me like a baby. So I left to live with my dad. But I got tired
of looking after him, so I've come back home. Things are better. I think
she missed me and she probably likes having a man around the place.

Connell *et al.* (1982: 98) have described the mutually supportive
home–school relationship between a ruling-class boys' school and the
production of masculinity, in terms of a sort of synchronization of family,
school and student peer-group practices. In contrast, at Parnell School,
which had a predominantly working-class student population, new
middle-class mothers did not automatically affirm and legitimate the
school's authority. They challenged dominant school gender practices,
maintaining that recent socio-political changes were still absent from
secondary schools' curriculum and pedagogy. They argued that schools
were perpetuating the myth of a patriarchal British nuclear family. They
contrasted local schools' unreconstructed gender regimes with their sons'
participation in their own more democratic domestic arrangements. They
were particularly critical of authoritarian male teachers, who acted as
potentially damaging role models for their sons. However, they felt that
new forms of young masculinities worked out within the home were strong
enough to withstand the traditional patriarchal organization of schools.

Ms Bracey: Schools, I think particularly secondary schools, that are
male-dominated anyway, are living in the dark ages. They transmit ideas of
the nuclear family that have never actually existed. They have no idea of
the broad changes taking place outside their gates.

Ms Fraser: They should be teaching them feminist ideas. Like how feminism
has altered the rights of partners in marriage. Women are moving into
whole areas of work that have been male preserves and that means that
men will have to change. I think it's awful what Adam has to endure with
some of those men, but he's surviving.

As pointed out above, the middle-class male students' name, the Real
Englishmen, served as a triple signifier with reference to their parents'
political position on issues of gender, sexuality and ethnicity. These were
highly contentious issues that overtly underpinned the making of their
masculine identity. The latter is examined later in the chapter. Here, the
focus is on their critical and rather cynical views concerning their parents'
involvement in the reformation of sex/gender relations.

M.M.:   Why do you call yourselves the Real Englishmen?

Thomas: It's good isn't it.

M.M.:   What does it mean?

Ben: Lots of meanings. We just call ourselves the REMs, rapid eye movement. Pretty cool, yeah? We're living in a fantasy world away from the heavy issues, away from having consciences about everything in the fucking world.

Thomas: I can't remember really. We were fooling about one night, talking about our parents and all the crap liberal stuff that they talk about all the time. And someone just said, they can believe what ever the fuck they want, we're real men.

Richard: It's all the crap about being new men and sensitive and caring. Okay sharing the housework and things like that are fair. But it's all the sexual stuff, all the stuff not making girls sex objects. It's ridiculous. What are you supposed to do? Become gay? And then there's a problem with that if you do.

M.M.:   And would you see yourselves as different to other guys?

Richard: Well that's the point. Our parents made a big principle of sending us to a comp [comprehensive school] and we've got to deal with all these ugly heavy macho types. They're really crude bastards with the girls and everything and we're forced to be with them. Our parents didn't have to go through this. They went to grammar school.

M.M.:   So the name [Real Englishmen] was directed towards other kids as well?

Thomas: Oh yeah. It was to the machos as well. They all go round thinking that they're real men, getting women and all that. It's all talk. They're just wankers. So, we started taking the piss out of them, saying we're the real men.

M.M.:   Would you say it to the macho crowd?

Ben: Do we fuck? They'd batter us. There's some really nasty kids here. And this is where we're supposed to become new men!

M.M.:   Why do so many of you say your parents are dishonest.

Adam: Because they are so screwed up about what they are supposed to believe or say, that they can't say or do what they really want to. Middle-class parents are definitely more dishonest than working-class parents, and the kids don't know what to believe now either.

Robert: We have been emasculated. Our feminist mothers have taken away our masculinity. When I was younger my mum would sit around with her friends and say bad things about men all the time. And then someone would say what about black men. And then they had to be anti-racist, so black men weren't included. And they'd hang around with these guys, who treated them like shit. The guys couldn't have respect for them, they had no respect for themselves. And at the same time I was an anti-racist by the age of four. It just does your head in.

Daniel: Like my dad he's anti-sexist and feminist and all this. You know he goes shopping and takes the baby out on his back, any fucking baby will do. And at the same time you hear him talking when they're drunk at parties to some of his mates about having sexual affairs with women at work.

Richard: And they say, you lucky bastard because they know he can use his power at work to get off with women.

Simon: It's true. And then they'll turn off Benny Hill and make a big deal about page three. They're just old hippy shits.

There is a danger of reading the young middle-class men's accounts presented here as confirming the idea that '"progressive" child rearing produces ineffective, marginal, unproductive adults' (see Smart 1988: 233; Mac an Ghaill 1988a). Such a reading was prevalent among many of the male teaching staff at Parnell School, particularly the Professionals and the New Entrepreneurs. However, alternative readings are possible of a younger generational response to an inherited cultural legacy of gender reformation. These young people point out that such issues are far more complex than their parents 'rationally imagined'. Without wishing to generalize from this particular class fraction, they provide important criticisms – from the inside as it were – of a cultural world that progressive educators are attemping to construct. They illustrate the complexity of transforming male-dominated sex/gender systems in a wider social environment that appears to be threatened by such social change. At the same time, they point to the internal contradictions of the complex interrelationship of different forms of social divisions. More specifically, they graphically indicate the way in which the attempt to address one aspect of multi-oppressions has unintended consequences for other aspects (McCarthy 1990).

The male students' accounts of their parents' discussion of sex with them added an interesting class comparative perspective to this part of the study. Most of the working-class students claimed that at home there was little inter-generational talk about sex. They recalled defensive conversations with their parents that involved prohibitive warnings such as: 'be careful' and 'don't come home saying that you've got someone in trouble'. The Academic Achievers assumed that middle-class parents were more liberal and open on this issue. The Real Englishmen contested this. Returning to a critique of their parents' gender and sexual politics, they spoke of middle-class parents' heterosexual regulation of their sons. The Real Englishmen were particularly critical of their parents' emotional manipulation (Aggleton 1987a).

Robert: Like when Susan said yesterday that working-class parents are more repressed and middle-class parents more open. I don't agree. They're repressed in different ways. I think sexually the middle-class kids, some of them might sleep around more than working-class kids and their parents knowing about it and they may be freer in that. But emotionally, middle-class parents have really screwed their kids up.

Adam: They'll talk openly about sex and have sex manuals round the place. But then they exaggerate their heterosexuality like they'll say I'd never sodomize a woman, it's unnatural. That's a code that homosexuality isn't natural.

Daniel: That's true. I remember when some of our parents were talking, all right-on people of course, and they were discussing this young guy whose mother said had been raped but he said he had consented. And they said it must be worse for a boy than a girl to be raped. And all they were concerned about was if he would become gay. I couldn't believe it. So much for all the crap they gave us about rape is about power, so it was really about sex all the time.

Robert: The kids, the boys who were there thought it was typical of them that they would make a big deal of knowing gays and all that. But they'd go mad if we got close to one. Like my dad wondered about David [brother] being gay. He's really camp a lot of the time. Dad said that basically he was hetero and was going through a phase. I thought, he better be.

While the new middle-class parents would critically examine the class and gender dimensions of inter-generational relations, they resisted discussion of the influence of their own white English (Anglo) ethnicity (Pajaczkowska and Young 1992). It was very difficult to engage these parents with such questions. Their sons' interpretation of their parents' denial of English nationality, which had implications for the Real Englishmen's development of a masculine identity, is explored later in the chapter. In the following extract, an Irish working-class female student points to the cultural specificity of the power relations operating between white English parents and their children.

Niamh: English people see Irish fathers as keeping wives down and that they are all old-fashioned, and see them as being hard on their kids. Well, I think the main difference between Irish and English people is that the English don't like kids. I don't know, they seem weird to me.

M.M.:   Why do you say that?

Niamh: Well, last year I went on holiday with an English friend to Devon and the hotels and pubs said no children. They did, I swear. You'd never get that in Ireland. Here, they have one or two children, really spoil them but don't like anyone else's kids. And then I think that even their own kids don't respect them, so the parents can't really love them can they?

In developing a research design, I was particularly interested in focusing on how issues of sex/gender identity formation intersected with the different sets of power relations that are transported across different sites of experience (see Aggleton 1987a: 11). I had anticipated that my participation in family networks and part-time work would be key arenas. I also expected the social relations of class, 'race' and ethnicity to be significant. However, unexpectedly, white English ethnicity became a central research focus. This is now examined.

White English ethnicity, racism and sexuality

There is a growing body of evidence that points to the 'contradictions, ambivalences and resistances of the popular cultures of racism amongst white youth' (Rattansi 1992: 33; also see Billig 1978; Cohen 1989b). However, at school policy level, there often remains an assumption that white racism is a homogeneous social phenomenon. As argued above, until recently equal opportunity policies have tended to focus exclusively on black ethnic minorities.[9] In so doing, white ethnicity has tended to be absent from critical analysis. Brah (1992: 134) has written very persuasively of the need to problematize the racialization of white subjectivity. I decided to make the white ethnic majority the object of my research, not only in terms of racial responses to others but also by focusing upon the problematic nature of white English ethnicity for a dominant majority in a post-imperial period. What emerges from this approach is the range of fractured and contradictory white male responses to issues of 'race' and racism. More specifically, I found that in exploring from within their own cultural logic the young men's construction of dominant white English ethnicities, I began to trace the links between schooling, nationalism and masculine identities (see Parker *et al.* 1992).

Equally important, much anti-racist school practice continues to emphasize a structural mono-causal perspective. Macdonald *et al.* (1989: 348) have shown the limitations of these simple models of power that assume we can understand racism without looking at its complex intermeshing with class and gender relations.[10] In a comprehensive critique of what they call moral anti-racism, Macdonald *et al.* are particularly critical of the unintended effects of excluding white students and their parents from responsibility for anti-racist education. Parnell School also operated with a reductionist approach that had counter-productive effects, with white students claiming that black students were receiving special treatment. It is important here to note the way in which a school policy can unintendingly serve to accentuate forms of white ethnicity (and sexism) (Hollands 1990: 9). It is such unintended consequences that have been the object of pernicious tabloid press campaigns throughout the 1980s against the legitimacy of anti-oppressive educational policies. Of specific concern here is white English male students' responses to anti-racist policies and the interconnections with the institutional development of white masculine identities. In highlighting these links, Macdonald *et al.* (1989: 143) poignantly ask: 'Did Ahmed Ullah die at the cross-roads where the power of masculinity, male dominance, violence and racism intersect?'

Hollands (1990: 171–2) provides one of the most sophisticated accounts of white working-class forms of racism within a post-school site, emphasizing the fragmented and diverse responses influenced by age, gender and more specific intra-class identities. After delineating a number of working-class transitions into work among young trainees, he sets out to explore the different forms of white racism that they have adopted. He draws on Cohen's (1986a,b) anti-racist work in schools, in which he distinguishes between three main class codes: an aristocratic code of 'breeding', a bougeois/democratic variant which provides a scientific reading, and a working-class proletarian code with its emphasis on inheritance of labour power and territoriality. The latter position, while also invoking bourgeois and nationalistic variations, is taken up primarily by the manual labour lads. He explains how England's economic decline disproportionately affects this group, resulting in their stronger self-interest in maintaining a 'white identity', even though black people are not responsible for the crisis. In contrast, the liberal position, with its more subtle and middle-class appeal, was more likely to be adopted by the upwardly mobile young men. Finally, he suggests that a left-labourist perspective of racism was being developed by a group he called the politicos. I have found Cohen's and Hollands' frameworks very helpful in understanding how racialized white English masculinities were set up by students within secondary schools.

At Parnell School, a highly complex racialized map of student inter-ethnic relations was being constructed, from which individual racial behaviour could not simplistically be read or predicted. During the research, the white male students illustrated the generational and intra-class specificity of racist discourses, challenging conceptions of a unitary working-class inheritance. Different sectors of male students, selectively drawing on racist constructs, offered diverse and inconsistent explanations (Gramsci 1971). Among the working-class students, the white Macho Lads tended to adopt a proletarian stance, showing more continuity with their parents than other peer groups, with particular references to their fathers' arguments that 'blacks had taken our jobs' and 'taken over our area'. The white Academic Achievers and New Enterprisers, adopting a more liberal perspective, challenged this interpretation, claiming that black people could not be held responsible for mass youth unemployment. A number of interrelated elements can be noted here. Black students' orientation to school and the accompanying masculine identities was of particular salience for the white English male students' responses to them. Also important, as John, a white Macho Lad indicates below, is that unlike their fathers, these students have gone to the same schools as black students. This is not to imply that such contact necessarily leads to a decrease in white racist perceptions. However, the point to stress is that the institutional inter-ethnic relations played out among the young men has a historical contingency with its own set of social dynamics (Jones 1988).

John: I used to be a right little Nazi.
M.M.:   How come?
John: Probably my dad the most. He just hates blacks and Asians. He always has. My mom is always telling him not to be so bad.
M.M.:   So how did you change?
John: I don't know. You hang around with them all the time. Like the ones in our gang, they'd do anything for you. I mean we just stick together. We always get into trouble together. Like the teachers always pick on us, so we stick together more.
M.M.:   What about the black and Asian kids you don't hang around with?
John: Well, they're all the same as the white pricks, sucking up to the teachers. You couldn't trust one of them. Our Asian mates say themselves that the Asians are the worst, the slyest. But they go their way and we go ours, en it?
Mark: Some of the bad nutters here are the Asian kids. But really they're just as bad as the white kids in the bottom classes and the blacks. They just

stand around threatening people, especially the little kids. They have to be tough all the time causing trouble, you know. But probably a main difference is that there's always been more Asians in the top classes. So you hang around with them more. We've got more in common, to talk about and that. The bright ones have more in common. It's not really about colour. Like we're all friends in the top set and hang round together.

Much has been written by white middle-class social scientists about male working-class youth forms of racism. However, middle-class young men have remained invisible. At Parnell School, the latter group provided a most revealing perspective on institutional inter-ethnic relations. Like Aggleton's (1987a) Spatown Rebels, the Real Englishmen differentiated themselves from other student sub-groups on the basis of what they were not. At the same time, the Real Englishmen were in the process of constructing a positive ethnic identity. At times, their talk of nationality appeared obsessive. They explained the significance of their name with reference to white English ethnicity. More specifically, they were developing a young masculine identity against their parents' denial and suppression of English nationality and nationalism. They pointed to the need for a local sense of ethnic belonging that notions of internationalism failed to provide.

Adam: It's like we can't be English, English men, be proud of being English. I argue about this with my dad all the time. He just dismisses it saying it's all constructed and we should all be internationalists.
M.M.: Why is it important to you?
Adam: Because it's unfair. All the Asian kids and the black kids, they can be Asian or black. They can be proud of their countries.
M.M.: Do you think of yourselves as racist?
Adam: No. No. That's what the teachers try and tell you, they try and force on you if you say anything, try to make you feel guilty like them. But we're not talking about colour. We're talking about culture.
Richard: English culture. And if you talk about the English flag or whatever, anything to do with Englishness, they call you a little Fascist.

In my discussions with the parents, they often appeared to either conflate 'race' and ethnicity or to subsume the latter under the former. They displayed a contradictory response to ethnic difference, acknowledging ethnic minorities but refusing to concede their own ethnic majority status. Some of the parents spoke of their sons going through a phase, as part of a broader adolescent search for an adult male identity.

Mr Stone: Adam reminds me of myself. Just trying out different things. He's very bright and the younger generation should challenge the older one. Adam and his friends at this age have very strong feelings. At times they try to shock us as parents. Quite healthy for young men. It's part of the process of their gaining their own independence.
Ms Taylor: You see them identifying with the Union Jack and talking a lot about English nationality. It's all tied up with the Falklands fiasco that ignited new forms of extreme nationalism in this country. Some of the parents wonder if we've produced little Fascists. But they'll come out of

this surer of themselves. At other times, like when we visit Europe, Ben's very much at home as a European.

White students in all the peer groups were critical of their primary and secondary schools' anti-racist practices. Working-class male students appealed to varying forms of what Cohen (1988) refers to as the 'nationalism of the neighbourhood', with the white Macho Lads emphasizing 'defending our territory'. The Real Englishmen, in their defence of what they saw as a declining English masculine identity, nostalgically appealed to the demise of 'English culture'. White students often complained that the teachers responded to their complaints about what they perceived as black racism, with crude catechetical slogans such as 'whites are the problem' or 'all whites are racists'. The Real Englishmen were also critical of their teachers and parents for generalizing across generations about responsibility for the legacy of historical forms of white racism.

Thomas: It's the same as the anti-sexist stuff. Our parents are always on about anti-racism and all this. And it's the same here. I always remember when we first came here and we were doing paintings and we suddenly realized you got more marks if you did multicultural ones.

Ben: The teachers and our parents when they talk about racism always say white people mustn't be racist to blacks. That's fine. But they won't say anything when Asians and black kids are racist to each other.

Adam: And how come they keep on saying that racialism is really bad but we've had a load of hassle from black and Asian kids. The ones in the lowest sets the most, the nutters, and no-one says anything about that. Well why is that okay?

Adam: But no-one asks about us. The older generation don't ask what it's like for us who have to live with a lot of black kids who don't like us. No-one says to black kids, you have to like the whites. They'll tell them to fuck off.

M.M.: Do you think that it's the same thing for you and for black kids?

Richard: Well that's what the teachers come back with, only whites can be racist. It's crap, all the imperialist stuff. But the younger ones, we didn't cause that did we?

The Real Englishmen raise a critical issue that is often absent from anti-racist programmes – the question of how English ethnicity fits into the complex configuration of inter-ethnic interpersonal relations at school level. Furthermore, implicitly they raise questions about whether we can begin to construct modern forms of progressive English national identity to counter the New Right's appropriation of the discourse of nationality with its projected atavistic representations of the strong British state. In such a process, it may be possible to work through the question of why 'there ain't no black in the Union Jack' (Gilroy 1987). Hall (1992: 258), writing of current shifts in black cultural politics, refers to this title and suggests that: 'Fifteen years ago we didn't care, or at least I didn't care, whether there was any black in the Union Jack. Now not only do we care, we must.' (See Hooks 1991.)

Rattansi (1992) has outlined the contextual contingency of racialized discourses, arguing that shifting alliances and points of tension may emerge from different arenas. He writes:

> of the ambivalences generated for many white youth by the attractions of Afro-Caribbean, Afro-American and African musical forms, and their admirations for some aggressive forms of Afro-Caribbean masculinity, have resulted in alliances in particular schools and neighbourhoods between white and Afro-Caribbean youth against Asian youth, where in some schools black–white conflicts remain submerged the dominant form of racist insult occurs between different ethnic minority groups, for instance Asian and Afro-Caribbean or Cypriot and Vietnamese.
>
> (Rattansi 1992: 27)

At Parnell School, similar inter-ethnic shifting tensions and alliances were present within a highly contingent and continually changing situation. For example, there was no fixed pattern of white or black inter-ethnic response in the different year groups. Rather, different student sub-groups assigned high status to particular individuals or peer groups in which different hierarchies of masculinity were competitively negotiated and acted out. During the research period, this was highlighted in relation to English-born Asian Macho Lads racially insulting year seven students who had recently arrived in the school from Pakistan.

Student inter-ethnic relations were a mixture of 'race'-specific elements and a broader range of social and psychic phenomena located within the school and linked to other social arenas. They involved specific emotional investments and cultural attachments around popular cultural forms, such as music and sport. This is a long way from the fixed ethnic categories of much conventional equal opportunities discourse on the racialization of schools. Below, two black sixth-form students explain the inter-ethnic student complexity and ambiguity at Parnell School.[11]

Carlton: Like all the stuff we read on blacks in schools don't even begin to get at what is going on. They talk of blacks, Asians and whites and then ask them what they think of each other. It's crazy. Like here with black culture, the kids' language, cussing and that, their cool movement, the hairstyles, the music and the clothes, you see the Asians and the white kids really getting into it, deeply into it, right. But at the same time some of these Asians and whites will have racist views about blacks. And it's the same with the blacks about the others. It's really a mix up and difficult to work out, you know what I mean?

Rajinder: You see there's a lot of sexuality in there. The African Caribbeans are seen as better at football and that's really important in this school for making a reputation. And it's the same with dancing, again the black kids are seen as the best. And the white kids and the Asians are jealous because they think that the girls will really prefer the black kids. So, the "race" thing gets all mixed up with other things that are important to young kids.

Fanon (1967: 160) has suggested that 'if one wants to understand the racial situation psychoanalytically . . . as it is experienced by individual consciousness, considerable importance must be given to sexual phenomena'. As Rajinder suggests, the complexity and contingency of the student inter-ethnic relations at Parnell School appeared most visible in relation to sexuality. This was made most explicit by the Macho Lads. The white Macho Lads adopted a range of contradictory racial and sexual discourses. At one level, there was a strong public masculine identification with the Asian and African Caribbean Macho Lads. The peer group constructed a hierarchy of sexual prowess in which they positioned themselves as the most successful with young women. This self-representation was worked out against white and black conformist students, who they publicly derided for their assumed sexual inexperience. At another level, individual white Macho Lads privately spoke to me – with more confidence outside of school – of the African Caribbean Macho Lads' perceived heterosexual success with young white women as illegitimate. At other times, white female students from Parnell School were labelled as 'slags' by white male students if they were seen with African Caribbeans or Asians from other schools, who were constructed as 'monstrous others' (Fanon 1967; Willis 1977).

Jim: Some of the white girls at that school let themselves be treated like doormats by the black kids. And some of them even go off with the "Pakis".

Similar contradictions operated with the African Caribbean Macho Lads, who combined a public solidarity with the white Macho Lads and privately a general criticism of white men's sexuality. They positioned themselves as sexually superior both to white and Asian students and to conformist black students. More specifically, they spoke of themselves as the main producers of popular style, which they claimed made them attractive to young women. This could not be simply read in terms of youthful boasting. The African Caribbeans appropriated discursive themes from dominant ambivalent white student representations, in which black male students' behaviour was over-sexualized. As for some white male teachers, this consisted of contradictory cultural investments, of desire and jealousy in the highly exaggerated ascription to the black Macho Lads of stylish resistance, sporting skills and 'having a reputation with girls'.

In order to enhance and amplify their own masculinity, the black and white Macho Lads were overtly sexist to young women and female staff, and aggressive to male students who did not live up to their prescribed masculine norms. They adopted a number of collective social practices in their attempt to regulate and normalize sex/gender boundaries. The black Macho Lads were particularly vindictive to African Caribbean academic students, who overtly distanced themselves from their anti-school strategies. In response, the black Macho Lads labelled them 'botty men' (a homophobic comment). As Mercer and Julien (1988: 112) point out, a further contradiction in subordinated black masculinities occurs, 'when black men subjectively internalise and incorporate aspects of the dominant definitions of masculinity in order to contest the conditions of dependency and powerlessness which racism and racial oppression enforce'. Ironically, the black Macho Lads, in distancing themselves from the racist school structures, adopted survival strategies of hyper-masculine heterosexuality that threatened other African Caribbean students, adding further barriers to their gaining academic success. Consequently, this made it more difficult for academic black students to gain social mobility via a professional job and the accompanying middle-class mode of masculinity. At the same time, white teachers' typifications of 'black male aggression' were reinforced (Gillborn 1990).

Summary

This chapter has explored the complex processes of learning to become a heterosexual within a secondary school context. Of strategic importance here is the ubiquitous male peer-group networks with their obsessive rites of passage, through which proof of their masculinity is acted out. The chapter illustrates the way in which the combined effects of new vocationalism, new training regimes, regendered local labour markets and changing family forms have impacted on the construction of diverse modes of student masculinity within a secondary school arena. The analysis of the developing sex/gender identities was placed within complex sets of power relations with particular reference to class, 'race' and ethnicity. This chapter has tended to emphasize the external social structures of schooling and masculinity. Chapter 3 will continue the critique of earlier male academic representations of young men's schooling, focusing in more detail on the internal dynamics of their psycho-sexual development.

3

Sexuality: Learning to become a heterosexual man at school

Introduction

> Since men are born into male bodies, but not into the successful accomplishment of culturally appropriate versions of masculinity, becoming a man is a complex process of learning and doing within shifting sets of social constraints.
>
> Holland *et al.* (1993: 2)

> If sex does not limit gender, then perhaps there are genders, ways of culturally interpreting the sexed body that is no way restricted to the apparent duality of sex.
>
> (Butler 1990: 112)

In the last chapter, I spoke of the limits of typologies. My own student typologies were constructed from the range of young men's cultural practices as a heuristic device to highlight different modes of heterosexual masculine identity. I found that they were not appropriate for the following sections, in which I explore from a male student perspective, the commonalities of what constitutes male heterosexuality within a school context. The student narratives contain shifting emphases of conflicting desires, anxieties, fears and confusions. They speak openly about relations with the school authorities, parents and young women, on a broad agenda that includes male bonding, hidden emotions and fantasies. However, there is little acknowledgement from them of the individual and collective institutional power that is ascribed to them as heterosexual males. What emerges is the development of a range of masculine subjectivities, which are experienced as transitional gender and sexual identities. In this chapter, I shall first set out the general pattern of what it means for these male students to be heterosexual. Then, I shall examine in more detail the specific dynamics of how this is played out.

What constitutes young men's heterosexuality?

I set out to examine the constitutive cultural elements of heterosexual male students' subjectivity within Parnell School. These elements, which consisted of contradictory forms of compulsory heterosexuality, misogyny and homophobia, were marked by contextual ambivalence and contingency. My focus was the complex interplay of these cultural elements as institutionally specific forms of gendered and sexual power. More particularly, I sought to explore how they were operationalized as key defining processes in sexual boundary maintenance, policing and legitimization of male heterosexual identities. In order to understand how students attempted to learn the sex/gender codes that conferred hegemonic masculinity, it was necessary to bring together social and psychic structures. What emerged as of particular salience was the way in which heterosexual male students were involved in a double relationship, of traducing the 'other', including women and gays (external relations), at the same time as expelling femininity and homosexuality from within themselves (internal relations). These were the complex and contradictory processes within which heterosexual male student apprenticeships were developed within a secondary school context (Hollway 1984a, b; Dollimore 1992; Middleton 1992).

Arnot (1984) examines the links between male compulsory heterosexuality and the masculine processes of dissociation from femininity. She argues that in a male-dominated society femininity is ascribed; in contrast, masculinity and manhood have to be 'achieved in a permanent process of struggle and confirmation'. She adds that it is not surprising:

> that it is boys who are more prone to construct and use gender categories. Not only do they have more at stake in such a system of classification (i.e. male power) but also they have to try and achieve manhood through a process of distancing women and femininity from themselves and maintaining the hierarchy of social superiority of masculinity by devaluing the female world.
>
> (Arnot 1984: 145)

A main argument in this book is that students are active makers of sex/gender identities, in which they have complex social and psychic investments (Connell *et al*. 1982: 77). Much of this work takes place at a collective level within the informal world of male peer groups, where specific subject positions are inhabited. In contrast to the processes of desexualization found within the official curriculum, sex and sexuality were compulsively and competitively discussed and played out between and within male and female student peer groups. Observing the 'sexual hustle and bustle' of classroom and playground life made clear the limits of state agencies' surveillance and control of youth populations. The pervasiveness of the categorical imperatives to act like heterosexual men circumscribed the peer groups' everyday cultural practices. Sexual orientation was seen as a primary source of identity and of social behaviour. Without accepting his critical stance, male students would agree with Foucault (1979) that sex has become 'the truth of our being'.

Amerjit: In year ten there was a new kid and he had a massive dick and they used to call him cock of the year. Do you get it? He had a big dick and he was seen as the strongest in his year. There was a lot of rumours that he was famous around here. Some called him a pervert because it was so big. And kids were jealous saying it's what you do with it that matters, not the size.

Mark: Lots of kids hate having a shower 'coz everyone knows whether you've got a big prick or a small one. Some kids really show off. You know, "I've got the biggest prick in the whole school".

Noel: I did different things. I used to try to get out of PE. A lot of kids do. When I was thirteen I had a tiny plonker and I used to just rush into and out of the showers, just quickly drop your towel and not even get wet sometimes. Then the PE teacher at that time would make you go back in. Everyone called him a poof. I fucking hated it, everyone standing around in the nuddy. I can still remember it. It could give you nightmares. And like I'd always go into the shithouse to have a piss, not the urinals if there was a crowd in the bogs. And I still do.

Most of the young men publicly associated sex exclusively with vaginal penetration (Holland *et al.* 1993: 6). There was an emphasis on the activity of male sex, with little acknowledgement of sharing needs with young women. As female students pointed out, many of these phallocentric young men displayed an obsession with talk of penis size, uncontrollable urges and sexual potency. The young women were highly critical of male students' obsessive and competitive talk about their 'little plonkers'. The following discussion took place as part of a project on gender representation in school texts. Working through the texts, female students objected to the construction of gender differences around the conventional active–passive dichotomy ascribed to masculinity and femininity. In response, some of the male students challenged them, arguing that these differences were based on fixed, biologically given sexual differences. This then developed into a critical encounter that highlighted the different gender and sexual anxieties of both the male and female students (Litewka 1977).

Joanne: You lot are obsessed with your knobs.

Liza: That's true, you never stop talking about your penises. Like, "it's so long, I can wrap it round my leg three times".

Stephen: Well you lot are always on about your weight.

Peter: At least we're joking. You lot are serious. You get mad if we say that you are fat.

Gaynor: Well, ninty-nine per cent of people are not going to see your plonkers, people see us.
Stephen: How many diets have you been on?
Liza: Well, that's for myself. It makes me feel better if I'm slim.
Joanne: But all your talk is crap. It's just to prove you're better than your mates. Why don't you all get together and measure your little plonkers.

One aspect of the research in this area was to examine how the male students learned the discursive codes and conventions of sex-talk and the resulting positioning of dominant and subordinate masculinities and femininities (see Lee 1993). In questionnaires on male topics of conversation, sex was consistently identified as of major significance. What emerged from further interviews and observation was that the purpose of male heterosexual sex-talk was not mono-functional. This confirms Cohen's (in Wood 1984: 82) useful suggestion that sex-talk has several functions, including, for example, that it may be confessional, seductive, therapeutic or educative. Wood (ibid.) adds: 'It is important to note that, depending on circumstance, one mode may stand for or promote another. Confessional talk may be seductive in some contexts, for instance.'

Graham: You have to be careful with girls. It's not like talking with your mates. Like you have to work out if they want you to be romantic or tough. If they want the romantic type, you tell them things about yourself, be open and that. A lot of girls love that kind of talk. It really gets them going.
M.M.:   Where do you learn that you have to talk in different ways?
Graham: I don't know, when you put it like that. I've got older brothers and I share a bedroom with them and when I was younger, I would hear them talking about their girlfriends. So I learnt a lot from them, not with advice and that, just listening to their experiences. I think that's why people say I'm mature for my age with girls.

Like Westwood (1990: 60), I was interested in the 'way masculinities are played out and validated for other men'. At Parnell School, one of the main functions of the young men's sex-talk was publicly to validate their masculinity to their male friends. This collective peer identity affirmation often manifested itself in terms of highly ritualistic obsessive discourses. In striving for masculinity they told and retold each other performance stories (Holland *et al.* 1990: 15). Their sexual narratives carried the predictable misogynous boasting and exaggeration of past heterosexual conquests and male heroic fantasies, in which women were represented as passive objects of male sexual urges, needs and desires. These male 'fictions' appeared to be crucial elements in setting the parameters of the prescriptive and proscriptive sex/gender boundaries that served to police schoolboys' performance by making them act like men (Brittan and Maynard 1984).

In the next chapter, female students critically describe their experience of male students' misogynous social practices. I found that my transcriptions failed to convey the full force of the underpinning institutional male misogyny and attempted domination in some of the young men's accounts of the objectification of women's bodies, through their use of sexist slang.[1] Wood (1984) manages to capture the specificity of the nature and function of a group of young mens' use of sex-talk. He writes:

> It is doubtful whether the existence of such terms [sexist slang] *per se* can be too simply linked to a patriarchal system, however old that system may be. Rather it is the tone, context and use to which they are attemptedly put, that makes sexual slang part of sexist talk. In terms of the developing sexism of the centre it is the use of terms for parts of the body *combined with* the intent to assess the girls in crude and superficial ways that constitutes the element of attempted domination.
>
> (Wood 1984: 58; original emphasis)

Although there was much student policing of sex/gender boundaries at Parnell School, it was not predictable which of the male students' social practices would be categorized by different peer groups as feminine or masculine. It was contingent on specific location and most significantly on individual male students' established sexual reputations. In other words, it was not predictable who could do what, when and to whom. There was a certain contextual fluidity in the construction of ascribed meanings that mediated the institutional signifiers of what it means to be masculine or feminine within the school and across other sites. This is illustrated in the following accounts by Ashwin, who during the research period shifted his masculine identity from a Macho Lad to an Academic Achiever, and Simon, a Real Englishman, who was ambivalent about his sexual orientation and preference.

Ashwin: Yes, I have gone from a warrior to a wimp. Smiths' fan and books and all that but it's funny how people see me. I could be seen as a right "poofter". But I've still got my old reputation with the gang I was with, of being hard. So I suppose they wouldn't see me as soft.

M.M.: When you say you didn't talk a lot about sex with the gang. How come that you got away with it?

Ashwin: Because I used to do other things.

M.M.: Such as?

Ashwin: Knocking off stuff and that, getting into fights, standing up to the teachers.

M.M.: So talking about sex or fighting might mean the same thing?

Ashwin: Yes, to look big to your mates. You have to prove yourself all the time. And it's different things in different groups. Like everyone can look at a street gang and say, oh yeah, all their behaviour is about being hard. But in the top sets it's the same in a way, getting the best marks and all that. That would be seen as "poofter" stuff to the gang but is acceptable to the top set lot. But it's still about beating other people, doing better than them, and you're shamed up if the girls get better marks. That would be real slack. You have to prove you're better than them and the other boys.

Simon: I think of myself as asexual, I suppose . . . with my friends. I can get away with a lot more, what a lot of people might call feminine behaviour and depending on where we are and it's easier now we are in the sixth form.

M.M.:   Did anything else make it easier?

Simon: It's easier when you're doing drama than with the macho boys in PE. It's easier at an alternative gig than at the nightclubs with the riff-raff. I would probably get away with acting more feminine or camp because I'm the joker in the group. It sounds a bit trite but I think it's because I make them laugh. Also, people may be afraid to verbally attack me because I'm known for my sarcastic humour ... I've never thought about it before but it may be I've developed the sarcasm to protect myself.

Alongside the heterosexual male students' practices of compulsory heterosexuality and misogyny, many of them displayed virulent public modes of homophobia. In trying to understand what was going on here, I found Rutherford's (1990) analysis useful. Drawing on the work of Derrida, Rutherford describes the inner logic of the psychic relations of domination:

> Binarism operates in the same way as splitting and projection: the centre expels its anxieties, contradictions and irrationalities onto the subordinate term, filling it with the antithesis of its own identity; the Other, in its very alienness, simply mirrors and represents what is deeply familiar to the centre, but projected outside of itself. It is in these processes and representations of marginality that the violence, antagonisms and aversions that are at the core of the dominant discourses and identities become manifest – racism, homophobia, misogyny and class contempt are the products of this frontier.
>
> (Rutherford 1990: 22)

Heterosexual male students at Parnell School adopted discourses of naturalization, in which homosexuality was constructed as a form of disability (Franklin *et al*. 1991). The students' own fantasies of men sleeping together 'made them feel sick'. This involved specific class cultural forms with intra-class differences. There was a tendency for many of the working-class males to adopt a heterosexual superiority/gay inferiority couplet. While for many of the heterosexual middle-class males it was frequently expressed in a more liberal discourse of gay men as intrinsically different rather than necessarily inferior to straight men; sharing their parents' view of gays as 'victims' rather than 'social problems'. The Real Englishmen combined a publicly confident discursive position in discussing homosexuality with an individual defensive stance. Among many of the Asian and African Caribbean working-class male students there was a tendency to identify homosexuality as a Western or white social phenomenon. Significantly, most of the male students never referred to lesbians when talking about homosexuality (Kitzinger 1990).

Ashwin: If I was gay, I would try to change. I'm not against gays as long as they don't touch me.

Bob: If homosexual people are there you have to change. You can't talk normal. Like if you see an attractive girl, you can't say, look she's attractive, he would feel embarrassed. Like if a handicapped person was there, you wouldn't talk about having a game of football because that would make them feel bad. Your basic characteristics, like whether you're homosexual or not makes you how you are. You can't get on together. I mean I couldn't get on with one.

As one of the sixth-form gay students pointed out, Bob was unaware of the irony of his own obsessive worship of male heroes, such as James Dean and Marlon Brando, that he publicly displayed in his style of dress.

Jim: I just hate "bum boys". When I think of them, it makes me want to puke. When I see two guys holding hands or pecking each other on the cheek, I have to turn away. I feel dead sick.
M.M.: Have you ever seen gays doing this?
Jim: No. But if I did I would. They must be looking at you, undressing you in their minds. They're just sick.
M.M.: Why do you feel gays are so bad?
Jim: They just are. It's a strong feeling inside of me, inside any normal people.
M.M.: I don't have that feeling.
Jim: Well it's different with you, you talk with all sorts of people and you're soft. Like the kids all say, you always take the black kids' side and the teachers are afraid of you.
M.M.: I don't understand what you're saying.
Jim: It's like you look after the weak ones, so you've probably been affected by it and you see things different.
Adam: We are all transsexuals but I personally don't want to sleep with men.
Simon: You'd hear your parents talking about Freud and bisexuals. I suppose sexuality depends on environment.

Two points emerge here. First, throughout the research such comments as Jim's perception of me as 'soft' seemed to operate as a code that served to legitimate how we could engage in this personal 'non-masculine' mode of talk. Second, in arguing that male heterosexuality is constituted by contextual ambivalence to homosexuality, this is not to imply that overt forms of public homophobia were not pervasive throughout Parnell School, as Jim illustrates above. As the gay students in the next chapter indicate, they had different responses to these different class cultural forms of homophobia. However, the more liberal stance, suggested by Adam and Simon above, was not necessarily interpreted as less problematic for them. For some gay students, it was a more invidious form of patronization, with the middle-class heterosexual males, such as the Real Englishmen, appropriating gay style, while publicly affirming their 'hetero identity' (Frith 1992: 181).

In Chapter 1, a key question that emerged was how masculine heterosexuality as a highly fragile socially constructed phenomenon becomes fixed as an apparently stable, unitary category. It was suggested that schools alongside other institutions attempt to administer, regulate and reify unstable sex/gender categories. More specifically, this administration, regulation and reification of sex/gender boundaries is institutionalized through the interrelated social and discursive practices of staffroom, classroom and playground microcultures. Lesley Hall (1991: 20), in her study of the hidden history of heterosexual men's fears and failures, provides evidence to reveal the 'considerable tensions between the ideals set up and the lived experience of men as they perceived it, and that the "normal" male and male sexuality were more problematic than they are usually assumed to be'. As indicated above, her argument finds a resonance with young heterosexual male students at Parnell School.

I have set out the general pattern of how the male students at Parnell School learn to be men in terms of the three constitutive elements of compulsory heterosexuality, misogyny and homophobia. In the following sections, I shall examine in more detail the specific dynamics of how this is played out in relation to my claim that these cultural elements are marked by contextual ambivalence and contingency.

'Just all mixed up' – Fragile masculine subjectivities: What do young heterosexual men want?

The last two chapters have explored the specific gender regime in operation at Parnell School and the masculine subject positions that it made available to the students. Its emphasis was on external social structures. Here, I wish to concentrate on the cultural production of adolescent masculine sexual identities, focusing on psychosexual dynamics. Connell *et al.* (1982: 174–5) have described the way in which:

> The high school enters the picture at a very important stage of psychosexual development, and its impact on the construction of gender has to be understood in this light. The masculinizing and femininizing practices within it . . . are in important respects responses to psychosexual diversity and its fluidity in early adolescence. The school certainly doesn't brainwash kids into a stereotype . . . But its intervention has a lot to do with the hierarchy constructed among different kinds of masculinity and femininity; and at the same time, the relations that are constructed between boys and girls.

Methodologically, one of the main difficulties of studying school masculinities was that the social context seemed to be critically significant in influencing how, what and when the young men (and male teachers) felt they could or would say to me (see Bhavnani 1991). In the next chapter, female students discuss similar male student responses, with widely contrasting private and public stances in different domains. Recently, a number of studies have suggested the need to examine how men experience masculinity and describe the ways it is problematic for them (see Metcalf and Humphries 1985). Askew and Ross (1988: 14) have critically assessed the formation of young men's subjectivities, with a specific focus on their experience of pressures to be male within the school arena. At Parnell School, the problematic nature of young men's heterosexuality manifested itself in terms of peer group pressures, ambiguities, confusions and contradictions. In short, the empirical research pointed to the need to address 'sexuality and its discontents' for heterosexual male students (Weeks 1989).

Earlier ethnographic work has recorded how working-class male sub-cultural school groups have been successful in collectively helping to resolve their institutional subordination. For example, the African Caribbean 'Rasta Heads' in *Young Gifted and Black* (Mac an Ghaill 1988c) were aware that their projected machismo image to those in authority had won concessions from their teachers. However, male ethnographers have been more reticent in researching the bleaker side of male peer-group life. Holland *et al.* (1993) have captured the tensions and contradictions of the pleasures and perils of the male peer group, that while affirming male power also creates an unsupportive competitive environment that serves to make individuals highly vulnerable. They argue that:

> It might seem reasonable to asssume that young men talk together in groups to express comaraderie and gain support. It appears from the accounts of the young men in this study . . . that such talk can be very unsupportive for the individual. In these groups, young men are subjected to teasing, having the mickey taken, and forms of collective pressure to express and define themselves in a particular way in order to prove their manhood. Aggression too can be seen in the negative labelling of those who fall short, or whose sexual claims are not believed – "wimps", "wallies" and "wankers". What the group does seem to support is a particular concept of hegemonic heterosexual masculinity, and separation from effeminacy, or homosexuality.
>
> (Holland *et al.* 1993: 12–13)

At Parnell School, similar processes to those reported by Holland *et al.* were in place. Peer-group networks acted as key local cultural sites, within which specific forms of masculinity were inhabited. In the following accounts, which were recorded in individual interviews, male students describe the adolescent loneliness and confusion that many of them experienced with their 'mates'. During the research, they reflected on their difficulty in expressing personal feelings with each other, resulting from their learning to hide from others and themselves what they felt (Tolson 1977). One of the main themes that emerged out of the heterosexual male students' accounts was their emotional illiteracy. In personal interviews, they frequently returned to two connected issues: first, that there was no safe space within which they could talk about how they felt; second, that the absence of an emotional language greatly influenced the development of their sexual identities (Williams 1977).

Daniel: We've never really talked to each other about anything, you know anything important. Like when Patrick's father died, none of us could really talk to him. I had one talk when he was really sad but we never talked again. You see if you were really open, well you just couldn't trust another bloke that the next day that he wouldn't tell everyone and then that would be the end of you.

Tony: You can't talk to men intelligently, only to women. You are talking to men seriously for a while, then they see a girl and say to each other, I'd give her eight out of ten.

Frank: I don't think girls put you down as much as blokes. Like when I said, sexual fantasy, all the blokes jump on you.

Wayne: You can't trust girls because of what they expect from you, of how you're supposed to act, you know. And you can't be honest with your mates because they'll probably tell other people.

Tony: Listening to the lyrics of The Smiths or The Cure about loneliness and relationships breaking up, they're not singing about themselves, they're married, they're singing about you. But I don't think you could ever talk about this to anyone, even though you're all feeling the same thing.

Nevertheless, these experiences are not necessarily determinant in the formation of young masculine subjectivities. For example, Graham combined a public high-status reputation among his peers of being one of the most sexually successful students in having girlfriends, with a private stance that questioned his peer group's sexual assumptions. It may be added that his final comments, which were representative of many male students with whom I have worked, illustrate the complexity of creating the conditions in which young men can actively participate in sex/sexuality education programmes in English schools.

Graham: I think kissing and hugging a man is okay but not anything more, no caressing or getting too close.

M.M.: Why?

Graham: Because only girls should do that. What if you get aroused? Then you might get used to a bloke doing it and you might not be able to do it with a girl.

M.M.: So a man could get you aroused?

Graham: Yes, not as easy as a girl. I have erections all the time, sometimes on the bus, once at a football match. I was so embarrassed.

M.M.: Have you talked to anyone about this?

Graham: Never. That's the trouble.

M.M.: Are you surprised you can talk so openly?

Graham: In a way yes, but then again, I think a lot of boys would like to talk but who do you talk to? Like these two girls said to me and my friends, you're not very close like us. And it's true girls are closer. They're allowed to be closer, aren't they? If I said anything like this to my mates, they'd think I was a "poofter". I mean you just couldn't.

M.M.: What about other people?

Graham: Like who? My parents wouldn't know what I'm talking about. And girls aren't going to want to hear this sort of thing. I mean it scares me when I think about it.

One of the main difficulties in the research was working through a central dichotomy in many of the young men's lives, namely, their projection of a public confident masculinity and their reporting to me their private anxieties and insecurities. Of particular significance here was their learning the masculine code of splitting sexual practices from emotional feelings. Wood (1984: 83–4) points to the insecurity men experience in the process of acknowledging their 'more feminine side'. He suggests that one element of this gender ideology is men's uncontrollable need for sex and that this may lead to the fusion of sex and affection, with the result that men do not know how to behave. At Parnell School, most of the young men appeared to find it difficult to talk about male affection in relation to sex. In interviews, they defensively could not or would not talk to me about how they might be linked (see Hollway 1984a,b). This is an interesting finding with respect to the issue of adult men refusing to take responsibility for the emotional side of their lives. Unexpectedly, while discussing male–female relations, one of the students spoke of his emotional relationship with a male friend.

William: We (a friend) wanked each other one night when we were really drunk. Then later on when I saw him, he said that he had a girlfriend. I knew he hadn't. We just had to move apart because we got too close.
M.M.: How do you feel about that?
William: Oh fuck it, it was ridiculous. I don't know. I'm not a '"bender" or anything. I don't give a fuck about the sex. I know some girls now and that. But I wish we were still mates. It's great to be close, you know what I mean, really close just to one person and just the two of you know.

As Mark explains below, this dichotomization of sex and emotions involved accentuated processes of gendered and sexualized practices. It manifested itself in terms of distancing oneself externally from any association with femininity and internally from a 'feminized' masculinity that was imputed to boys. It is important to emphasize that these external and internal processes took varied class and ethnic cultural forms in different sites, such as the home, the peer group and the workplace.

Mark: I'd say I'm one hundred per cent heterosexual from the waist down and seventy per cent from the waist up.
M.M.: What do you mean?
Mark: Well you know, I'm a right randy bastard, always thinking about how I can get it away. Just thinking of screwing all the time. I can't help it. My girlfriend says I'm sex mad. But at other times, she says, I'm soft like a girl and I can be very emotional and caring. She reckons the only woman I'll ever love is my mum and I'll just want girls for sex.
Bob: I don't know really. I never used to be like this. There's a lot of pressure from your mates and probably the worst for me was my dad and brothers calling me "poof" 'coz I used to do a lot of things around the house with mum. I used to like cooking. It's funny, I don't do them any more but I'm still very close to her, the most really.

The next section indicates the limits of making generalizations in social class terms about male students' relations with their mothers. However, I was surprised by the frequency with which some working-class male students spoke to me privately of their emotional closeness to their mothers. As indicated in the last chapter, this contrasted with the new middle-class Real Englishmen, who directed much hostility to their mothers and fathers.

Rutherford (1990: 25), locating children at the base of modern hierarchically ordered societies, claims that they suffer most pain, humiliation and shame in relation to their parents. At Parnell School, male students and their parents spoke at length about inter-generational difficulties. At times, it seemed as if members of the same family were talking about different experiences. I was surprised at the young men's explanations of why they felt their parents didn't love them. McRobbie (1984) provides an insight into the unintended deep emotional hurt felt by these young men. She claims that:

> Hugging is partly what links fantasies about the self with the need to prove oneself to another. It looks back to childhood and the desire to win parental approval: look what I've done! Aren't I clever! Not surprisingly this latter dimension makes the pleasures of hugging problematic . . . The hug is both the recognition and the reassurance, the parental reward, the sign of absolute affection. No wonder it has such resonance in memory and in expressions of desire.
>
> (McRobbie 1984: 159)

A number of male students spoke of the fact that their parents weren't physically close to them and that they differentiated emotionally between them and their sisters.

Tony: I can never remember my mum or dad ever kissing me as a child. Maybe on exceptional occasions. They never tucked me in at night. There was none of those close feelings expressed with me not like my sister. And then I think that you can go one way or the other. Either hate being touched or like me love being hugged and hugging people.
M.M.:   To your parents?
Tony: No, not with them. I suppose when you think of it, there's few people that you can hug. Like none of my male friends except when we're drunk and maybe one or two if we're on our own.
Frank: I think in families the girls are closer to their mums and dads. But boys, who can they be close to? Like in our family and all my friends, the parents wouldn't be close to their kids. I don't know why. Like my dad spends all his time in the pub with his mates. Why doesn't he want to be with me? Why doesn't he say that he loves me? Fuck it, I don't know. It does my head in.
M.M.:   Could you say this to him?
Frank: No. I couldn't. We couldn't get close, we hardly ever talk. I think my sisters do with my mum. But I've never talked with anyone about real things, true things, in my whole life.

Ashwin: I just want to be loved but girls never seem to want this. It's the same at home, my mum is closer to my sisters. If there's rows or anything, they always gang up on me.

Stephen: I've never got on with my dad. Before he left, he was always onto me, getting at me in little ways. He was terrible to me and my mum. He was always saying I was too weak and he wanted a strong son. So him and my brother got on good and he took him with him.

M.M.:   So how did you cope?

Stephen: I don't know really. My mum got me into body building and eating the right food, so I feel a bit better now, and the girls like my muscles!

One of the most emotionally demanding aspects of the research was listening to the students' relations with their parents. At early stages in the research, I was surprised at the male students' openness and vulnerability in disclosing to me what were highly personal feelings and memories. Throughout the study, they frequently returned to these central issues in their lives. The methodological and ethical issues involved here are discussed in Chapter 6.

Hearn (1988: 9) suggests that in critically examining men's experience, we 'may need to indicate how things are for men, how complex, contradictory and multi-layered. For example, men's relations with each other may be part competition, part fear, part solidarity, part longing.' This has specific meanings for a subordinated younger generation located within a state institution, in which processes of normalization and regulation of masculine sexuality are integral features (Skeggs 1991: 129). As indicated above for heterosexual male students at Parnell School, sexual boundary maintenance, policing and control were definitive peer-group cultural practices. In Chapter 5, gay male students challenge the conventional sexual polarities that maintain clear-cut boundaries between heterosexuality and homosexuality. They suggest that there is a 'private' world in which their straight friends act out a more ambivalent sexuality, marked by elements of confusion, repression, denial and projection onto the 'other'. A small number of heterosexual male students provided support for this view, that sexual transgressions occurred more frequently than is often assumed.

Robert: We are all a bit gay. It depends what you mean by gay. Whether you like the person as a friend, admire him or want to sleep with him … A lot of the sixth-form kids here like certain clothes and music that started off with gays, you know.

Andy: I think everyone goes through a phase of it.

M.M.:   At what age?

Andy: When you're becoming aware of sex, from twelve on, certainly at fifteen and sixteen.

M.M.:   Did you go through it?

Andy: Yes, in a way, a bit. Like looking at a male and thinking I like his hairstyle, his clothes and he's got a good body. That's a bit gay isn't it?

M.M.:   But no-one I meet claims to have gone through the phase.

Andy: But they're not aware of it, are they? You don't give it that label. But you go through a stage of confusion looking for your sexuality. I know I like women. I am fully heterosexual.

These comments make very interesting reading in relation to the most recent media presentation of 'finding the gay gene', with its dominant assumption of essentialist sexual categories (McKie 1993). The young men here suggest that it may be more appropriate to think of human sexuality in terms of a continuum rather than a rigid dichotomy between heterosexuality and homosexuality.

Fear and desire: 'You can't win with girls!'

Cockburn (1987: 44) writes of the need for conceptualizations of male and female behaviour, in terms of 'dealing with, modifying or resisting definitions threatened by the opposite sex, within an overall rampant culture of heterosexuality'. In talking with the young men about sex and sexuality, what emerges is a picture of complex inner-dramas of individual insecurity and low self-esteem. In relation to young women, many of them feel, shy, inadequate and unable to cope with the demands of initiating and maintaining 'a relationship with a girl'. There is a feeling of immense pressure from peers with whom the collectively fantasized heterosexual ideal is constructed (Holland *et al.* 1993). Dominant prescriptive male representations of what men are supposed to be and their constant banter among themselves of 'getting girls' is fundamentally contradicted by their experience of feeling unable to make (sexual) contact with young women. Following Wood (1984: 75), many of the male students seemed to be developing relations with young women in the contradictory terms of: 'a mixture of pursuit, disinterest, patronisation, fear and fixation'. Their individual lack of confidence, manifested in terms of highly defensive talk among themselves about young women, served to hide from the young men the gendered and sexual cultural forms of power that are ascribed to them as heterosexual males. The dominant response of the young men at Parnell School was similar to that reported by Holland *et al.* (1993). They write of:

> Spotty youths not fancied by girls, boys who lack social skills of confidence, whose sexual technique appears to them inept, who lack knowledge of women's bodies and feelings, risk their manhood. Fear of failure to achieve masculinity is a fear of lack of potency both personally and socially (Tiefer, 1987). It encourages resistance through subcultural variants of masculinity and also boasting of exploits, aggression, competition, homophobia, racism and the general subordination of women, as young men set out to prove themselves.
>
> (Holland *et al.* 1993: 2)

Frank: You want girls more than anything. You know we are always chasing them. But I don't know, when you're with them you get tired. Then Miss Ryan [teacher] is always saying that the girls are pressurized by the boys but I think it's a load of crap. We have all the pressure of having to get off with girls and asking them out.

Gilroy: That's true. It's the girls who have all the power. Like they have the choice and can make you look a prat in front of your mates. If they see someone they fancy they just chuck you for him and he might even be your friend. They're always causing trouble, are you with me?

Paul: You can't trust them [young women]. They talk to all their mates saying he's not very good and all. And they're really bitchy towards you and there's nothing you can do, 'coz you can't really hit a girl. And even if you did hit a girl you'd get expelled, but when they do it it's all right. They cry to the teachers, saying he called me names. It's just not fair.

Edward: Even with the intelligent ones, you say stupid things, like they're the only one in the world and all that and they'll do anything for you. And then they think they're in love! Girls, the way they think, everything about them is different. My older brother reckons all they want to do is to tie you down. I just can't understand them.

Stephen: I've never asked a girl out. The only times have been when they have asked me. I just can't talk to girls. I have to pretend to be someone else for a while and then when I relax, they see what I'm really like, they get bored, saying that they want to have fun and a good time, not talk serious all the time. So, they dump me.

Wolpe (1988: 174) found in her study of sexuality and schooling that male students tended to spend much time together in the peer groups, even when they had girlfriends. She suggests that further investigation is required to establish whether the cause is male students' slower development or fear of handling a relationship with young women or other factors. Nevertheless, earlier in her study, Wolpe (1988: 164) suggests that: 'the boys' lack of experience and their ineptitude may well account for their tendency to spend more time together with each other while pretending disinterest in girls'. In group interviews at Parnell School, female students questioned the male students about the gender exclusivity of their relations with other males.

M.M.:   Why do you spend so much time together with the lads?

Frank: Well girls stick together, don't they?

Amerjit: I've never really thought about it. It's true. Because we have more things in common.

Smita: Like what?

Frank: Just things that you talk about, things you enjoy together.

Smita: How do you know that we don't talk about these things? The only difference that I can see is things like you all get in cars together and hassling girls.

When I asked the young men why they chose to spend so much time together, most of them were hostile, feeling that the question had homosexual connotations. It was self-evident to them that as heterosexuals they preferred to be with young women. In further interviews, most of the students accepted that they did choose to spend much of their time with male friends. Ironically, young women were one of the main topics of the young men's conversation. Nevertheless, as their social practices demonstrated, they preferred to talk *about* them rather than spending time *with* them. They offered varied explanations for their 'choice'.

Noel: Boys would prefer to be with girls than with their mates but there's pressure from mates not to. Like when I'm in the car with three of my friends and they ask me if I'm pissed off and I say yeah. I would rather be with my girlfriend and so would they. But they take the piss out of you and pretend they wouldn't. It's mad. There's even pressure from your mates not to spend time with one other male. Somehow you have to be with the gang.

Tony: I think the school makes it that way that you spend more time with . boys, the subjects and everything. And the way that teachers treat girls and boys differently.

As suggested above, this is a relatively under-researched area. Hence, there may be a danger in empirical work on the interplay of schooling, sexuality and masculinity to focus on mono-causal explanations of what are, to the researcher, often highly paradoxical and confusing cultural practices. Noel's and Tony's comments imply the multidimensionality of this complex area.

In critically examining what constituted young male heterosexual subjectivity, I explored with the students the dynamics of same-sex male behaviour. They spoke of a hidden masculine code within which men could exhibit positive emotions to male friends, while intuitively knowing the difference between male and female physical contact (Aggleton 1987a).

Edward: Sometimes we get called "bum boys" by the hard kids if we go round putting our arms around each other. But you know that it's different if you put your arm around a bloke than a girl, don't you? You do it in a male way to a bloke that both of you would instinctively know.

M.M.:   How is it different?

Andy: You would feel something about being with a woman. I can get close to a man but it's different with a woman, you feel a closeness, a sexual closeness.

Nava (1984) writes of the different forms of regulation that exist for young men and women, that are lived out through their relationships to each other. She notes that:

> The dominance exercised by boys over girls is rooted . . . in their ability to enforce the boundaries between femininity and masculinity . . . These boundaries are secured by them through harassment, through the policing of sexuality – to maintain a double standard – and through the branding of gender unorthodoxy (of activity, initiative and independence) as unfeminine and undesirable.
>
> (Nava 1984: 14)

There was much evidence of these oppressive processes at Parnell School and, as Nava suggests, the manner in which they operated was quite complex. At one level, many of the young men made a distinction between 'their girlfriends' and 'other girls'. The former were positioned within discourses of male protection and respect. The working-class male students' accounts were reminiscent of their talk about their mothers. For the young men, the category 'other girls' appeared to signify the legitimation of a more overt set of sexual relations of harassment. However, these differential responses were not clear-cut, and contextual shifts made it difficult to identify the underlying male peer-group rules. In the following extracts, the young men explain their differential responses to their 'girlfriends' and male friends. Male peer networks set out to define the parameters within which the young men operated and had their own internal logic of surveillance and control. The young men commented that young women would come and go but 'your mates' were always with you. These young men's practices would support Connell's (1987) argument that male heterosexual ambivalence towards women should not be read as an aberration, but rather as an intrinsic aspect of what constitutes hegemonic masculinity. He writes:

> In this sense hegemonic masculinity must embody a successful collective strategy in relation to women. Given the complexity of gender relations no simple or uniform strategy is possible: a "mix" is necessary. So hegemonic masculinity can contain at the same time, quite consistently, openings towards domesticity and openings towards violence, towards misogyny and towards heterosexual attraction.
>
> (Connell 1987: 185–6)

Noel: On the first instinct you're interested in looks, then other things later on, like having a laugh. You're with your girl and you think she's like a pot of gold. Like my mates are jealous of me with my girlfriend and she keeps on at me about them. Sometimes it's difficult to keep everyone happy.

Stephen: When you're trying to pick a girl up, then yes, if you're out with your mates, you would spend more time with her to chat her up. But if she's a more regular girlfriend and you're out with her and your mates come in, yes you would spend more time with them and she would go into the background.

M.M.:   Why is that?

Wayne: It's just normal. Girls are important but a particular girl isn't going to be around long is she? You always come back to your mates in the end, don't you?

M.M.:   What do the young women think?

William: Some accept it. Others are unreasonable and go off moaning, which just shows you we're better off without her.

M.M.:   Don't you think it's fair they act like that?

Stephen: Most girls know the score, the others will only give you trouble, believe me.

In interviews with young women, they confirmed these male assumptions and the resulting gender interaction and social closure. In the next chapter, they discuss the meanings of this male camaraderie. They were highly critical of the fact that for young women, men appeared to be important in a way that women were not in men's lives.

Popular cultural consumption: Some day my prince/princess will come along[2]

Corrigan (1978: 151), in his study of the schooling of the male working-class *Smash Street Kids*, has pointed to the range of contradictory positions they may occupy as actual and potential labour and consumers. He maintains that this results in ideological, and occasionally material, room to express age-related cultural differences. He found that pop culture represented an arena that the students felt belonged to them more than powerful state employees, such as teachers. More recently, Hollands (1990: 148) has written of the continuing connection between consumption, the construction of differential youth identities and varied transitions into adult life. He emphasizes that these 'identities include not only gender and racial influences but are also linked quite closely to intra-class orientations towards the work sphere and subcultural styles'. Similarly at Parnell School, the consumption sphere was intimately linked to the formation of a range of intra-class masculinities and femininities. At the microcultural level, student peer groups, clothes, haircuts, trainers, sports bags, bikes and video games were key signifiers that marked out gender and sexual status. Possession of these highly desired commodities served as an index of high-status masculinity and femininity. Intense gender surveillance was a major student practice involving deeply felt and articulated cultural investments.

Darren (Macho Lad):   A lot of the girls would prefer us because we dress the best and are always the first to get the new fashions. The teachers hate us of course. They're always getting at us for something, like when we shaved our heads and we were the first to have tram lines in our hair. The teachers would prefer the snobs, who dress like tramps with their boots and their long coats.

Tony (Academic Achiever):   Like I said before, there's a lot of gangs in this place. You can tell them by the clothes they wear. The worst gang is the trainer and shell suit lot. They go round as if they're really it, as though all the girls are after them. I don't know what girl would be seen dead with them. They're just prickheads.

Adam (Real Englishman):   Most of them here are into all the commercial crap, no imagination. Just like sheep, getting clothes from up town in the big shops, the latest fashion that's advertised. Like they wouldn't even know about different styles.

Reading through the history of school ethnographies, it seems that during the last decade there appears to have emerged what might be called the 'feminization of male youth cultures', with hair, skin and clothes becoming male focal concerns on a much larger scale, which includes younger age groups. This provides an interesting example of the historical specificity of the changing categorization of femininity and masculinity expressed in youth styles. Male students' sex/gender identities are formed against an older generation's surveillance and social regulation. This was highlighted in relation to their fathers and male teachers, who found the imputed forms of femininity, which they ascribed to the young men's behaviour, highly problematic.

Andy: The way me and my brother dresses causes real problems with my dad. He thinks wearing long hair and an earring, people will think I'm a "poof". He just hasn't got a clue. My older brother says it's because he's getting old and is jealous and he's got no control over us anymore. I mean with our clothes and that.

Edward: The men teachers they're always taking the piss. Like when we're changing after games, the teachers will say, "come on girls we haven't got time for you to put your make-up on". Because we're using gel or something.

John Hill: The teachers, especially the men teachers, are always on at us saying, "don't forget to do your nails" or they show you up in front of your mates by saying, "Has anyone seen Hill's new dress?" Just because we wear good gear and want to look smart.

Some of the male teachers were particularly vindictive to the Macho Lads, challenging the latter's contradictory practices, that of 'hard men' compulsively concerned with their personal appearance. These teachers challenged what they saw as the increased narcissism of male students. Interestingly, they represented the students' involvement in youth style in sexual terms. In contrast, the male students defended themselves from a generational perspective.

Mr West: I don't think it's healthy for boys to be over-concerned with their personal appearance. I just can't understand their obsession with looking in mirrors and the way they're always at their hair.

Bob: The teachers, a lot of the men teachers, they think they're really funny because they take the piss. They say things like: "So you lot think you're hard, then how come you're dressed up like nancies?" Things like that, just to get you going.

M.M.: And what do you do?

Bob: Well, they only do it if you're on your own away from your mates and there's not much you can do. You couldn't tell them about looking smart. They're just too old to understand. Most of the teachers dress like tramps. The same old clothes every day. One of the kids sees the teachers around his way out of school and he said, "they wear the same clothes that they wear at school". So you can't expect much can you?

The everyday masculinity of popular culture manifested itself in terms of the male students' strong identification with and involvement in the 'male' social world of football, music (including a number of the students being in bands), action films, videos and computer games. One of the main surprises during the research was discovering the masculine exclusivity of the heterosexual male students' social fantasies. I examined this in relation to a number of masculinizing cultural practices. Football was one of the most important of these cultural practices for many working-class male students at Parnell School. It is very difficult to portray the complex emotional intensity of the game of football for them (see Parker 1992).[3]

Frank: You sometimes just dream of being adopted by a famous footballer and he trains you to play for England.
Jim: At the match [football], it's just the best feeling in the world, being with your mates and feeling good.
Stephen: It's what keeps you going all the week, seeing the lads out there. It's great on a Saturday getting ready for the game, going round to get your mates. And you all feel really proud, you know, "we're the city boys". And people move out of your way on the street.
Leon: When you're out playing a game, wearing the [football] strip, you feel really strong. You know at school you're bossed about and at home, but when the game starts you're really free.

Hornby (1992), writing of his childhood experiences as a football fan, notes the advantages of the football ground for a divorced father and himself. He recalls memories of this key working-class social drama:

> Saturday afternoons in North London gave us a context in which we could be together. We could talk when we wanted, the football gave us something to talk about (and anyway the silences weren't oppressive) and the days had a structure, a routine. The Arsenal pitch was to be our lawn . . . the Gunners' fishbar on Blackstock Road our kitchen; and the West Stand our home.
>
> (Hornby 1992: 4)

White working-class fathers described the significance of football in terms of class cultural continuity in a rapidly changing local community. Implicit in their accounts of 'the game' was the safe space it provided for inter-generational male bonding rituals between fathers and their sons. An important element here was that the common language of football facilitated an emotional familial exchange to take place, that for young working-class men was a much welcomed exception to normal relations with their fathers.

Mr Davies: For generations, fathers have taken their sons to the football [matches]. There's been a lot of changes around here. You'd hardly recognize the place in the last twenty years. They're bringing in all this American stuff. But you can't beat taking the kids down the game, listening to all the great names and meeting all the old characters. It's all you've got to hold onto.
Mr Bridges: It's terrible for the kids round here. There's nothing for them. The Tories have destroyed the jobs. And everyone is moaning about the

kids, but it's not their fault. Lads will be lads, we were. But there's nowhere for them to learn how to grow up. Like in foreign countries they have initiation for the young lads. But with the jobs gone, there's nothing down for our kids. They're not going off to university or anything, are they? And I know it might sound silly to you but I think that the Saturday game is one of the few things left, that brings different generations together and everyone enjoying it.

Middle-class male students tended to romanticize working-class male students' relations with their fathers. One of them, Daniel, was a keen footballer. In the following account, he exemplifies his peer group's perception of their own relations with their fathers, many of whom did not live with them.

Daniel: Our fathers have all this hippie crap about being sensitive men. They want to be at the baby's birth and all that kind of thing. Well, I wish they were like the [working-class] kids' fathers here, taking them down the football match and just talking to them. The middle-class have all this repression, so if your parents take you to a sport event you can't enjoy it. It has to be educational. It's like you say about middle-class parents turning the whole world into school.

Summary

In this chapter, I have developed recent work in this area, examining the complexity of adolescents' psychosexual development of masculine hetero-sexual identity. The focus has been on the public and private dichotomy of working-class and middle-class boys learning to be men, while policing sex/gender boundaries. I noted in the Introduction that gay male students directed me to make more problematic the issue of male heterosexuality. This chapter has explored the different aspects of how male students learn to be heterosexual within a secondary school context. I have examined the three cultural interconnected constitutive elements of compulsory hetero-sexuality, misogyny and homophobia.

4

Young women's experiences of teacher and student masculinities

This is a paradigm of how differences are institutionalised and reinforced throughout social life – from work practices ("sexual harassment") to street conventions ("wolf whistles") to routine rituals in bars and other social activities. Despite all the changes that have taken place . . . male sexuality as culturally defined provides the norm and, not surprisingly, female sexuality continues to be the problem. Males in *becoming* men, take up positions in power relations in which they acquire the ability to define women.

Weeks (1986: 60)

I was reading *The Women's Room* at home, and I thought that's just the way it is. Especially at school the girls have no space of their own. I think that's what gets the boys so angry, when we spend a lot of time in the toilets. It's the one place they can't come in and take over.

(Paula, student)

Introduction

This chapter explores young heterosexual women's experiences of teacher and student masculinities at Parnell School. It provides empirical evidence of female–male social relations in a key cultural site of adolescents' sex/gender formation. The young women identify the significance of male power at personal and institutional levels within the school system and its links with the wider society, including home, leisure and work relations. They offer a sophisticated analysis of the sex/gender structuring of these arenas, demonstrating that they are neither 'mere victims' or 'supergirls' of current institutional sex/gender regimes (Chigwada 1987). They recall a range of responses, that are class, 'race'/ethnic and age specific, including highly flexible forms of cooperation, negotiation, survival and resistance to teacher and student masculinities (Gillborn 1990: 71).

Key issues in this chapter include: the sexual division of labour, the remasculinization of the new vocationalist curriculum at Parnell School, male teacher discourses, the use of public spaces, talk of boys and men, future waged and domestic labour and cultural contestations, disruptions and resistances. This ouline suggests a rather wide-ranging discussion that may present problems for the reader. However, as indicated in the Introduction, I have held on to this framework in order to illustrate the institutional complexity of young women's experiences of, and responses to, teacher and student masculinities, which pervasively circumscribe their school lives.

There is a danger in a male researcher writing on gender relations, that the inclusion of one chapter on young women reads as a rather perfunctory exercise. My specific focus in this book is with the cultural production of masculinities, within the context of a rapidly changing English secondary school system. This chapter is not a case study that seeks to identify what constitutes student femininities to match my investigation of masculine youth formations. Such work has been carried out elsewhere and informs my theoretical and methodological stance.[1] These feminist texts have posited that femininity is a constitutive element in the cultural production of school masculinities (MacDonald 1981). For example, as Cockburn (1987: 43–4) argues in a highly salient critique of sub-cultural analysis of young people, which emphasizes the interrelatedness of female and male peer groups:

> We need a conception of male and female subcultures as related, two facets of a single unitary phenomenon. Just as masculine and feminine are complementary parts of a single gender system, so girls' and boys' subcultures are in reality only two aspects of one subculture, with different implications for the sexes. It was fair enough to propose that girls' culture was not merely marginal to boys: girls had something going for them and what the girls did and thought and felt was cultural and specific. But it is not enough to interpolate a "girls' subculture". Girls lived their lives that were complementary to, in relation to, and mutilated by, those of the "lads". We need to understand young men's culture as gendered, relational and entailing a certain form of femininity. It is sometimes suggested that, through the subculture of femininity, girls and women "contribute to their own oppression". They do not. What contributes to their oppression is living on the dark side of a gendered youth subculture, male dominated and male-advantaging.

The male gay students' accounts of the interplay of schooling and masculinity unexpectedly involved a restructuring of my research design.

In the original research formulation, I had under-theorized the key issue of sexuality and, more specifically, the complex power structure of hetero-sexism. In contrast, my reading of feminist methodology and my own earlier empirical work led me to expect that female students and teachers would be key contributors to a critical exploration of school masculinities.[2] This was certainly the case. In examining the heterosexual young women's perspectives on school masculinities, they pointed to the need to go beyond the interpersonal level, to a more comprehensive theoretical framework that begins to explore the effects of and responses to the institutionalization of masculinity. Most importantly, they highlighted a major absence in the male teachers' and students' accounts at Parnell School, that of the operation of sexual micropolitical power relations. It is suggested in this study that contemporary school masculinities are a complex, problematic social phenomenon. These young women help us to understand the specificity of the production of masculine identities at the local level of the school. Like the young male gays in Chapter 5, the heterosexual female students occupy a critical social position from which to speak of masculini-ties and their cultural and political impact on their lives and future socio-sexual destinies. Heward (1991: 36–7), writing of the conventional subsuming of gender in studies of social class, notes that:

> In recent years concern has grown in a number of academic disciplines with the tautology of these conceptualisations and at-tempts are being made to coin understandings and explanations for the way that power is associated with certain groups of men – white upper-class heterosexuals rather than blacks and gays. Accounting for the consistent exclusion of women from power has been the subject of much feminist work and attempts are now underway to forge more satisfying explanations than the universality of patriarchy.

Such an approach is developed by Wolpe (1988), who provides a most refreshing account of schooling, disciplinary control and sexuality.[3] Moving away from passive notions of over-determined student gender socialization to the more dynamic conception of social positioning, she sets out to reassert multidimensional factors into feminist accounts of young girls' education. More specifically, she challenges such work as that of Mahony (1985), which she sees as adopting a gender reductionist stance, claiming that patriarchy overrides all other forms of relationships in determining women's subordination. Wolpe acknowledges the successes of such work in challenging girls' and women's 'invisibility' and the resulting classroom inequalities. However, she notes the inadequacy of this approach, maintaining that 'the differentiated forms of male power can only be accounted for by analysis which takes into consideration the specific conditions which gives rise to these situations' (Wolpe 1988: 11). She cites the differentiation that exists in relation to class and 'race', within the home and the labour market. In short, she is claiming that the specificity of young women's education cannot be understood outside of sets of internal and external structures. A similar argument is presented here in relation to female students at Parnell School. Such an analysis may help to make clear the relative autonomy of cultural production processes operating within a wider social reproduction framework. In so doing, this may help us to explore the contextual contingency of gender formation produced in this cultural site. In turn, this may provide a purchase on the search for possibilities of making political interventions, which would include male teacher and student support for feminist practices.

The young women's peer groups

At an early stage of my research, I set out to delineate a range of young women's experiences of masculinities, with particular reference to the research participants' class and ethnic social positioning. At Parnell School, there did not seem to be female peer groups equivalent to those of the young men reported in Chapter 2. McRobbie (1980) and Davies (1984) have illustrated how female peer relationships do not follow the masculine route. As Griffin (1988) persuasively argues, the 'gang of lads' model is inappropriate in exploring the cultural production of school femininities. Furthermore, such studies cannot and should not be reductively read in simplistic terms of young women's reactions to masculinity. Most importantly, Griffin (1985b) emphasizes in her study of young women that there were no necessary links between 'pro-' and 'anti-school' attitudes, friendship patterns and future jobs. She continues: 'It was less important to identify particular girls as "good girls" or "troublemakers", than to understand the meanings associated with these categories and the ways that they were used to distinguish between groups of students by teachers and the young women themselves' (Griffin 1985b: 16). Consequently, at the planning stage of the research, I prepared questionnaires for female students in years 10 and 11 that I found useful in signalling their own areas of concern. At later stages in the study, I also found school diaries informative concerning the development of different femininities within a secondary school context.

However, at Parnell School, there was a group of black and white working-class young women who called themselves 'The Posse', who adopted a more 'masculine' student response to schooling. They displayed a 'highly visible group identity' (Gillborn 1990: 69) and were perceived by most teachers as the worst behaved female student group in the school. They were in the lowest two sets and spent much of their leisure time together in and outside of school. Some of them were publicly identified by peers and teachers as the 'girlfriends' of the Macho Lads. One of them, Linda, explains the significance of their name.

Linda: There's a lot of posses ['gangs'] in this school. A lot of the boys are in them. But we are *The Posse*. The teachers have to check us out all the time. And even a lot of the boys are afraid of us.

M.M.:   How did you get together?
Linda: It just happened. We live on the estate, went to the same primary
  schools, things like that. When we came here, we just moved together and
  we got a reputation as a bad group. They put us all in the low classes, so
  that gives us more time together and we go round to each other's houses.
M.M.:   What's the best things about being in The Posse?
Linda: People can't just boss you around like they could if you are on your
  own. We stand up to the boys. They won't mess with us. And it's just
  good because school is so boring. It's something to do and you look after
  each other. If I have any problems, I'd talk about them with my mates.

The Posse constituted a critical social group at Parnell School, in that
their gender transgressions were highly visible and served to challenge the
conventional institutional arrangements that placed female students in
subordinate positions. The teachers tended to see groups and relations
within the school in isolation from the rest of society. Adopting discourses
of cultural deficit, the teachers tended to pathologize the young women's
behaviour in terms of individual deviancy. However, The Posse was not
merely an alienated school sub-cultural group. Their social practices need
to be located within a wider social setting. Like the Macho Lads, they came
from a large working-class housing estate, which was built by the council in
the 1960s. It had suffered mass deprivation during the last twenty years
with high rates of structural adult and youth unemployment. Among the
teachers, it had a notorious reputation as a place of violent crime and
'problem one-parent families'. Their group identity based on a strong sense
of collective solidarity was developed within this wider social arena.

Young women 'taking on' the domestic division of labour

Nava (1984, 1992) has written how, for girls, against a background of
'labouring in the home, pleasing and serving others, their girlhood merges
into womanhood'. In questionnaires and interviews with female students
at Parnell School, domestic responsibilities were frequently critically cited.
They reported a wide range of experiences of the domestic division of
labour in their homes (Griffin 1985b; Cockburn 1987; Smart 1992). For the
young women, the main explanation for this was the influence of different
family forms. A high proportion of them had experience of living in
lone-parent, mother-headed families. Many working-class students assumed that gender relations were 'more equal' in middle-class homes.
Among the middle-class young women, it was suggested that their
mothers' feminism informed their domestic arrangements. The young
women's main argument was that they shared an unfair burden of
'managing things and people in their homes' compared to their brothers
and fathers who merely 'helped out'. However, they maintained that there
were different generational responses to the disruption of conventional
forms of domestic femininity and masculinity, with a tendency for the

younger generation to be more assertive in challenging traditional expectations. Female students argued that teachers refused to acknowledge that their domistic responsibilities influenced school work.

Dawn: That's one of the main things you learn as a girl, you have to look after other people. Like at home my older sister brought me up and now I'm the one looking after my gran.

M.M.:   Why do you think that is?

Julie: It's true what that girl said in the discussion. I never thought of it before. Girls have to look after men all their lives. My dad and brothers can do nothing for themselves. We have bad rows about it. My mom says there's not much you can do about it but me and my sisters argue with them and my brothers are changing a bit.

Sam: I think a lot of the new men types, like my mom's partner, they talk about sharing domestic responsibilities. But you know that it's not true. In fact like all these things what's different about middle-class fellas compared to other men is that they are more dishonest.

M.M.:   And would that be true for all middle-class men?

Sam: It's probably changing with boys our age. I think that it's different with my brother because my mum and me have different expectations about what men should do. He does a lot more of the housework. But you have to keep at him to do it. It's also because he's younger than me. It will be interesting to see if he changes when he's in his own place with a girlfriend.

I will now explore the gender dynamics of recent curriculum changes in relation to female students' experiences of and responses to the new vocationalism.

The remasculinization of the new vocational curriculum: The production and marginalization of femininities

Stanworth's (1981: 58) influential study of schooling and gender divisions in the 1980s reported that: 'girls may follow the same curriculum as boys – may sit side by side with boys in classes taught by the same teachers – and yet emerge from school with the implicit understanding that the world is a man's world, in which women can and should take second place'. One aspect of my study was to examine if female students in the 1990s reported a similar picture to that of Stanworth. As part of the overall theoretical framework of this study, it is argued that schools produce a range of masculinities and femininities. Each of the chapters in this book provides evidence to support Gilbert and Taylor's (1991: 10) argument that, at a broad cultural level, the promoted institutionalized modes of masculinity and femininity constructed in everyday social practices, provide the basis for women's subordination. In Chapter 2, it was suggested that the curriculum is a key institutional process that produces different masculine subject positions that the students come to inhabit. Feminist research has highlighted the differential gendered access to curricular and pedagogical resources for female and male students (Skeggs 1992).

My specific focus was the effects of the new vocationalism embedded in the entrepreneurial curriculum and the resulting restratification. I explored the repositioning of female students in the remasculinization of the curriculum, as a key element of the 're-formation' of schooling that has taken place with recent educational policy changes. In interviews with male teachers, I was particularly interested in the under-representation of female students in the new route of social mobility, which was created for 'high-achieving' students located in the emerging high-status technological and commercial subject areas, such as business studies, technology and computer studies. The main argument of the male teachers who taught these subjects was the conventional assertion that male students on the basis of 'natural' gender differences chose these courses. The curriculum coordinator explained to me that a high-status vocational curriculum sector was currently of specific pedagogical and commercial significance. First, at a time of high unemployment among the local male population, it was important to provide young men with the necessary hi-tech skills needed for a rapidly changing workplace. Second, high-quality vocational courses were very popular with parents and male students and would serve to enhance the school's reputation in the local area.

M.M.:   Why do you think that there are so few girls doing IT [Information Technology]?
Mr Jones: Well obviously the boys are naturally more interested. I personally think it's a shame because we have tried different things to get them in.
M.M.:   When you say that boys are more naturally interested, what do you mean by that?
Mr Jones: Well you know it's a boys' area. Traditionally, they have chosen the area. They have more interest in machines, technical matters. It fits in more with their lives, I suppose.
M.M.:   Would you be surprised if I told you that female students here would disagree with you.
Mr Jones: I'd respond, well, they would wouldn't they! No, I think you'll find that what I say applies to most of the girls here and you can't generalize from one or two with different views that the girls might have. That's a big danger of not doing a more scientific, a more objective study where you look at a wide range of views, but of course I don't have to tell you that.
Mr Griffiths: We have worked hard at creating top quality vocational courses. It's terrible for the kids around here. Work has disappeared. A lot of their fathers aren't working and it will be the same for them unless we get it right on training for these kids, kitting them out with the transferable skills. These are the windows of opportunity for the future, and it's an uncertain future for all of us.
M.M.:   Have you created these courses for any particular groups of students?
Mr Griffiths: What do you mean? Obviously it's not for the top set, the academic groups. But apart from that, no. I'd say a lot of the kids are from families that are keen that they get on and they are our more supportive

parents, more ambitious for their kids. I'd say these are the kids that would have gone on to do apprenticeships, ten, fifteen years ago. And with all the competition between schools now, I think quality courses are particularly attractive to our parents.

M.M.:   There seems to be very few female students in these classes.

Mr Griffiths: Oh, yes. Some of the women, the women teachers, comment on this. But as I've explained to them, it's not about being sexist.

M.M.:   But the male students are getting a lot of the resources.

Mr Griffiths: Like I explain to the women teachers, we have a major problem in this country and you only have to look around here to see it. Large numbers of the boys are leaving school and not finding work, some of them unemployable. Work is the finishing school for our kids, for the boys. It gives them the discipline, helps them to settle down to future responsibilities of planning for a family.

M.M.:   What about female students?

Mr Griffiths: Of course they're important as well. But they have alternatives that the boys don't have. Around here more girls are getting jobs than boys. I don't mean this as being against women. But it's in all our interests and most definitely the girls' own interest that boys have work. Like I say, it's a major crisis in the inner-cities, young men hanging around with nothing to do. They can't value themselves. They can't have respect for themselves because if they haven't work then who are they? Who's going to even look at them? How do they plan for the future when they haven't got a stake in any future? Girls aren't going to be interested in a future with them, are they?

As Gleeson (1983) has pointed out, one of the effects of new vocationalism has been to make visible the hidden curriculum of schooling. The female students were aware of the regendering of the curriculum and offered varied explanations for their being 'locked out' from benefiting from recent changes at Parnell School. The Posse emphasized that current curriculum exclusionary mechanisms were a continuation of the institutional marginalization and alienation that was directed towards them and the Macho Lads because of their refusal to accept teacher authoritarianism and their rejection of the social discipline of the new vocationalism. For the working-class socially mobile female students, the curricular social closure was read in more explicit gender terms. They felt that the new vocationalist curriculum could in principle be open to female and male students but that in a masculine dominated co-educational school, the changes operated to add further barriers to the traditional masculine subject areas, which offered future opportunities in the labour market.

Smita: Teachers keep on about all the money spent on the place. Well, we haven't got anything out of it. It's just the same for us in the low classes. They say it's our behaviour. We're too bad to be allowed into the high classes. You're supposed to accept the teachers bossing you around whenever they feel like it. When we ask if we can use the new computers, they say no because we have the wrong attitude.

Tanisha: The teachers try and push you into low things like typing and they call it office skills and all this crap. And the same with the boys we hang around with, they hate them for sticking up for themselves.

M.M.: Why is that?

Tanisha: You see the teachers only like the snobs in this school. They think we're low class because we come from the estate. My dad said they treated him the same at school. The teachers even hate it when they see us having a laugh with you. You're supposed to look down on us.

Nicola: The teachers say we have to improve our presentation skills and all this rubbish.

M.M.: What does that mean?

Nicola: Don't ask me. I don't know. They've got all this stuff about profiles where you write up things about yourself for employers. But it's none of their business. And the teachers talk about you, in interviews telling employers you promise to do anything. You see there's no jobs so you're supposed to go on your knees to them. No way.

Susan: It's nearly all boys in the top classes in the new courses. But girls could do just as well. They just won't let us in, and if you're in the class, the boys just treat you horrible and the teachers let them get away with it.

Shahida: We've told some of the teachers in PSE lessons, when they ask you what you think of the school, that we should be allowed to use the computers more. It would help us just the same as the boys when you go out for jobs.

M.M.: What do the teachers say?

Shahida: Some of the women teachers agree but there's not much they can do. But most of the teachers just take the boys' side even though they don't admit it. When Miss Harrison asked about single-sex lessons, the other teachers went mad. But on new courses, it's nearly all boys and no-one says that's wrong.

Natalie: The teachers, especially the ones in CDT and business studies, say that girls weren't interested. And we had a big discussion and so they set up a computer club for girls. And when the boys took over, the teachers said, see the girls aren't interested, so they thought they were proved right!

M.M.: So, what happened?

Natalie: The usual. In fact it's got worse in the last few years. My mum's on the governors and she asked, why is all the new equipment been used by boys? And the teachers said they've tried to change girls' attitude to technology but it hasn't been very successful. But my mum asked them if they've thought of changing the way they teach the subjects instead of always trying to change the girls.

In the recently restructured new vocationalist curriculum at Parnell School, working-class young women were directed into low-level courses that focused upon the 'construction of caring subjectivities'. Skeggs (1988: 142) argues that 'this process, through which students come to identify themselves as practical, caring and responsible is also structured by the culture of familialism'. Beechey (1985: 99) has described familial ideology in terms of a system of beliefs and practices which:

(1) describe a particular kinship system and set of living arrangements (the coresident nuclear family) and assert that this form of family is universal and normatively desirable, and
(2) assert that the form of sexual division of labour in which the woman is housewife and mother and primarily located within the

private world of the family, and the man is wage-earner and bread-winner and primarily located in the "public" world of paid work, is universal and normatively desirable.

Senior management justified the new vocationalist courses for young women who were in low sets, in terms of their future domestic and occupational value. The young women contested the naturalization of their domestic apprenticeship and transition to labour and marriage markets. In so doing, they made visible the gendered cultural gap between themselves and male teachers.

Mr Spencer: I know we might be accused of being old-fashioned, I hear from my daughters at the grammar about their school. But it's different here. A lot of these girls, the ones in the low sets, they will be married at a young age and they need to have the appropriate skills to cope. But it's not only that, the jobs that they will be getting are in the areas of personal caring, and some of them are very good at it.

Mr Best: Well let's be honest, a lot of them aren't even going to get married. So, it's even more important we train them for parenthood, isn't it?

Mr Middleton: These girls lack confidence. A lot of them have problem backgrounds. They will tell you the care courses we have devised for them give them back that confidence. It tells them they can be as good as any of the high-flyers here. The new vocational courses have given them new skills and most importantly confidence in themselves that comes from acquiring those skills.

Kelly: The teachers told us to write down what we had learned from the caring course. I told him nothing. And then he said what about all the stuff you learned about child care. What a stupid man. I couldn't even begin to tell him, that's not learning, I do all that at home. I have to look after my younger brother and sister.

Kerry: When he [teacher] asked me what I had learnt, I told him, "I've learned that you are trying to make us housewives". He went mad, saying that we were learning lots of new skills. That's rubbish, it's just common sense; to us anyway. They should be teaching us things that will help us to get a real job. But once they've taught you how to read and write, that's it, isn't it really?

As feminist research has shown, teacher discourses and male academic representations of working-class young women have served to marginalize their experiences and make invisible their responses to schooling (Griffin 1993). The young women above illustrate the gap between policy intention and its local mediation in schools. Despite central government's current rhetoric of student entitlement and empowerment, new vocationalism is premised on the assumption that students are not active curriculum makers. At Parnell School, this in turn was premised on a deficit model of black and white working-class students, which precluded the teachers from engaging with the young women's knowledges, experiences and feelings. Mr Spencer's patronizing comments illustrate the different social worlds that most of the male teachers and working-class young women inhabited.

Their differering accounts of the new vocationalist courses reminded me of earlier work I had done with young women on a Certificate of Pre-Vocational Education (CPVE) course at a sixth-form college. One of the young African Caribbean women, Marie, a 'pro-education' student, was offered a three-week placement at a local community centre working with young children. The community leader praised her 'professional competence in dealing with difficult underprivileged children'. It was assumed by Marie's teachers that she had gained this competence from the 'services to people' component of CPVE. In fact, she had missed these lessons, which she claimed were irrelevant. As Marie pointed out, she acquired an understanding of 'underprivileged children' by living with them. She was the eldest daughter of seven children and her father had been unemployed for three years. Her teachers had compiled a personal profile of her, which included the above information. However, in response, she was categorized as 'one of the underprivileged children', with little capacity or potential (Mac an Ghaill 1988b: 123–4).

Similar assumptions concerning black and white working-class young women were in operation at Parnell School. It is also interesting to note here that though these young women reject the label 'feminist' to describe their response to these teacher assumptions, nevertheless they display a feminist sensibility in challenging the institutional allocation of working-class young women to highly gendered labour and domestic markets.

So far, I have delineated the general patterns involved in the interplay between the new vocationalism curriculum and the location of female students. Now I will focus on their experiences of and responses to male teacher discourses in helping to shape specific feminine identities.

Male teacher discourses: The social administration and regulation of 'good' and 'bad' girls

In this study, I have chosen to focus primarily on male teachers, in line with my interest in examining female students' experience of school masculinities. However, this is not to suggest that there was predictable, unproblematic positive gender identification between female students and female teachers. Some white and some black young women empathized with younger female teachers. For other students, class and ethnic peer affiliations were significant social variables in shaping their interaction with middle-class female teachers, who were evaluated primarily in terms of their professional function of social regulation. However, female students did receive positive affirmation of their developing feminine identity from some female teachers, albeit often in a strained manner.

Smita: A teacher is a teacher at the end of the day. When she's with the other teachers, who's side is she going to take? I don't think she'll be on the kids side, do you?

Maxine: She's not like the other teachers. You can talk to her and she'll

listen. And she'll say things like, "when I was at school, I used to feel like
you". She just helps you with things that may be bothering you.
M.M.:   Why is she different to other teachers?
Maxine: It's just the way she is. Maybe because she's younger than the
others and knows things more about us.

In a recent study of schooling and masculinity, Parker (1992) summar-
izes the early concerns of liberal feminist educational research. He writes:

> feminist work discussing gender relations in schools has been
> essentially geared towards the domination of boys within the
> everyday processes of mixed schooling, both in terms of how they
> monopolize teacher attention, and govern social and/or physical
> space . . . Additionally, specific concern has been expressed over the
> greater educational attainment levels and opportunities open to boys
> in particular subjects (mainly in science), in comparison to girls of a
> similar age.
>
> (Parker 1992: 3–4)

Much of this academic writing has emphasized the polarized school
behavioural practices of female and male students. Most of the male
teachers at Parnell School worked with a common-sense pedagogical
assumption that male students caused more trouble and were more difficult
than female students to discipline, though as is illustrated below in the
discussion of bullying, these views were not consistently held. From my
own observations around the school, teacher–student relations appeared
to be more complicated than that suggested by this 'commonsense'
consensus. In my field notes I had recorded many incidents in which young
women were disciplined. Furthermore, in discussions with 'anti-school'
working-class female students, they challenged this dominant official
perception, claiming that teachers frequently 'told them off' and 'showed
them up' for being 'trouble-makers'. What emerges here is the question of
the young women's apparent 'invisibility' as disciplinary problems. At one
level, what appears to be happening is that, when a male student becomes a
disciplinary problem, it is seen by male teachers as a frequent attribute of
'adolescent masculinity'. However, classroom disruptions caused by
female students tend to be seen as individual acts of deviancy which do not
challenge the teachers' idea of 'adolescent femininity'. One consequence of
this was that a disproportionate amount of the school's resources were
allocated to male students, who were positioned as a threat to the
institution. More recent research in this area provides some clues to these
apparent confusions regarding conventional school representations of
adolescent femininity and masculinity.

Carlen *et al.* (1992) provide a historical account of state institutional
administration and control of girls and young women. Writing of the
gendered modes of regulation for young female truants, they report that:

> For well over a century, the sexualization of all types of troublesome
> behaviour committed by young females has been a central constituent

of the discursive technologies whereby a gender discipline has been systematically imposed on adolescent girls . . . The sexuality/gender/ sexualization axis of social control, whereby deviations from any gender conventions are stigmatized as being evidence of a distorted sexuality (the girl is a "slag" or "butch" . . . or both!), is not only the site of a punitive regulation. It is also an all-pervasive mode of preventative regulation which can inhibit not only women's sexuality . . . but also their use of public space . . . the successful presentation of self . . . and the acquisition of effective self and social knowledge . . . While young women remain within the conventions of family, home, school, workplace or male-related domesticity they are usually seen to be gender-controlled and are accordingly treated as being invisible . . . These assessments (of deviant girls as "cases for care") are constituted not only within conventional constructions of female sexuality and femininity, but also within individualized typifications drawn from class and racist stereotypes.

(Carlen *et al.* 1992: 102–103)

Gilbert and Taylor's (1991) work helps to conceptualize current female students' accounts of their experience and contestation of contradictory male teacher discourses and representations. They have brought together research on cultures of femininity, providing a wide range of evidence which demonstrates the complex conflicts that young women experience, as a result of the contradictory messages they receive concerning 'appropriate femininity'. They identify three interrelated contradictory discourses, the domesticity/paid work conflict, the 'slags or drags' conflict (Lees 1986) and adolescence/femininity conflict (Hudson 1984), that they argue serve to shape female students' futures in paid work, marriage and motherhood. Hudson's (1984) work is particularly helpful here. She maintains that young women have to develop a feminine identity within the context of the 'masculine' construct of adolescence:

All our images of the adolescent . . . the restless, searching youth, the Hamlet figure; the sower of wild oats, the tester of growing powers – these are masculine images. This is the basis of many of the conflicts posed by the coexistence of adolescence and femininity: if adolescence is characterised by masculine constructs, then any attempts by girls to satisfy society's demands of them *qua* adolescence are bound to involve them in displaying not only lack of maturity (since adolescence is dichotomised with maturity), but also lack of femininity.

At Parnell School, the male teachers' differential social regulation of female and male students was a key element of the students' social positioning. This institutional construction and moral regulation of feminine and masculine student subjectivities was lived out within separate academic and informal spheres (Griffin 1985b; Walkerdine 1990a). As pointed out in Chapter 1, there was in operation at Parnell School a wide range of disciplinary instruments that were highly gendered. Male teachers argued that school gender divisions, manifested in classroom registration, school uniform, male/female subjects and different modes of discipline, signified natural biologically based differences that were simply encoded in institutional arrangements (Wolpe 1988). For many of the young women, the teachers' emphasis on natural differences was experienced as forms of social and academic subordination and closure. They were critical of male teachers' disciplinary inconsistencies, which frequently and arbitrarily shifted between demands that as young women they should be more mature and complaints that they were 'growing up too fast'. They also spoke of the ambiguity of male teachers' differential disciplining of male students and the accompanying teacher–student male bonding that cut across age and cultural barriers, manifested in terms of the common language of male subjects, sports and television programmes. (It should be added that I also spent much time with the male students celebrating our projected male fantasy popular cultural heroes.)

Julie: The teachers like Mr Williams are always having a go at our group. They keep moaning about the way we dress or if we're running down the corridor or if we're walking too slow, they'll tell us off for not walking like girls should. Mr Gaine [deputy-head] has about a hundred rules just for girls. They're always trying to rule your life.

Nihla: I don't think men teachers know how to treat girls. Like they'll say one day why don't you grow up, if you're messing about. Then the next day if you've got make-up on or something, they'll say you're acting too grown up. I'm sure we confuse them. But they wouldn't think they confuse us; one day do this, the next day the opposite, especially when they're in a mood.

Ann Marie: Like the men teachers say they treat boys harder and they do in a way. But there's still a togetherness about the way they behave.

Dawn: That's especially in things like PE. Some of us go to the matches [football], but the teachers, the men teachers would never talk to us like that.

M.M.:   Like what?

Dawn: It's like they're in a club and girls can't join. The men teachers are the same sometimes even with Miss Eagleton [PE teacher]. Sometimes I really feel sorry for her.

Niamh: One minute they're telling the boys off and the next they're talking together in a close way about telly programmes and football. They're always on about football.

Sharon: If the men teachers are telling boys off, you know what I mean, it's a bit of a game with both of them being macho, you know, the hard man. But it's not a game with girls.

M.M.:   Why is that?

Sharon: Because we are supposed to be mature, to be more mature than the boys.

M.M.:   And are you?

Sharon: Yes, in a way and then again, we have to be. But not in the way the teachers think. We want to have a laugh as well. School's boring for us as well. You've got to have a laugh or you'd die, wouldn't you?

As indicated in Chapter 1, Walkerdine (1984) has provided an innovative framework which goes beyond simple models of school socialization, in which female students are the subject of negative expectations and labelling. She maintains that what is of particular importance is the need to understand the relationship between those practices which define appropriate femininity and masculinity, while at the same time producing subject positions to occupy. She continues:

> So it is not the case of unitary identities, but a question of those practices which channel psychic conflicts and contradictions in particular ways. "Good girls" are not always good – but where and how is there badness lived? What is the struggle which results from the attempt to be or live a unitary identity? Much work is necessary to engage such questions. But we might begin by exploring how different positions are produced and understood . . . We might also look at the practices of schooling which produce positions for girls and claim to know the truth of such girls as singular beings: with personalities, intelligence and so on.
>
> (Walkerdine 1984: 182)

The female students highlighted one of the major contradictions of male teachers' dominant perceptions, that male students were behaviourally more difficult to cope with than females. In interviews with male teachers, they confirmed the validity of the young women's argument. In so doing, they revealed the inconsistencies of their disciplinary position. While refusing to accept that their masculinity was a significant variable in their interaction with female students, nevertheless they claimed to be able to identify with the 'straightforwardness of boys who know the rules'.

Julie: If you look at the boys we hang around with, they are seen as really bad by a lot of teachers. But when the teachers act hard, the boys do the same and then they sort it out some way. But with us when we get the teachers going, they don't know what to do.

Claudette: The teachers say we are the worst behaved in the school and you hear them saying to each other, "I don't know what to do with this lot, I've tried everything".

M.M.:   What about the men teachers?

Claudette: Well, in a way most of the women teachers are softer, except one or two. But even the hard men teachers, they don't know what to do when we ignore them. You see they would rather you shouted back and all that.

M.M.:   So, what happens?

Claudette: They call us things like sullen. You know then that it's really getting to them.

Mr Maynard: Yes, it's true the boys are thought of as the worst behaved, but I think a lot of us would say that if a girl goes bad she will be a lot worse.

Mr McArther: With the lads, most of them, you can have a good row and you both respect it in a way. You both know the rules. But with girls, it's hard to know what they're thinking. I suppose that's why a boys' school is easier in a lot of ways.

M.M.:   Do you think it's got anything to do with being a male teacher?

Mr McArther: No, certainly not. The women teachers often have it worse than us. No, it foxes me. Boys tend to be more straightforward, even the real rogues. They'll argue their case but they know who's in charge. But the girls are very stubborn. To be honest, I can never understand them. But then, I've been married for twenty years and I've never understood my wife's mind.

M.M.:   Do you think, she might think the same about you?

Mr McArther: That's a good question. But the facts are, I know we're not supposed to say this these days, but women's minds are a mystery to me. I've always got on better with my daughters than my wife has, but I can't say I actually understand what they're on about much of the time.

During the research, male teachers often commented upon their confusion concerning how female students' responded to their 'little jokes'. Stanworth (1983: 22) has suggested that what may appear from a male teacher's perspective as 'incidental to the real business of teaching', contributes most forcefully to the reinforcing of classroom gender divisions:

> For example, in the sixth form department where my research was conducted, male teachers often interspersed their lectures with good-natured jokes of a mildly flirtatious sort. "Good heavens, Jane, I didn't realise that you had legs!" (addressed to a pupil who appears for the first time that year in a skirt) is a typical remark: while jokes about role reversal, humorous appeals to "we men v. you girls", and mild sexual innuendoes are used to promote a "friendly" atmosphere in the classroom.

These were common pedagogical practices at Parnell School. The female students in the top sets were highly critical of male teachers' patronization, in systematically highlighting gender differences in relation to academic achievement. They argued that teachers, in attempting to motivate male students by humiliating them for being 'beaten by a girl', used them as a gendered resource to draw upon. These misogynous male teacher discursive practices acted as highly effective academic and disciplinary mechanisms in the policing of masculine boundaries. The female students pointed to the way in which these mechanisms took differentiated forms in relation to male students' position in the school's stratification system. This was an example of how different femininities were produced in relation to the hierarchy of masculinities at Parnell School. In the highly competitive academic arena, 'high-achieving' young women experienced specific pedagogical exclusionary mechanisms, which served to undermine their confidence. In terms of the distribution of academic knowledge, this strategy was prevalent in the high-status masculine subjects of science and mathematics. For young women in low sets, the discursive practices of teacher misogyny took a more disciplinary emphasis. For example, attributing feminine characteristics to troublesome male students in the low sets was a common disciplinary male teacher practice.

Helen: The men teachers are always at it. Showing you up if you get higher marks than the boys in tests. They say they are only joking but they never do it to the boys. What's funny is that the boys are supposed to be better than us, so they have to make us feel bad if we come higher.
Sharon: The men teachers are always shaming up the boys, saying that they're acting like girls, and if the boys are being soft, the teachers say, "I'll get you two married off".

In discussions with male teachers about sex/gender typifications, they found it easier to prescribe how female students shouldn't behave rather than how they should. Sex/gender boundary maintenance was most explicitly expressed in proscriptive terms that 'girls shouldn't act like boys'. At times, male teachers working within the single discourse of gender used moral imperatives of 'appropriate femininity'. However, at other times, in their management and administration of femininity, male teachers were involved in increased surveillance and control of white and black working-class female students, who were seen as 'threatening the new successful image of the school in the local area'. It was this sector of female students that was seen as producing threatening unbounded femininities, described by male teachers in terms of acting like 'tomboys' rather than 'normal' girls. Here, two working-class young women illustrate the cultural specificity and complexity of feminine identity formation, in relation to institutional gendered discourses of 'race' and ethnicity (Caplan 1987; Fraser 1989; Hooks 1991).

Nihla: It's funny the teachers think, oh you're a typical oppressed Asian girl and all that. But at home I'm a real tomboy. I wear jeans most of the time, play football with my brother and cousins and go around in cars.
M.M.:   And at school?
Nihla: At school they try to make you act like their stereotype of a girl, and for us they have a stereotype of the Asian girl, all quiet and passive. I don't know why they feel threatened if girls act differently. It's like they blame us for not acting like Asian girls. But it's not us that's the problem. We're just not living up to their stereotypes because it doesn't mean anything to us.
Niamh: It's been the same for me. I was brought up on a farm in Ireland and in a lot of ways the differences in school between boys and girls was less than in England.
M.M.:   Like what things are different?
Niamh: At home it's just normal for me to go round with my brothers but at school the teachers say, "you're acting more like a boy, no-one will respect you". They say I'm rough and run around the playground too much shouting. In Ireland you had more freedom in school. My ma says the English are funny about these things. I don't know.
M.M.:   Is that all the teachers?
Niamh: No, to be fair, Miss Ware is different. She's good. She's more like

me, and the kids call her a lesbian even though they know she's married and has a child. It's because she's a grown up "tomboy". You know, can look after herself and thinks for herself, not falling over stupid men.

In looking at male teacher discourses in relation to the construction and regulation of femininities, I have emphasized the need to locate these practices in their specific contexts, in which shifting, contradictory typifications operate. A continuing tension throughout the study was placing this contextual specificity within the broader institutional pattern of a patriarchal social order. The next section, which includes discussion of sexual abuse, makes more explicit the dominant conventional gender divisions and heterosexual arrangements with which the young women at Parnell School had to negotiate. An important element that served as a key marker of femininity and masculinity was the gendered and sexual use of public space.

School public spaces: The construction and mediation of sex/gender relations of dominance and subordination

A main argument in this study is that the school microcultures of management, teachers and students are key formal and informal infrastructural sites through which sex/gender regimes are structured and mediated. It is often not realized by teachers and parents how significant informal sites are in students' daily lives. In this research, both female and male students identified the playground as a particularly important sphere within which student cultures are organized and lived out. It is also a crucial arena with its own gender regime, within which students construct a hierarchically ordered range of masculinities and femininities. As with the staffroom and classroom, the playground has its own rules, routines and regulations. At Parnell School, this was part of the students' informal world which was regulated by non-teaching staff, with teachers tending to exist outside of a social world of student talk, with its main themes of gossip, clothes, music and girlfriends/boyfriends. Here, the adult division of labour reflected the 'high culture'/popular culture split that pervaded the social relations of the school, with most teachers not actively engaging with the students' sub-cultural lives. As the support staff reported in Chapter 1, working-class mothers had primary responsibility for controlling this area.

Lavern: I don't think that teachers realize how important the playground is for pupils. They're battlegrounds for getting a reputation. Gangs of tough kids rule and make life really bad for a lot of other kids, especially if you're seen as different.

Recently, the issue of school bullying has emerged as a key concern among educational commentators. For example, Marland (1992: 20) writes of:

The fastest-growing suicide rate, according to the Samaritans' latest figures, is among the under-25s – up by 41 per cent in the last decade. Of all young suicides, four-fifths are male. But of all those attempted, four-fifths are female: one girl in a hundred aged 15–19 attempts suicide every year. Many young people are vulnerable, and none of us can know what will tip an individual over the edge. But clearly bullying is an important factor. Traditional views about bullying have underplayed its verbal aspects, preferring to think of it mainly as physical violence. Yet verbal taunts often play a key part in a child's decision to commit suicide.

Most of this commentary has not engaged with feminist, anti-racist, lesbian and gay educational research (Mahony 1985; Gillborn 1990; Harris 1990). Most significantly, a popular discourse has been constructed that serves to depoliticize the sexual and racial violence taking place at the microcultural level of the playground and classroom. This is most graphically illustrated in relation to the popular media response to the inquiry, *Murder in the Playground*, that reported on the death of Ahmed Iqbal Ullah at Burnage High School in 1986 (MacDonald *et al.* 1989). Feminist scholarship in critiquing male ethnographic work on schooling and masculinity has argued that anti-school male student behaviour cannot reductively be read as simply a product of resistance, but also acts as a 'legitimation and articulation of power and subordination' (Skeggs 1991; see also Walkerdine 1990a; McRobbie 1991). This research has established that widespread forms of sexual harassment and abuse are experienced by female students and teachers (Lees 1986; Holly 1989b).

Heward (1991: 38) has described public school bullying as a 'power struggle in which those seeking to dominate demonstrate their superior power by successfully designating themselves strong and another individual or group weak, and then ensure these designations are accepted by the rest of the house'. Currently, the dominant official explanation of bullying excludes the dimension of power, appealing to a mixture of conventional psychology and 'common sense', which seeks explanations and remedies primarily in terms of deviant individuals. In the following accounts, working-class young women provide an alternative analysis that links bullying to wider issues of the distribution of sexual power between adults and young people. A number of students who were from lone-parent families challenged the current moral panic, orchestrated by central government and played out in the media, which blames 'single mothers' for the increase in male violence. For them, a major cause of violence was poverty and, in their experience, it was women and more specifically their mothers who suffered the most from poverty, while having primary responsibilty for child care.

Kerry: We had an assembly on bullying. But they only talked about the kids. That is bad I know, but teachers wouldn't admit that they bully as well. But they can get away with it. And that's just the same outside of school.

M.M.:   Like what?

Nicola: Grown-ups can do what they like. Like I told you, when my friend was getting battered by her dad, what could she do? If you call the police, they don't want to know or they come and they batter your dad. So, it just goes on. When you think of it, the only thing that adults know is how to beat each other up. They wouldn't tell you that in assembly!

Michelle: We were talking in PSE [personal and social education] about all the abuse in families. Marie, she always gets people going, she said, it was better without fathers and the teacher was really mad because she's always saying how wonderful family life is. But she's not married. And the boys started shouting at Marie that she hated men.

M.M.:   So, what happened?

Michelle: They wouldn't listen to her. But she was right in a way. Like some of us don't live with our dads and we were talking, saying how can they blame single mothers? How can they blame women, when it's men that do all the violence?

Tanisha: They've always done it to black people, to black women. They say, we have too many kids and then can't control them.

M.M.:   How do you think these views come about?

Tanisha: Well obviously racism. You see like we are more likely not to be able to get good jobs and houses, so we're going to be more poor. And it's easy to pick on poor people and say they're more violent and all the rest of it. And then the police can do whatever they want to us, can't they?

Claire: I can't see how they can say women are to blame. If you look at our moms, they don't have much money but they do everything for us. Like my mom goes to work and she does everything for my brothers and me to get on. So, it seems stupid to say she's causing all the violence, doesn't it?

For most of the teachers, 'tough' white and black working-class male students were positioned as the main threat to other students. Many of the female and male students held a similar perspective. However, The Posse provided an alternative reading to this dominant view, which they linked to their own inter-personal relations with male teachers and working-class male peers, particularly the Macho Lads. Without condoning the young men's abuse, they described their ambivalent sympathy with subordinated black and white masculinities in a state institution that 'forces them to take on being tough'. They were also critical of the recent commercialization of the school, with the increased pressure on them and their male peers 'not to spoil the school's image'. The working-class young women's analysis challenged the teachers' confused accounts that contradictorily slipped backwards and forwards between discourses of gender, class and racial deficiency in their explanations of playground bullying. At times it was 'adolescent boys' who were the problem, whereas at other times they directed their discourse of deficit to particular sectors of white and black working-class students, suggesting that 'these girls [The Posse] were as bad as the boys'. Male teachers, in naturalizing young men's behaviour, failed to acknowledge the institutional power invested in masculinity with the accompanying social positioning of femininity. At the same time, they obscured working-class female students' insights into the contextual complexities of subordinated black and white working-class masculinities located within a middle-class institution.

Mr Taggart: You see it more clearly in an all-boys' school. You have to feel sorry for the lads, with all that youthful energy that we are keeping down all day. But of course that doesn't excuse they're going beyond the limits we set. That's why they need firm discipline to help them to learn to control their natural boisterousness. And that's a lot more difficult for a lot of boys here with no father figure at home. Like I say, you can understand why they go so wild when they're with us.

Mr Wall: The girls here are just as bad as the lads. In fact some of them are much worse. The idea that all boys are bullies and all girls are victims is arid nonsense. It's the way the trendies talk here.

Linda: The teachers make them that way. Like they are always picking on John and his posse. The teachers are always really trying to put them down.

M.M.:   Like what kind of things?

Linda: Well just lately the head and the teachers have been really telling us off and even more with John's posse. They have their little talks with them after school, saying that it's really important not to let the school down. And you must be prouder of this school than the others round here.

M.M.:   What do think of that?

Linda: We're not worried about other schools and nor should the teachers. They should look after this school. They've done it up last year, so they can't wait to kick us out, so they can have a smart school.

M.M.:   Why?

Linda: Everyone picks on John and them but no-one says how the teachers hate them. Like the teachers spend all their time with the kids in the top sets. They've done the school up but it's still a dump because we haven't got anything good out of it. Just the same old boring work and more moaning all the time.

M.M.:   How do the teachers treat John?

Linda: When John came in year eight, I remember he worked hard but then he got into the low sets. And then it's just rubbish. If you're in the lowest set they won't let you get into the computer stuff. John is one of the best in the school at computer games. Like they've got all this new equipment and new buildings but it's for the snobs in the top sets. So, they pick on him and he has to defend himself. A lot of the teachers are scared of him, even the men teachers.

M.M.:   Why?

Linda: Because he acts really hard. But he's not really. It's just an act but the teachers are too stupid to know that.

Tanisha: Well something must be going on in this place because I can tell you as a fact that the kids the teachers really pick on are different out of school. So, it must be the school's fault some of the way.

M.M.:   Why do you blame the school?

Tanisha: Like we said before, the teachers here have the worst stereotypes for the black kids, for the boys, even worse than for us. So, what can they do. They have to protect themselves.

M.M.:   But that doesn't happen to all black lads, does it?

Tanisha: No, that's true. But you look at Gilroy and them and they are stuck in the bottom class and what's this school done for them? At assembly they keep saying, we've built this new school for you, but they're worse than the police, keeping us away from the new buildings. They haven't even got a job in this country for them, you know what I mean? And they keep on about all the new courses will get us good training. They don't know what they're talking about.

These young women highlighted the methodological complexity of collecting and selecting research participants' accounts relating to the operation of sex/gender codes. In questionnaires and in diary reports a wide range of female students had identified male student use of public space as a major problem for them. However, in framing my questions about their experience of playground bullying, The Posse interpreted my focus as reinforcing the dominant teacher perspective, that operated exclusively to blame the Macho Lads. In response, they provided a highly persuasive explanation of how 'tough' middle-class male teachers helped to produce 'tough' working-class male students. However, in defending their male peers against the teachers, they were not uncritical of the former's masculine practices that operated against them.

As pointed out above, feminist research has documented the wide range of overt and covert forms of abuse operating within different sites (Hearn and Parkin 1987; Jones and Mahony 1989). Nava's (1984: 12) work in youth centres indicates how the policing of heterosexual femininity takes place outside the home through the interaction of young women and men:

> the regulation of girls is enforced largely by *boys* through reference to a notion of femininity which incorporates particular modes of sexual behaviour, deference and compliance . . . In this culture outside the home, girls are observers of boys' activity and *guardians* of girls' passivity. The ability to exercise this control does not usually reside in the individual boy. Such power is located in groups of boys (and girls) who, through reference to certain discourses and categories – like "slag" and "poof" – are able to ensure "appropriate" masculine and feminine behaviour.

At Parnell School, male students' sexual harassment and the resulting social closure was a major concern of female students. They developed their feminine identities within the context of teachers and students acting out their masculinity in terms of its constitutive elements of objectification, fixation and conquest (Litewka 1977). There was much evidence of the constant pressure and surveillance that the young women were under 'to conform to accepted sexual divisions and heterosexual arrangements that exist and are constantly reinforced among adolescents through language, ritual and interaction' (Weeks 1986: 59). Of specific concern for the female students at Parnell School was the everyday 'ordinary' practices of being the object of male teachers' and male students' gaze.

Sam: The men teachers are as bad as the boys, always having a go at you.
Claire: Some of the men teachers are really dirty, really looking at girls with piercing eyes.
Shahida: Some of the teachers fancy themselves as big Romeos. They go round flirting with the attractive girls and it just makes you sick. But you can't say anything or they'll say you're making it up or they'll blame you for starting it.
Maxine: Some of the boys are really rough, always trying to grope you, always getting at you.
Susan: If you just walk past a group of boys, they're all calling out sexual things and insulting you badly. Saying one of them has been with your mother.
Sharon: It's worse if you've been out with someone and it's over. You walk past and they're shouting out things really loud, badmouthing you. Like things about the way you look or the boy makes up things about what you're supposed to have done with him.
Ann Marie: You know it's just so they can look big to their mates but it still makes you feel really bad inside. And sometimes the boy's gang will follow you round just being stupid and threatening you.

Lees (1986) describes graphically the significance of the concept of 'reputation' in structuring women's sexuality as part of the wider construction of gender positioning. She argues that:

> While everyone knows a slag and stereotypically depicts her as someone who sleeps around, this stereotype bears no relation to girls to whom the term is applied . . . What is important is the existence of the category rather than the identification of certain girls . . . All unattached girls have to be constantly aware that the category slag may be applied to them. There is no hard and fast distinction between the categories since the status is always disputable, the gossip often unreliable, the criteria obscure.
>
> (Lees 1986: 36)

At Parnell School, the term 'slag' was a complex concept with shifting meanings, which were frequently used by young men and women. At times, the term tended to be a sexually explicit insult, while on other occasions it was used as a general term of abuse (Cowie and Lees 1981). As the young women made clear, it was also a key discursive concept through which male students' ambiguous misogyny operated to position women as sexually despised and at the same time sexually desired. For the female students, a key aspect of male teachers' collusion with male students was their refusal to take sexual harassment seriously. If they complained about being called 'slags', male teachers would desexualize male students' comments, claiming that they were not intended as an attack upon the young women's sexual reputation.

Vicki: The boys are always at it calling girls slags. But it's funny because they shout out, "I've had her and her" and all that. And they're really

horrible to us but you know that the girls they call slags the most, they
want the most.

M.M.:   Would you tell teachers about this?

Vicki: Some of the girls would tell the women teachers. Some that you can
trust. But nearly all the men teachers take the boys' side and say, "they're
just having a laugh". But you know, don't you when it's a laugh and when
it's serious.

It was within the context of such official processes of normalizing public
modes of masculine heterosexuality that feminine sexuality was institutionally regulated. This policing and control of sexuality operated
pervasively through male teachers' denial of the politics of female
appearance and reputation and the implicit sets of power relations that were
inscribed within the young women's everyday school interaction with male
teachers and students. In the following accounts, young women discuss the
ambiguities and confusions of constructing a feminine identity within the
constraints of dominant modes of masculinity.

Kelly: I feel so insecure lately.

M.M.:   Why's that?

Kelly: People are noticing me, taking notice of me, boys are. And I want
them to, but at the same time it makes me feel bad how they all look. I
want to be noticed but want to be able to decide how I respond to them.
And most of the time I feel they won't let me . . . I'd like Pete to want to
be with me and leave it at that, but he won't. Boys just won't, will they?

Debbie: Why can't men just like us for what we are?

Julie: I think they do in a way but it's for later when they marry; now they
just want to be seen with the best looking one.

Ann Marie: I feel really slack with Mary. She doesn't get boys looking at
her much and asking her out. I feel sorry for her.

Natalie: I don't think any girl feels attractive all the time. Sometimes you
will and then at other times your mood changes completely and you don't
feel attractive.

These comments are most revealing in relation to the heterosexual male
students' comments in the last chapter, providing evidence of the cultural
gap between these male and female students that schools help to structure
and maintain.

Talking of boys and men: 'Getting an education'/'getting a man'

In describing the complex interrelationship of young people's social
positioning across different sites, Cockburn (1987: 40) speaks of the
multi-faceted social significance of developing a sex/gender identity:

It is not just the simple fact of sex, the existence of male and female,
nor is it just the cultural phenomenon of gender that is important in

the lives of 16–17 year olds. It is actively sexual relationships. Sexual relations are not merely physical, they are cultural and gendered. Gender relations are thus a powerful link between the different phases of an individual's life: they mesh her [his] relationships to production, consumption, to recreation, to love and desire in a seamless fabric. Getting and maintaining an approriate gender identity goes on within all these spheres. It goes on at home, on the street, on the dance-floor, and it goes on at work. Success or failure in this respect in one sphere embellishes one's image and chances in others.

Male teachers at Parnell School appeared to be unaware of this interconnectedness between school and wider social spheres, in which feminine and masculine subjectivities are negotiated. Rather, many of them pathologized female students' social relations with male students. They were aware that among groups of young women, there was talk of 'not speaking to a friend because she was going out with an ex-boyfriend'. Also during the research, young women were reported to senior management on a number of occasions for fights involving disputes over boyfriends. For male teachers, these incidents reinforced their pejorative images and representations of young women as jealous, vulnerable and insecure. They were particularly critical of working-class female students, who they associated with 'troublesome' working-class males, such as the Macho Lads. These teachers justified their perception of female students in terms of the latter's own assumed classification of young women into a crude 'good girls' and 'slags' dichotomy.

Mr Mills: We try very hard to explain to the girls that it's important that they don't get a bad reputation, especially with the rougher types of boys we have here.

Mr Jones: Often, of course they won't listen. I find it very effective to remind them what other girls will think of them. Young people are very rigid in their thinking, very moralistic. I tell them quite honestly, either you're going to be seen as respectable or as someone who's loose. And these labels stick.

Many of the young women went to great lengths to distance themselves from being labelled 'slags' or 'being slack'. Some of them appeared to share the male teachers' evaluative dichotomy, ascribing similar negative characteristics to other female students. However, most of them operated with a more complex evaluative system, marked by contextual contradictions and inconsistencies. For example, they made a distinction between their friends' behaviour and 'other girls'. It was the latter group who were more likely to be labelled 'slack', for being involved with male students, although they appeared to display similar behaviour to that of their friends. Furthermore, the cultural gap between middle-class male teachers and working-class female students prevented the former from appreciating the sophisticated student explanation of the generational attraction of the Macho Lads' masculinity, which included unintended outcomes of the teachers' relations with 'anti-school' young men.

Julie: Some of the girls here are stupid, really slack. They'd go after any lad. But that's not many. Then you get the quiet ones and then there's us, who go round with the boys a lot.

M.M.:   How would the different groups be seen?

Vicki: It depends. Some girls get called really bad names because they're always flirting. But then if you take us, sometimes we'll call each other bad names. But other times you think, well if the boys can do it why can't we?

M.M.:   Is it very different for boys?

Vicki: You must be joking. Things are a lot easier for boys. And it's funny, because boys are allowed to have lots of girlfriends. In fact they have to in this school or they'd be called a "poof". But if the girls aren't supposed to go out with boys, then who are all the boys going to go out with? They'll have to go out with each other! [Laughs]

Smita: The reason why girls choose the macho ones is not because they prefer them because they're tough or rough. They're really bad at times. But it's more because they're the ones who stop the teachers getting their own way all the time. And they are looked up to.

M.M.:   By whom?

Smita: Everyone. They're the ones that the teachers have to check out. Even if it's only telling them off all the time, the teachers know that they're important. And it can give you a good feeling to be with someone who people are talking about all the time. It's just more fun when school is so boring. And if the teacher knows you're going out with one of them, they would think twice about getting at us.

Emma: Girls aren't stupid. Sometimes you make a mistake going out with a boy. But most of the time the girl is getting something out of it. And other people can say you're mad to be going out with a boy, but you know what he means to you and when that stops you get rid of him.

M.M.:   Is there different ways of treating boys?

Emma: Of course, it's different when you first go out with him and then it changes when you're together for a bit. And if you become known as boyfriend and girlfriend you would act different again. But all those times you might be getting different things. Like for some girls, it's being with the most attractive one in the class, some like the romantic types, or he might protect you or spend money on you, like the older boys do.

Hameeda: It's different for Asian girls. They don't have to be so concerned all the time with getting a boyfriend. But this is changing with some girls in this school going more like the English girls.

As pointed out above, working-class female students did not admire the Macho Lads' hyper-masculinity in itself, but perceived it as a legitimate defence against authoritarian male teachers. In turn, the young women had a cultural investment in this defensive male student response, which was read as gaining space for them as 'anti-school' females. At a wider level, young women spoke of adopting varied responses to young men depending on their emotional investment in them. Asian female students felt that there was less pressure upon them 'to get a boyfriend', though some of them were adopting the 'Western trend' (Griffin 1985b: 62).

One of the young women's main issues of contention was male teachers' collusion with the prescribed and proscribed sexual double standard, that placed them 'in a no-win situation'. As they suggested, male teachers' moralistic warnings about 'getting a bad reputation' operated within a decontextualized situation that did not acknowledge the rampant male heterosexuality that pervasively circumscribed much of their lives. This political decontextualization, which served to make invisible sexual power relations from which male teachers benefited, provided a masculine logic in which young women were blamed for the sexual harassment that was directed against them. This was most clearly illustrated for a group of female students when one of them got into a fight defending herself against sexual harassment by a male student. In the following account, young women discuss male teachers' collusion with male students.

Michelle: When it comes to it, teachers are not going to be unbiased. Like when Joan was attacked, a lot of the men teachers really blamed her for having a short skirt and wearing make-up.
M.M.:   What did they say?
Michelle: Well they come right out with it. They start off by telling the boy off. Then they get you and warn you that the short skirt and all that may cause these things, even though he doesn't agree with it happening.
Shahida: Yes, and this is for your own sake. But really the teachers are just taking the boys' side, aren't they. They must think we're stupid or something.
M.M.:   Would many of you report a thing like that again?
Maxine: No way. You get into more trouble yourself.
Claire: Trouble is that's probably what they want, when you think of it. I don't know what I would do.

Another main issue that emerged in the interviews with female students was the way in which male teachers reductively spoke of sexual harassment as an student inter-peer problem, thus making themselves absent from their own narratives. As young women pointed out, male teachers were highly significant in regulating female sexuality, which included coded warnings about the threat of pregnancy, which were selectively given to them but not male students. When I took these issues back to male teachers, they initially adopted strategies of denial. Later in the research, some of them did admit that schools were arenas in which teacher and student sexualities are played out. However, they tended to explain these relations exclusively in personal interactionist terms. In their privatization of sexuality, they underplayed its complex social and pychic power structure, within which schooling serves to legitimate the promotion and celebration of specific forms of male and female sexual identities, with the accompanying institutional positions as normal and natural. Furthermore, although they claimed that they responded to female students' sexualization of classroom situations, there was no reference to the promotion of a dominant form of masculinity that for female students and teachers was a central element of the school's gender regime.

Kelly: We asked Mr Cooper why they only talk to girls about getting pregnant. It's as if the boys had nothing to do with it and they're the ones who are forcing themselves onto girls.

Kerry: You see the men teachers make the rules for us, don't they? The rules are for boys and girls but some of them affect us the most. They are more prejudiced to the boys, letting them get away with more.

M.M.:   Like what?

Sharon: The men teachers are more strict with us, with what we wear, everything, the way you walk, talk, even smile: They say you're supposed to do these things like a lady. They mean do it for them.

Kelly: The men teachers always pretend that they're different to the boys, you know that they are the adults. They think girls are stupid. But we see the way they look up and down the women teachers, and how they spend more time with the attractive girls. We know the ones who are flirting but they would never admit it. In fact the boys would be more honest.

Mr Turner: Yes, sometimes a pretty girl will flash her eyelids at you and she knows you will be a bit lenient. But of course, you mustn't let these things go too far. These girls can be very manipulative.

M.M.:   Do you think it's always on the student's side?

Mr Turner: Oh yes. They might even say things about the men here. You have to be very careful these days. Watch yourself all the time.

M.M.:   What do mean, they might say things?

Mr Turner: New teachers, for example; some of these girls here are right little madams. They will use all their feminine charms. I tell the younger teachers when they arrive to watch out for this sort of thing.

These defensive comments were a frequent theme in male teacher narratives of their interaction with female students, which sought to disguise and displace their responsibility for existing sexual power relations, by representing themselves as potential victims of 'feminine charms'. Such accounts radically differed from those presented by the young women at Parnell School, who found male teacher and student mechanisms of surveillance and control to be a constant strain and constraint on their lives.

It was within this context of dominant social and discursive gendered practices, that adolescent heterosexual feminine identities were actively worked out within the sexual cultures of peer networks (Bhavnani 1991; Holland 1993). For many of the female students, compulsory schooling had little intrinsic meaning. There were a range of orientations to the official curriculum and varying degrees of cultural investment in creating informal leisure spaces. Griffin (1985b: 59), writing of the importance of leisure in the lives of young women, notes that: 'It was the area in which pressures to get a boyfriend were most intense. Getting a boyfriend was seen as proof of young women's "normal" heterosexuality and more "grown up" femininity.' Similarly at Parnell School, there was intense pressure on young women to get a boyfriend. In questionnaires, they reported that boys were a main topic of conversation. However, there were a range of strategies involved in female students' public stances to male students. Members of The Posse, from the security of their peer group, and some middle-class students adopted a highly visible position. But most of the young women were more covertly involved in thinking through, with the help of a best friend, how to translate 'fancying a boy' to 'having the courage to do something about it'. They also often had to negotiate their way through the desired young man's peer group, with whom he continued to associate 'even when he was going out with his girlfriend'.

Debbie: It's probably diffferent for us [new middle-class] than for a lot of the girls here. We'd meet boys in different places, not just at school and you'd just let them know you're interested in going out with them.
M.M.:   How would they know you were interested in them?
Debbie: Well it depends. Start flirting a bit. A friend might tell them you fancy them or just go up and ask them out.
Nicola: I don't know why boys have to stay with their friends if they're going out with you. Wherever Joe goes his gang follows him. I mean girls would never behave like that.
M.M.:   So, what do you do?
Nicola: You might have arguments about it, if you're going out long enough. But then you might just have to accept it. They seem to want to be with their friends all the time.
Claire: I don't know if boys are shyer than girls. They seem to get tired of you and want to go back and talk to the boys.

In discussing the tensions between 'getting an education' and 'getting a man', the female students compared single-sex and co-education schools. Parnell School is located in a local education authority, in which schools are highly stratified on class, gender and 'race' lines. For many of the young women in the lowest sets, single-sex schools were regarded as elitest. Hence, whatever the disadvantages of co-educational schools, it did not appear as though there was a real alternative. The female students in the lower sets spoke more favourably of the social advantages of co-education, both in terms of 'more fun' and 'meeting boys'. The female students claimed that coping with male students was easier now they were in year eleven than in earlier years when they experienced more widespread teasing. A number of them spoke of female friends who had established reputations that served to protect them from male students. Sophie was one of the physically biggest female students in year eleven and one of the school's best athletes. She felt that she and her friends could 'look after themselves'.

Michelle: The girls at Woodbridge [a single-sex school] are really snobby. They wouldn't even talk to you, not that you would want to talk to them. I had a friend who left and went there and she's a real pain now. She's even changed the way she talks, do you know what I mean?
Sharon: If you went to a girls' school, you'd never meet any boys, you'd never get a boyfriend. You see the girls at the grammar [a single-sex school]. They don't even know how to behave with a boy. They're all over any boy they can get.
Lavern: It's better with the boys in the class. You can have a laugh with them. They're more fun than just girls.
Sophie: If you asked me when I first came to the school, I would say I would rather go to a girls' school. A lot of the boys are still horrible to us

but it's changed a lot in another way. We're more grown up and can stand up to the boys, especially if you're bigger than them.

Smita: Well some girls will say that boys are loud and mess about too much. But a lot of the boys in our class would be afraid of Kelly. She'd batter them. So, its okay for us. If they get on my nerves, I give them a bad stare or cuss them down. They know they can only go so far.

The young women's ambivalence to having 'the boys around' appeared to change as the study progressed. At an early exploratory stage of the research, when these students were in year ten, they were more positive. Throughout the study, the young women claimed that they preferred 'older boys'. However, towards the end of year eleven, there was more emphasis on their male peers' immaturity. Among themselves they recounted fantasy stories about female students' older brothers and sixth-form male students (see Wolpe 1988).

Vicki: You just grow up and you look at the boys in our class, they're okay for a laugh but not to go out with.
M.M.:   What's the difference?
Kerry: It's like we're always saying, for one thing, girls are more mature. Older boys are more fun. They know how to treat you better than the boys in our class. You just grow out of them. Year nine girls are more interested in them.

These accounts serve to illustrate the limitations of the over-rationalized male teacher discourses indicated throughout this section. Working with unitary categories of subjectivity, these discourses position young women in situations in which it is assumed that they are failing to make rational decisions about their futures because of their emotional attachments to male students. It should be added that from a different perspective, most of the equal opportunities work at Parnell School operated on a shared ideological terrain. There was much talk of the need to provide 'strong role models' with which female students could identify. The young women here point to the need for a more comprehensive framework within which to understand their experience of schooling and masculinity. Most important-ly, they suggest the complexity of the personal and collective gendered investments of young women that cannot be read reductively in terms of either/or choices about 'getting a good education' rather than 'getting a man'. The next section will explore this theme further, in examining the young women's preparation for their post-school work and sexual destinies.

Future waged and domestic labour: The feminization of the local workforce

Griffin (1985b) has provided an insightful analysis of the complexity of the socio-sexual destiny of female students. Writing of the social and economic pressures on young women in relation to waged and domestic labour, she has described the simultaneous positions that they occupy in the sexual, marriage and labour markets:

> The sexual marketplace values women according to their perceived attractiveness to men, with youth at a particular premium. In leisure time this could be measured by young women's ability to get a boyfriend (or boyfriends). In the workplace it might refer to their fulfilment of the non-technical side of the office or shop jobs: developing a particular mode of sexy service with a smile . . . The marriage market covers pressures to get and keep a man, with the role of devoted wife and mother presented as women's primary function and biologically ordained destiny.
>
> (Griffin 1985b: 187–8)

At Parnell School, formal careers advice tended not to address the specific gender dynamics of female students' transition from school to these three markets. Informally, there was much ridicule from male teachers and disinterest from female teachers concerning female–male student relations, which were of central concern to the young women. There appeared to be little awareness by the teachers that the informal student networks were a key arena in the development of student sexual identities and future social destinies. Adopting a discourse of deficit, the male teachers spoke of black and white working-class young women 'in search of a boyfriend as a breadwinner' in contrast to the 'bright girls', who postponed their attachment to young men and concentrated on their future careers. These male perceptions of young women find a resonance in the dated 'transition from school to work' literature, which has a history of privileging and celebrating representations of white male rites of passage (Griffin 1985b, 1993). Contradictorily, the male teachers privately represented the female students as occupying a position of dependency, in seeking a male breadwinner, while at the same time they were publicly critical of female students, who they claimed were finding it easier than the male students to get jobs in the local area.

Mr Allen: It's very difficult with a lot of the low-ability girls we have here to get them motivated. They're more interested in chatting up the boys. You see them dolling themselves up for them. They seem more interested in getting hitched than education. I suppose they see them as a better investment for the future than a job.

M.M.:   Do many of the female students get jobs when they leave?

Mr Allen: It's picked up for the girls, even the low-ability ones. We get feedback that more of them than the boys are getting jobs or training.

M.M.:   Why do you think that the female students are investing in the boys, if the boys are more likely to be unemployed?

Mr Allen: Well you've got a point there. I never thought about that. Then again, these girls often don't make much sense to us or themselves, I would have thought.

One of the major complaints of working-class female students was that male teachers positively discriminated in favour of preparing male students for training and work. The young women claimed that, in turn, male students colluded with these practices, arguing that men should have priority in the allocation of scarce jobs in the local area. The young women challenged these views, claiming that they should not have to compensate for central government's failure to provide jobs for all young people. However, despite their experience of various forms of gender discrimination, in which male students' post-school destinies were privileged, working-class young women were sympathetic to the future work situation of their male peers. For many of them, this was informed by domestic experience of fathers and brothers being unemployed or working irregularly. These working-class young women's accounts find a resonance with Northern Irish working-class young women's experiences of living with a future of broken transitions into adulthood, in which they support unemployed boyfriends and husbands (Willis 1985; Holland 1988; Gillespie *et al.*, 1992).

Maxine: The men teachers don't really care about us [female students]. They're more worried about boys having jobs.
Kerry: They keep telling you to be realistic.
M.M.:   What do they mean?
Kerry: That means taking crap, and then the men teachers say you should be grateful even the boys aren't getting jobs. Well that's not our fault, is it?
Julie: The boys say they should have jobs first and then if there's any left over we can have them. But the girls don't think like that. The government should make jobs for everyone.
Linda: Nearly everyone we know round here has been unemployed sometime. It's terrible, all the rows at home and everything. I think it's no wonder all the kids are getting battered by their fathers. It's just terrible, if that's all you've got to look forward to. You can see it with a lot of the boys round here. They've just got no future and it's not their fault. But the teachers are wrong, it's not the girls' fault either.

Recent work, such as that by Weis (1991: 144–50), has challenged earlier feminist research which suggested that female students adopt a marginalized wage-labour identity. There has been a tendency in such work to set up dichotomies in which young women are assumed to be orientated either to careers or love marriages. As argued in Chapter 2, at the time of the research, structural changes had taken place in the school/waged-labour couplet that were not reflected in the schools' career advice system. These changes include the cumulative effects of the globalization of capital, the changing nature of labour processes and local labour markets, new school and work technologies, changing family forms, the feminization and racialization of poverty, the decline of the trade union movement and the success of feminist political struggle (Cockburn 1985; Phizaklea 1990; Walby 1990; Rees 1992).

By the 1990s, a socio-economic, legal and political reconstitution of young people is taking place within the training regimes of central government youth schemes, which have important implications for gender identity formation (Hollands 1990). This reconstitution was mediated at Parnell School within a local economy in which the disappearing 'masculine' manufacturing base was being displaced by an increase in the traditional 'feminine' service sector. In response to the perceived feminization of the local workforce, male students were appropriating former 'feminine' work skills, thus redefining the sexual division of labour in their part-time jobs in the service sector. Exploring the position of young women at Parnell School suggested the need for a more comprehensive conceptual map of the school/waged-labour couplet, which would take account of the increasingly complex and fractured differentiated regional experiences of state, workplace and domestic changes. I was particularly interested in examining how young women were responding to this gender restructuring of work, in relation to the interconnections between waged labour, future family life and the formation of feminine and masculine identities.

Within this socio-economic sphere, new femininities and masculinities are being materially and socially refashioned, opening up fresh possibilities in the changing private–public patriarchal worlds which the young women at Parnell School inhabit culturally (Holland 1988; Walby 1990; Lees 1993). In the following accounts, they make clear the ambiguities of these changing gender relations in their transition from school to future waged and domestic labour. The young women argued that male teachers were romanticizing the position of working-class women at work. For a high proportion of female students, in lone-parent families or with unemployed fathers, their immediate domestic experience of the feminization of the local workforce was of high levels of poverty. However, they felt that increased opportunities for women in the service sector of local labour markets might help to challenge the isolation of 'being stuck at home all day'. They also thought that part-time work might offer greater flexibility to women with childcare responsibilities. At the same time, they were realistic about the poor pay and conditions of the expanding market of part-time jobs. Some of the young women suggested that the increased number of women involved in waged labour might lead to changes in the domestic division of labour, with men taking greater responsibility for what conventionally was seen as 'women's work'. Others were less optimistic, particularly with reference to childcare responsibilities.

Niamh: I think a lot of men teachers are old-fashioned because they talk as
    if most women don't go out to work. But nearly all of us here, our moms
    work. They have to or we'd starve. It's not a big deal.
Julie: A lot of the teachers here, especially in careers, talk about all these
    women getting jobs as if it's great. But they don't tell you that the
    employers want you because they can pay you less, boss you around more
    and they want girls who look nice.
Shahida: The men teachers don't know anything about us, about our

families. When they talk of women's jobs, they're talking about lawyers, and doctors and teachers, not ordinary working women. My mom has gone back to work and it's really slavery the money she's getting.

M.M.:   Why do you think that is?

Claire: They've always paid Irish women nothing for doing all the cleaning. You see her with her friends, they haven't got much money. And she wouldn't even ever get promoted. All the women in charge are English. She says the Irish and black women have always been pushed to the bottom. So, what are the teachers talking about?

Sharon: It might be a good thing if more and more women went to work because that would give them a bit of life for themselves. But the trouble is when they come home, if they have to do all the housework as well.

M.M.:   Do you think things will change in the future?

Nicola: I hope so. My mom's nearly dead. She does two part-time jobs and my dad hasn't worked for ages. But really if you look at it, he only does little things at home. Like he's not become a house husband, like that boy was talking about the other day, there's no such thing.

Kelly: If you take our class. A lot of the boys might not get work. But I can't see them doing the housework and especially not looking after the kids, can you?

As I suggested for the male students, 'work experience' organized by the school might similarly be read for female students as an indication of the development of future trajectories into employment. Writing of the gendered two-track central government youth training schemes, Cockburn (1987: 12) has noted:

> My previous work and that of other researchers on the labour process has suggested that occupational "choice" is governed by a strong reality principle. In particular, people know that jobs are, in a sense gendered as they themselves are. Women know full well that certain jobs are "for" them and that if they seek to do jobs that are "for" men they will experience, at worst, hostility and ridicule, and, at best, discomfort and a persistent pressure to step back into line. Male and female act on each other, sustaining gender complementarity and difference.

This reality principle was reinforced by working-class young women's work placements. They described the continuities and discontinuities of their experience of school and workplace masculinities. One important difference was their unfamiliarity with the sexual regulation and control of the 'real world' of the workplace. Another important theme in their accounts of work placement was the gendered processes of infantilism that returned them to being 'treated like little girls'. This was of particular significance for these young women whose fantasies of future work centred around a transition to an adulthood of economic independence, that would serve to legitimate a lessening of their domestic responsibilities for others. Paid labour was also seen as enabling them to increase their spending

power on consumer goods, such as clothes, make-up, music and magazines, which provided a highly valued cultural space in which to live out
individual and collective feminine identities.

Lina: I thought a lot of men teachers here were bad but it was worse on
    our placement. The bloke at training scheme in charge of us kept calling us
    love and things like that. And you don't really know what to do. Like at
    school, you're with all your mates, so you can take the piss out of the
    teachers.

Michelle: They do things like putting their arm around you as if they know
    you or own you. They think that they can get away with this because we
    are only girls on the training scheme. You should be judged as a person
    not because they're frustrated. They think they can use you.

Ann Marie: I think what surprised me the most about the training was that
    they treat you worse than at school. I thought there they'd accept you as
    more grown up and you'd act more grown up. But it was actually worse,
    telling you to make tea for them or whatever rubbish jobs they wanted
    doing. They wouldn't treat a boy like that, would they?

Lavern: I've done shop work, part-time, but somehow I thought that real
    work would be different. It was worse. You didn't have your mates. I was
    thinking of leaving school straight away to try and get a bit of money and
    that but I'm not sure now.

Sharon: The same for me. I thought if I was doing a proper job like my
    brother, I'd get away with more at home like him and spend more time on
    things I like doing for myself. But work was terrible and at home nothing
    changed.

Listening to the young women's accounts of their work placements
highlighted the heterogeneity of the sub-cultural self-preparation for their
post-school socio-sexual destinies. Hollands (1990: 105), writing of the way
in which the traditional domestic apprenticeship pattern continues under
the surface of job 'choice' and training opportunities, describes the
different transitions into work for young women on the Youth Training
Scheme (YTS). He identifies three main orientations: 'glam' (glamorous)
jobs, paraprofessional/domestic work and factory jobs. Similar patterns
were developing among the female students at Parnell School, with
different orientations being highlighted following their return from work
placements.

One of the main issues to emerge in this part of the research was a critical
engagement with male teachers' suggestion that the new vocationalist
skilling programmes in operation at the school were opening up new career
opportunities for young women. The female students in the low sets, on
returning from work placements, strongly disagreed with their teachers'
inflated claims. These students who spoke of wishing 'to work with
people', chose jobs that 'would get them away from blokes bossing them
around'. At the same time, as Skeggs (1988: 139) found in her study of
gender reproduction in further education, the importance that these
students attached to appearance when talking of jobs, suggested that they

were aware that paid labour was also a potential 'marriage market', as well as a place where labour is performed. Other, socially mobile female students spoke of choosing hi-tech office work that provided a supportive, clean environment, in which they could develop a career that was not available to their mothers. They tended to be optimistic about the changing nature of local labour markets in relation to women's work, arguing that although teachers exaggerated the degree of the changes, there were opportunities for individual women 'to make something of their lives'.

There were varied responses to work placement from the female students in the top set. For the socially mobile working-class students, like their male peers, the Academic Achievers, it was dismissed as a distraction from their academic studies. In contrast, the new middle-class female students, like the Real Englishmen, enjoyed their placements, selecting work places that blurred the boundaries between work and leisure, in which they could socialize with friends while working. A group of these students were involved with a local community feminist group which produced videos of women's lives. They argued that single-sex occupational groups provided a supportive feminine sphere in which to develop work skills. They were enthusiastic about future careers in the media, theatre, art and design, and fashion (Aggleton 1987a).

Julie: The teachers are always talking about getting skills. It's a load of rubbish. All the places where they sent our class [the lowest set], you didn't need any skills. I don't think people at work would know what skills are. It's just common sense, what you've learnt at home, like looking after people and that.
Dawn: Before we went on placement, we talked together about getting somewhere that was nice to work in. So you could get out of the uniform and wear some nice clothes for a change.
M.M.: Do you think that it's very different for the boys?
Dawn: It's more important the way a woman looks. You have to look good and that's sexist really. Like on the placement, some of the men would say you're looking nice today. But in another way dressing up makes you feel better about yourself. It just makes you feel more confident.
Emma: It was brilliant with the community group. You could really enjoy it. Some of the girls here went to typical places like typing and child care. But we wanted something different, where we could be ourselves, something more real.

There is a danger in a book whose focus is female students' experience of school masculinities of reductively reading femininity as being over-deterministically shaped by teacher and student masculinities. Femininity should not be seen as simply complementary to masculinity. Rather, femininities are actively constructed within specific institutional arenas in relation to and against each other. Schools produce a range of feminine subject positions that students inhabit culturally. This is illustrated here by a group of white and black socially mobile working-class female students, who were in the top set at Parnell School. They pointed out that the main difference between themselves and new middle-class students was that the latter had the economic security of a parental network of social contacts in the labour market. For the working-class students, this provided middle-class students with a personal independence both from academic qualifications and marriage. In contrast, they felt that working-class female students in the low sets, in rejecting academic qualifications, were creating future conditions in which they would, like their mothers, be dependent upon husbands. The socially mobile young women distanced themselves from both these groups, highly valuing their own future career and domestic options (Bates and Riseborough 1993).

Susan: You can't compare us to the middle-class girls here. They've got it made. You see them hanging around with the boys, doing nothing and they'll still get good jobs. Their parents get them private teaching and they have all the contacts. There's a small group of us here from ordinary backgrounds and we'll get on because of ourselves, on our own effort. Our parents support us but they can't in the same way as the middle-class girls because they don't know the system.

Natalie: Sometimes I think the teachers prefer the middle-class girls to us because they remind them of their own daughters. Like some of the teachers know their parents and go to the same places at night. And they'd talk in class about this even though the girls try to hide it. They pretend to be rebels but they haven't got anything to rebel against. So they have to go to the extremes, posing all the time, getting into black music and the rest of it.

Dawn: A lot of the girls in the low classes don't care about working in class or doing homework and they'd never prepare for tests. They'll end up with nothing. You have to work hard if you're going to get anything in this life but they haven't learnt that. The work is worth it in the end because you'll get on.

Susan: Looking back some of us, like in our class, have made definite decisions about getting on. It will give you more opportunities about how you want to live your life. You can have a career and then get married later if you want to. But a lot of the girls in the low classes, they're from the estate, they don't see this, so they just end up the same as their parents on the dole with unemployed husbands. That's their future.

The combination of these suggested different school biographies and the changing conditions in the local economy appeared to be significant elements in a discussion on the future position of women in family life. It arose in a debate in a single-sex personal and social education lesson, in which new middle-class white female students defended the motion that marriage and the family were outdated patriarchal institutions that primarily served men's interest in oppressing women. The middle-class students, supported by socially mobile white and black working-class students, presented a strong case, and drawing on white feminist analysis they criticized the conventional nuclear family. Those who challenged the motion offered a range of arguments. For black and Irish working-class young women, extended family networks remained an important site strategically, both in terms of defence against racism and in providing a space for women to support each other. Among some of the white working-class English students, a main defence of the family was that there was not an alternative social framework within which to raise families. They also felt that the new middle-class young women tended to generalize about men, while in their experience young men after a period of adolescent unrest settled down to marriage and family life, from which both women and men could benefit. My representation of this debate reads as an overly rationalist account, in which the participants held consistent views. The situation was more complex than implied here, with shifting positions emerging as the debate progressed. In other words, the 'pro'- and 'anti'-family stances were contextually based and constituted a continuum rather than a rigid dichotomy. For example, in interviews with me, the Irish and black working-class young women who took part in the debate were highly critical of their own family's patriarchal practices.

Young women also spoke of the disruption of family life that accompanies unemployment. This had a historically specific local meaning for white English students, who have enjoyed relative stability in employment, offered by the former strong manufacturing base located in the West Midlands. This contrasted with the experiences of the black and Irish students, whose parents had shared a long history of migration, involving the break-up of their extended families. An important part of the political cultural rhetoric of all immigrant groups, black and white, that is transmitted to their children born in England, is that one day they will return 'home' to their country of origin. This is one of the main themes of traditional and contemporary music, which Irish working-class young women at Parnell School celebrated (Curtis 1985; Hickman 1986). They were actively involved in the Irish community's cultural activities and made regular visits to their extended families in Ireland. Many of them wished to find work there, feeling that it was 'a better place to bring up kids'.

Claire: We feel safer among our own, at the club [local Irish community centre] and places like that. My mom will let me out to dances at the Centre.
M.M.:   Is there a difference between Irish and English men?
Ann Marie: Well of course a lot of them are after the same thing. But English blokes are more aggressive. You just couldn't go to an English pub in town. They're just out looking for fights.
Niamh: My cousin was over from home [Ireland] and she said she couldn't believe why so many of the lads had tattoos. They look so ugly but they're all trying to look really tough.

There has been much criticism of resistance theory, both in terms of its theoretical and empirical value in understanding the experiences of subordinated groups (Giroux 1983). Diamond (1991: 160), who has critically developed earlier work on gender resistance to schooling, offers a theoretical framework within which she seeks to 'explicate the linkages between the individual action and structural dimensions of schooling'. I shall now examine the diverse responses of young women's contestation and resistance at Parnell School.

Cultural contestations, disruptions and resistances: Producing gender/sexual counter-discourses

Most recently, Griffin (1993), in her work on British and North American academic representations of young people's family life and sexuality, provides a critical evaluation of the reported range of young people's experiences. She (1993: 194) suggests that:

> In the feminist literature on sexual abuse and harassment, this tension between the construction of young women as victims or survivors was resolved in texts which represented young women as capable of adopting strategies of resistance, coping and/or survival (e.g. Halston, 1989). By the late 1980s many radical texts had jettisoned the discourse of resistance, representing young working-class people and young people of colour as trapped within a state of crisis by the late policies of Thatcher and Reagan. Other radical analyses addressed the debate between structure, culture and agency, and between subjects and texts (e.g. Roman and Christian-Smith 1988; Willis *et al.* 1990).

A number of studies (Griffin 1985b; Mac an Ghaill 1988c; Mirza 1992) have pointed out that the meanings of white and black female school conformity and deviance are more complex than the traditional ethnographic work on males has suggested.[4] At Parnell School, the male teachers' responses to student contestation of schooling was underpinned by conventional expectations of the bipolar gendered ascriptions of 'active' masculinity and passive 'femininity'. As Kessler *et al.* (1985: 226) have argued, overt resistance among young men may confirm and even exaggerate their masculinity, while the same behaviour among young women violates conventional femininity. At Parnell School, male teachers accommodated female student 'passive' contestation through discursive themes of naturalization. However, a major concern to the staff were the more overt forms that were most visibly expressed by The Posse, who adopted social practices which contested class-based gender representations. Earlier feminist research has illustrated the processes whereby state institutions construct young women's overt 'deviancy' as sexual (Jones 1985; Holly 1989a). While the research was being carried out, there was a heightened awareness of female students' active sexuality, as a result of a student pregnancy in a local school. This incident was discussed in terms of the effect it would have on the school's reputation in the local market.

Writing of the gendered contradictions involved in young women's resistance to schooling, Cockburn (1987: 44) has suggested that:

For girls, too, the possibilities are contradictory. Some use femininity itself (make-up, stylish or outlandish clothes) as a form of resistance to school and class authority . . . There is an alternative strategy available to girls however that rejects glamour altogether. It is an active resistance that undermines conventional femininity and challenges girls' subordination . . . Girls are continually testing out the boundaries of their confinement to get a sense of their possible power. We will see how one way girls have of doing this is to refuse "women's work" and women's domestic roles and make a bid for "men's work" and a space for women in men's world.

At Parnell School, the students adopted these modes of feminine resistance and contestation within specific contexts. There was a wide range of tactics of feminine disruption, solidarity and use of sexuality, developed in response to their social positioning as young women, which were expressed in specific class and ethnic cultural forms. The mode of masculine social regulation in operation, in such different sites as classrooms, corridors and the playground, offered varying opportunities to counter their institutionalized subordination. Equally significant, feminine forms of contestation were influenced by male teachers' disciplinary reputation. Young women, in collectively challenging school masculinities, sought to exploit individual male teacher weaknesses.

Julie: All the girls fancy the new English teacher. He's a real dishy geezer. It's really a laugh, it's so easy to make him embarrassed, asking him about virgins when we were reading the book in class.

M.M.: Why do you do that with him?

Julie: We always do it with new teachers before they learn the ropes. He's too young to be really horrible. And with him, well he's too attractive to be a teacher. Once he settles in, he'll be like the rest of the men teachers here, bossing you about all the time. So, we just get our own back while we can.

It is important to note, as Skeggs (1991) reminds us, that young women's contestation of state schooling is severely circumscribed by the school's institutional power, which enables it to act as a key gatekeeper to future economic and social destinies. She writes:

However, the students' willingness to use their limited power to challenge male sexuality is based on expedient cost–benefit judgements. It is dependent upon the place, the significance attributed to the males involved and the students' investments in the course. Their responses indicate the limits to which they are un/willing to compromise in order to gain their educational "ticket".

(Skeggs 1991: 134)

At Parnell School, female student investment in the formal curriculum was a key variable in shaping their contestation of schooling. However, the way in which school knowledge was appropriated and utilized for different purposes was not predictable and varied greatly (Hollands 1990: 71). For example, in a previous study of black students' schooling (Mac an Ghaill 1988c: 28), I identified a group of young women of Asian and African Caribbean parentage, the 'Black Sisters', who developed a specific mode of resistance within accommodation, which involved a pro-education/anti-school position (Fuller 1980; Anyon 1983). In the following extract, one of the students, Judith, illustrates this subtle survival strategy.

> With me like, I go into school and I listen to the teachers and I put down what they want. Christopher Columbus discovered America, I'll put it down, right. Cecil Rhodes, you know that great imperialist, he was a great man, I'll put it down. We did about the Elizabethans, how great they were. More European stuff; France, equality, liberty and fraternity, we'll put it all down. At that time, they had colonies, enslaving people. I'll put down that it was the mark of a new age, the Age of Enlightenment. It wasn't, but I'll put it down for them, so that we can tell them that black people are not stupid. In their terms, we can tell them that we can get on. In their terms, I come from one of the worst backgrounds but I am just saying to them, I can do it right, and shove your stereotypes up your anus.

A number of African Caribbean female students at Parnell School spoke of similar strategies of survival, making a distinction between technical and social school requirements. Like 'pro-school' students, they conformed to the technical demands made upon them, gaining high marks by completing class and home work. However, they did not automatically conform to the school's social demands, either in terms of appearance or appropriate behaviour to teachers. Like the Black Sisters, they adopted an overtly instrumental approach to schooling, in which white teachers were perceived as a means of acquiring qualifications. White teachers were not necessarily highly valued in themselves, in contrast to qualifications, which were invested with value in racial and gender terms.

> *Mr Middleton:*   I'd say a lot of teachers would say the black girls are the most difficult to handle. Obviously, I don't mean all of them. But it's difficult to know how they are going to behave. And not just those in the low classes. Sometimes I think that they don't really care what you think about them. They don't value your opinion of them.

As indicated in Chapter 2, at the time of the field research a moral panic was in the process of being constructed, in which African Caribbean males were being displaced by Muslim male students as the new 'folk devils'. At the same time, there was increased concern among the staff about an emerging group of 'troublesome' Asian female students. Writing of African Caribbean females in a comprehensive school Gillborn (1990: 69), describes the way in which:

> They adopted the role of "protectors" of younger Afro-Caribbean pupils (of both sexes) in the school: if they saw any argument or fight

involving a young Afro-Caribbean pupil and a peer of another ethnic origin, they would intervene – often in a physically aggressive way – to ensure the safety of the former. This role was extended to arguing with staff if a young Afro-Caribbean was being reprimanded.

At Parnell School, this function of 'protector' was adopted by young Asian women in defending recently arrived Asian students from attacks by male students. The teachers, working with a crude racially based disciplinary evaluatory system of students, failed to enquire about the specific meaning of the young Asian women's apparent 'bad behaviour' in being physically aggressive to male students.

Maxine: A lot of the time you write down the stuff for them [the teachers]. Well, for them because they have the power to pass and fail, yes. But you are really doing it for yourself because black people have done so bad in this system. So you have to be careful all the time that you are not another one that they fail.

Wendy: It's qualifications that matter out there. If you want to go on further in education, they're not going to say, "did you like your teacher?" They're going to say, "what qualifications, what grades have you got?"

M.M.:   Have you always wanted qualifications?

Wendy: No. I used to fool about a lot with my friends. Then we talked at home and I began to see. You need to work hard to prove that you can do it. And it's important because if you get a good education, you can be freer from men when you leave school. I look at my aunt and I really admire what she has done. She is really independent, working for herself and she has made it easier for our generation, hasn't she?

A number of researchers have noted the limits of young women's contestation of the normalization of masculinity that operate through processes of compulsory heterosexuality (Jones and Mahony 1989). Griffin (1985b: 59), in her study of white and black young women, found that 'heterosexuality was experienced as a freely chosen sexual preference: it was seen as "natural" and inevitable. Alternatives to heterosexuality (e.g. bisexuality, celibacy, lesbianism) were seen as deviant, abnormal and pathological.' Young women at Parnell School made similar comments. Some new middle-class young women discussed lesbianism in terms of a 'passing phase, sometimes chosen by women when they are between male partners'. The female students reported that lesbianism had never been mentioned in lessons while they were at the school (Epstein 1993). However, informally it was a major term of abuse. Cockburn (1987: 41) has described the discursive power of the term 'lezzie' in young women's self-policing of sexual boundaries:

Beyond "slag" and "drag" of course is another damaging label that can be attached to the girl who steps out of line: that of lesbian. It appears that it's only since the emergence of the new women's movement and active politicised lesbianism in the 1970s that "lezzie" has become a term of abuse in school culture. Now "lezzie" has joined "poofter" in the lexicon of insults used in classroom and playground. The universal slur on lesbians drives homosexual feelings underground, makes attachment to men compulsory and makes close and enduring friendships between girls difficult.

Finally, as Skeggs (1991: 134) suggests, a number of studies 'have shown how conversations about sexuality and potential boyfriends only occurred in safe places such as toilets (McRobbie and McCabe, 1981 and Griffin, 1982)'. She adds that: 'the single-sex classroom can be seen to be a similar "safe place"'. Throughout the research period at Parnell School, young women would often imply that 'much private talk' was taking place in 'safe places' that they had created for themselves. Occasionally, as Paula indicates in the opening comment to this chapter, female students would make explicit references to their use of such places. However, most of the time I was excluded from such talk.

Summary

These young women have provided an insightful review of school masculinities, clearly identifying and articulating the institutional power that is ascribed to male teachers and students. The chapter provides support for earlier feminist studies in this area, highlighting the diversity of young women's responses to schooling. The chapter also offers a critique of much current equal opportunities work, which has not made masculinity a critical focus. There are continuities between this chapter and the next, in which sixth-form gay male students discuss their experiences of secondary schooling. Both the heterosexual young women and the gay male students are in a position within which to provide critical perspectives on dominant modes of male heterosexuality at the local level of the school.

5

Schooling, sexuality and male power: Towards an emancipatory curriculum[1]

Introduction

> Sex now seemed a strange thing to me, a social rite that registered, even brought about shifts in the balance of power, but something that was more discussed than performed, a simple emission of fluid that somehow generated religious, social and economic consequences.
>
> (White 1983: 193)

> At school there's no such thing as sexuality, so it seems. Then one day you come out and say you're gay and then you find out that it's the most important thing in the world. The teachers try everything to change you. "It's a phase, you need psychiatric help, it's unnatural, it's against your religion, your parents won't accept you, your friends will reject you, you won't get a job." I've heard it all. I think that teachers feel more threatened by gays than by any other group.
>
> (Rajinder, student)

This chapter sets out to explore a group of gay male students' experiences of schooling and sexuality that are seen as complex, problematic and contradictory. They display a political awareness that is often absent in theories of sexuality. Furthermore, the students provide a critique of most research on education and gay sexuality which sets up young people as a 'problem' or as victims. Acknowledging the multiple determination of power upon and within state institutions, as Rajinder indicates above, central to their understanding are the heterosexist and homophobic power relations that circumscribe their lives. Such an understanding illustrates the potential for the development of critical educational explanations of what is going on in schools and colleges, which could serve to support progressive curriculum practices. This will be explored further in the next chapter.

This is a relatively under-researched area (Epstein, in press). The paucity of information concerning gay students' schooling is all the more serious at a time of increased and increasing state and media control, surveillance and criminalization of the gay community. This is made legislatively visible with the infamous Clause 28 of the 1988 Local Government Act now in place, the pernicious and crude Clause 25 of the 1991 Criminal Justice Bill and the proposed revision of Circular 11/87 in early 1993, later withdrawn. Here we see an attempt to outlaw the legitimacy of individual and community gay identity and return it to a pre-Wolfenden era. Such coercive legislative instruments of control have been accompanied by increased physical and verbal attacks on gays and lesbians.[2] Writing of the absence of what might be called the 'peculiarities of the English' in relation to the discussion or display of sex or sexuality, Harris (1990: 2) identifies:

> the emergence of three recent developments, all of which evolved outside the lesbian and gay lobby, which forced the issue of sexuality to the fore of political and educational debate. These are Section 28 ... the advent of HIV and AIDS, and the recent decision to transfer the responsibility of sex education to school governing bodies.

The young men involved in this two-year ethnographic study were aged between 16 and 19 years. They attended three institutions: the sixth-form at Parnell School, a sixth-form college and a college of further education, all situated in the Midlands. I taught three of them – Rajinder, Sean and Julian – all of whom were following A level courses. Within the school they were not known to be gay. They informed me that they were open to me about their sexuality because of my anti-homophobic stance. In lessons and in informal situations, I presented a pro-gay perspective. They introduced me to their friends, who in turn introduced me to their friends. We operated as an informal support group. As with the main study of Parnell School, much of the material was collected by observation, informal discussion and individual and group semi-structured interviews with the students. I also interviewed their parents, and their teachers at the three institutions they attended. In addition, they kept diaries and helped to construct question-naires that they took part in. The students were aware that I was studying the construction of masculinities. Rajinder and Sean suggested that I look at a gay perspective based on their school experiences. Skeggs (1988: 133) writes that her study:

> focussed on the tensions and contradictions that were part of the students' construction of subjectivity in relation to institutional and structural forms. For instance, it examined how the students attem-pted to gain some autonomy in an institutional and cultural situation which rendered them almost totally powerless and socially worthless.

Skeggs is writing about young women's experiences in further education. Interestingly, as is shown below, there are many parallels between the processes of marginalization and the creative responses of the young women in her study and the gay students here.

A major danger of making the young men the focus of this study is that it may serve unintendedly to reinforce the dominant 'commonsense' view of equating discussion of sexuality with gays as social problems or victims. For example, when I asked a number of sixth-form and further education teachers if I could interview their students about masculinity, I was informed that either there were no gays in their institutions or that they did not think it appropriate to discuss homosexuality, particularly in light of Clause 28. Such self-surveillance has been the specific and frequently misunderstood hidden state agenda developed during the last decade with the emergence of the New Right and the New Right moralism (Weeks 1989). Implicit in the teachers' responses was the assumption that dominant forms of heterosexual masculinity are unproblematic. They assumed that any research in this area implied a critique of masculinity, which for them could only mean a focus on gayness. Here, there is a resonance with feminist empirical research documenting the difficulty of interviewing men, which I encountered throughout my work on studying masculinity. Despite widespread evidence of male sexual abuse of women and girls and boys, these men remained cocooned within the collective security of the hegemonic sex/gender power relations operating upon and within modern institutions, such as schools. As Seidler (1989: 219) suggests: 'heterosexuality as a structured institution enforces the conception of "normality" that is taken for granted within the culture'. It was assumed by the teachers that as a male researcher I would collude in the reproduction of this invidious 'normality' that serves to mystify the mechanisms through which male heterosexual privilege and domination operate. Progressive male theorists of masculinity tend to over-emphasize the methodological advantages of men researching other men. Frequently absent from such accounts are the potential dangers of male collusion in the construction and representation of male practices (Canaan and Griffin 1990). Although I have political and theoretical doubts about exploring the young men's school experiences within this context, the primary reason for doing so is that they occupy a critical social location to challenge the above assumption, as part of a broader concern with the sexual structuring of schools and its interconnecting relation to other major organizing principles of schooling, namely, class, age, gender, 'race'/ethnicity and disability (see Haywood 1993).

As part of the study's collaborative approach, the students and I chose the following categorizations as the main areas of concern in this chapter: sex/sexuality education, essentialism–constructionism, sexual structuring–sexual typification ('the enemy within'), sex/gender regimes, and being gay (positive and creative).

Sex/sexuality education

Students enter schools as sexual and gendered subjects, having experienced wider formal and informal learning networks, central among which are their families, local labour markets, peer groups and the media. The students had received little formal sex education from their parents. For those that did discuss it with their parents, the emphasis was on biological aspects, which was heterosexist and assumed male dominance and power (Wolpe 1988). The main message was 'not to get girls into trouble'. At their schools they were presented with an equally narrow, negative perspective. Furthermore, sex education tended to be subsumed under other curricular areas, such as biology or personal and social education (see Wolpe 1977; Rance 1982; DES 1988a; Lee 1993; Thomson 1993).

In examining the quality and character of sex education in schools, Measor (1989: 38) found that: '[the] . . . teachers failed to address many of the issues most central to the pupils' concerns. Instead the sex education that they provided was derived from their own culture, and from their adult status.' The students reported a similar picture of ill-prepared, under-resourced lessons, that both lacked any sense of progression and were overly teacher-centred, with irrelevant information that was repeated frequently throughout their schooling. Ironically, at a time of much pedagogical rhetoric about student-centred teaching approaches and cross-curricular initiatives, there appears to be little movement among policy-makers or within schools to design whole-school programmes of effective sex education that starts with the students' experiences and needs. The transfer of responsibility for sex education to school governing bodies and the overloading of the subject-based National Curriculum offers little hope of change (DES 1989). (See Conclusion for discussion of the intro-duction of the Sex Education Amendment to the 1993 Education Act.)

Wolpe (1988: 100) argues that:

> The ideology on sex and sex education, and its relation to moral order, structure the official way in which sex and sexuality are handled within a school. Inspite of these discourses and the tendency for teachers to accept these seemingly unquestioningly, sexual issues are ever present but not necessarily recognised as such by teachers.

The students' school experiences support Wolpe's argument. On the one hand, they felt that in lessons sex and sexuality appeared to be absent, in contrast to its pervasiveness outside of lessons, particularly in upper secondary school and in their present institutions. On the other hand, they felt that it was not so much that sex and sexuality were absent from lessons, but rather that they tended to be 'invisible'; they did not get talked about. Nevertheless, they recognized that they were present in teacher–student and student–student relations within the classroom and the wider school.

Michael: It's like two separate worlds. In lessons sex is almost never talked about and outside of lessons it's a main topic of conversation. Most of my friends' parents never discuss sex with them. Mine certainly never did and school wasn't much better.

Julian: Sex is supposed to be good. But schools give you a totally negative view. It's all about making you feel guilty and making sure that you're not doing it. It's like they're talking about their own sexual habits and hang-ups because it doesn't mean much to the kids. We're not all screwing around. Teachers see sex as sexual intercourse, but the most we'll get up to is masturbation and fooling around together. But the men teachers you see were hypocrites, giving us the moral talk then forcing themselves onto the girls all the time and pretending it wasn't sexual. Teachers think kids are stupid!

The students became aware of the underlying dominant ideologies that structured their schooling. They described the narrow range of topics that were discussed in lessons and the overt and covert moral values that were transmitted within the context of normative/prescriptive accounts of the two-parent nuclear family lifestyle. They also spoke about what was excluded from their sex education lessons. They agreed with Aggleton *et al.* (1989: 42) that: 'Official prescriptions about sex education, as well as those materials readily available to parents and teachers, operate with an almost uniform commitment to heterosexuality, procreation and "traditional" role relationships between men and women.'

Sean: They [the teachers] don't talk about the differences between sexual love and other kinds of love. They don't talk about emotions and they don't encourage you to talk about your desires or how they come about. Most boys go through all their school life without ever discussing how they feel about other people. I mean in a positive way. All the aggression and anger is allowed and expected really, if you're a real man. That's why men are so emotionally under-developed. When you think about it, girls and boys come out of school like two separate tribes not really understanding each other and then they're expected to live together. It's not an accident it turns out that way; the school makes it like that.

Gerard: In some ways it's difficult for the teachers because it's not like normal lessons, when they're supposed to have the knowledge. With sex education a lot of them haven't got their own relationships sorted out. But they shouldn't keep on about the future and having babies and getting diseases. They should talk about how we feel now as we're going through the school. They create a whole lot of people living in separate little sexual worlds, who think that there's something wrong with them when everyone is going through the same thing.

The students' insights are particularly salient in identifying a major flaw in much recent progressive pedagogical practice in relation to gender oppression. This flaw is most surprising given the unique theoretical position of feminist work in England in successfully combining analysis and practice, structure and subjectivity, rationalism and empiricism (Barrett 1980; McRobbie 1991, 1990; Segal 1990; Nava 1992). An unintended effect of anti-sexist policy initiatives in focusing on the institutional structures of subordination has been the failure to incorporate a critical social psychology. This has led to an over-rationalist pedagogy employing a positivist epistemology. Here, there is an assumption of an *a priori* superiority that anti-sexist 'facts' are theoretically more adequate and efficacious explanations of gender relations than the logic provided by 'commonsense' feelings about gender and sexual differences (see Cohen 1987).[3] Schools are recreated as pre-Freudian landscapes in which there is an absence of individual intention, structure of feeling, emotional responses, repression, displacement and irrationality (Freud 1933; Mitchell 1975; Lacan 1977; Chodorow 1978). We are returned to a Kantian world in which it is assumed 'that our lives can be lived by reason alone and that through determination . . . we can struggle against our inclinations, to live according to the pattern that we have set ourselves through reason' (Seidler 1990: 219).

In criticizing conventional programmes of sex education, the students are challenging the structures and practices involved in the desexualization of school life, in which not only is homosexuality excluded but by sleight of hand all aspects of sexuality other than the institutional form of the monogamous family structure is written out of the curriculum. They hoped that within their suggested framework, lesbian and gay issues could be introduced in a non-problematic form, thus enabling all students to feel confident to discuss their sexual and emotional development with self-selected teachers and students. Such an approach sharply contrasted with their own experiences of school, which are now examined.

Essentialism–constructionism

One of the main recent theoretical and political areas of concern within lesbian and gay studies has been the essentialist–constructionist debate.[4] Plummer (1989: 26) outlines these positions:

> Briefly essentialists assume that homosexuality has an essence; is found across societies and history as a universal form; and exists as a condition within us at birth or certainly very early in life. By contrast, constructionists assume that erotic and emotional attachments between people of the same sex are potentials in everybody but come to exist in fundamentally different ways, in different times and places. There is no transhistorical, transcultural universal essence of gayness.

Eight of the students were supportive of the constructionist position, while two of them were undecided. The students described the formation of their sexual identity as part of a wider process of adolescent development, with all its fluidity, experiments, displacements, transgressions and confusions. For them, sexuality could not be reduced to the conventional perception of a heterosexual–homosexual (straight–gay) continuum, on which each group's erotic and emotional attachments are demarcated clearly and unambiguously. They spoke of the contradictions of the public–private social worlds that gave them an insight into the complexity and confusion of young males' sexual coming of age. They have become experts at decoding the ambivalent social and sexual meanings of heterosexual behaviour involved in male bondings and rites of passage.

Michael: Everyone is confused about their sexuality when they are young. It's part of growing up for all boys that you get closer to your mates. Girls are allowed to express it more. I think that I am gay but I like women as well. I will probably get married but I think that there will be a part of me that will stay gay.

Sean: No-one can really say how they feel. One day you really fancy someone then it passes. Most blokes prefer to be with their male friends, including the straights. They have a better time with them, that's what they think. They prefer to talk about girls than talk with them. There's a lot of pressures on you to act that way and follow the crowd.

Adrian: A lot of people have got a hidden sexual past. Like when my dad heard that I was gay, he really threatened me, really bad. He was drunk and called me a bender and all that. Then next morning he came and told me that whatever I was I was still his son. And when he was younger he rolled sailors. I really respected him for that. He didn't have to tell me. My dad is the typical big macho man – on the outside.

Matthew: Everyone is a bit gay, especially when you're young. At college a lot of straight guys come up to you when they're on their own away from their friends and say, "my sister thinks you look like a model, or the girls in our class think that you've got a really good tan or I bet all the women are after you with your looks". They mean that they find you good looking or fancy you. But they couldn't admit it. Not just to you but to themselves.

Joseph: My sister was getting married to Pete and just before the wedding she found him in bed with his best friend. He told her that there was nothing in it; they didn't have sex or anything. His friend told me that they did. She was going to call the wedding off but I told her that it wasn't the sleeping together that was really the problem but because of Pete's emotional closeness to his friend. She eventually agreed that was really the threat. I doubt if Pete will ever sleep with him again. But even if he did, does that make him more gay than the feelings that they have for each other? There's no simple answers; feelings are more important than sex.

These young men were highly critical of the conventional conflation of sex and sexuality. They also challenged the reductionist classification and representation of male sexuality in terms of a bifurcation of an essentialist heterosexuality and homosexuality. They pointed to the precariousness of all sexualities, suggesting that gays are a vital part of straight male culture, with homosexuality always present in heterosexuality. James Baldwin (in Troupe 1989: 178–9), describing more graphically the latter's dependence on gays, points to the political significance of the male body, implying the Freudian insight that extreme personal and cultural antipathy is premised contradictorily on desire and need. He writes:

the society makes its will toward you very, very clear . . . these are far more complex than they want to realize. That's why I call them infantile. They have needs which for them are literally inexplicable. They don't dare look into the mirror. And that is why they need faggots. They've created faggots in order to act out a sexual fantasy on the body of another man and not take any responsibility for it. Do you see what I mean? I think it's very important for the male homosexual to recognize that he is a sexual target for other men, and that is why he is despised, and why he is called a faggot. He is called a faggot because other males need him.

(Troupe 1989: 178–9)

Sexual structuring–sexual typification: 'The enemy within'

Interviews with the students' teachers focused on the wider issue of masculinity and schooling. Male teachers made a point of informing me that they found the subject matter difficult to discuss. They were particularly reticent about discussing homosexuality, claiming that it was not relevant as a curriculum issue, although they stressed that there were 'a few effeminate boys each year in their institutions'. In contrast to the students, most of the male and female teachers' explanations of homosexuality were rooted in essentialism; that is, that gayness is a universal category into which people are born.

Plummer (1989: 28) informs us how meanings around homosexuality have changed in recent times: 'from a sick condition in the fifties, criminalised and medicalised, to a positive liberated identity in the seventies, to an AIDS-linked identity in the eighties'. The teachers selectively chose negative behavioural ascriptions as part of their social pathological discourse on gays. They employed a number of reactionary 'commonsense' representations of adolescent homosexuality, which included effeminate boys, mother-dominated males, arrested sexual development, predatory sexual practices, psychological sickness and disease-related behaviour. These images are resonant of nineteenth-century religious, legislative and medical discourses (Foucault 1979). They have been particularly pervasive in England throughout the 1980s with the political shift and appeal to authoritarian populism by the New Right moralists (Hall 1983; Watney 1993).

Most of the teachers operated with crude conceptions of straight–gay identities in terms of a superiority–inferiority couplet. Some of the liberal teachers, particularly those who worked in pastoral care posts, tended to emphasize sexual differences rather than sexual superiority. Nevertheless, all of them shared the dominant homophobic conception that heterosexuality is intrinsically different to homosexuality and that these sexual differences are primarily causal of social behaviour (see Barker, 1981, on the new racism). Furthermore, none of the teachers felt competent to counsel lesbian or gay young people. Many of them informed me that Clause 28 and the 1986 Education Act would prevent them from taking a positive curriculum approach to homosexuality.

The students have grown up in a society in which there are no positive images of gay or lesbian people. There is no acknowledgement of gay and lesbian history, sensibility, lifestyle and community. There is no recognition of gay or lesbian achievement. For example, the research showed that when texts written by gays or lesbians were read in class, no reference was made to the authors' sexual orientation. In fact, in lessons homosexuality was rarely discussed and, on the few occasions when it was introduced, it was presented in a negative way, most recently in relation to AIDS. A similar situation was found in curriculum analysis in North America (see Warren 1984; Johnson A. 1989).

For the students, this silence – reflecting that in the wider society – pervaded the whole of the formal curriculum, serving to reproduce and legitimate dominant heterosexual hierarchies. From this perspective, heterosexuality was presented as natural, normal and universal, simply because there are no alternative ways of being (Egerton 1986). The students emphasized the personal isolation, confusion, marginalization and alienation that this engendered. Most significantly, without a positive reference group, they tended to internalize ambivalent negative messages about themselves as gay men. These experiences are recalled by Lilley (1985: 18), who describes how:

> Some teachers remain to be convinced that the problem is a serious one. While giving a vague intellectual assent to the proposition of equal rights, they cannot feel that much harm is done. Let me assure them, and I can say this from my personal experience and my knowledge of scores of ex-pupils, that going through the school system as a gay person is a terrible ordeal, one full of loneliness, anxiety and isolation, and one suffered by a tenth of the population. The usual fears and worries of adolescence are magnified ten-fold.

Barrat (1986: 42, 56) makes a distinction between the psychological view of typification with its focus on individuals' attitudes, such as prejudice, and the sociological view that locates typifications within the wider context of society, and emphasizes the ideological function that they serve in reproducing dominant power relations. Referring to the work of Perkins (1979), Barrat (1986: 45) argues that: 'Even though we may not "believe" the stereotype [typification] it remains as part of our consciousness and works as a short-hand technique for conveying a complex idea.' Hooks (1992: 341) has described the 'inner logic' of stereotypes (typifications) as specific forms of representation:

> Stereotypes, however inaccurate, are one form of representation. Like fictions, they are created to serve as substitutions, standing in for what is real. They are there not to tell it like it is but to invite and

encourage pretence. They are a fantasy, a projection onto the Other
that makes them less threatening. Stereotypes abound where there is
distance. They are an invention, a pretence that one knows when the
steps that would make real knowing possible cannot be taken – are
not allowed.

It is argued here that the material and social construction of the 'modern
homosexual' in the 1990s is pregnant with symbolic meanings within the
collective heterosexual imagination, which is linked to the wider socio-
economic, historical, gender and moral order (Matthews 1989).

The students recalled how they have come to see that the absence of gays
and lesbians from the curriculum is not an arbitrary oversight, but a
systematic policy of omission. They felt that gays and lesbians had been
removed insidiously from school view. The students explained how they
have shifted from individual-based explanations of this removal with an
emphasis on sexuality as a problem, to socio-cultural-based explanations of
their sexual subordination, in which schools are seen as central to gay and
lesbian oppression. They have become aware of how dominant systems of
representation and typification, as Barrat suggests, function to maintain
wider power relations.

M.M.:   Why do you think that teachers have these views of gays?
Peter: Because they want to control you and to control how all people
behave. So they label us as bad and themselves as good. It's a bit like the
'cowboys and Indians' stereotypes, turning people against each other.
Rajinder: Gays and lesbians are seen as a big threat to this society. They are
seen by straight people as challenging the way that things are supposed to
happen. That is a man meets a woman, they settle down, get a house if
they can and live happily producing and bringing up the next generation.
Gays and lesbians are seen as a big threat to all of this. Male straights
fantasize that we are having a better time sexually than them and we aren't
even paying the price. We have sex and our freedom, that's the way they
see it. We are the enemy within.
M.M.:   Why is that?
Rajinder: Like I said, firstly because it allows an alternative lifestyle and
suggests that marriage is not the only way of living your life happily.
Secondly, it challenges ideas about what is normal. If I am living happily
with my boyfriend, then that can be seen to be normal for me. And then
straight people may see me as happier than them. So my lifestyle becomes a
threat to unhappy marriages and there's lots of them about. Lesbians are
even more of a threat because for a lot of women they would be better off
living with other women than straight men.
Colin: Also marriage controls women. They have to stay at home while their
husbands go out to work or at least they're supposed to or do both.
Joseph: Sexuality is very difficult to talk about. It's difficult to know what it
is really, when it's present and when it's not. I think that's why it's seen as
dangerous. Men and women have different positions in the world with men
who are supposed to be the rulers. Then we [gays] come along. I suppose
we are seen as a threat to that power. If there are different ways of being

men, then it may mean that there's different ways of being women that are equal. Then there are no set roles to justify why men must rule are there?

Joseph's comments reflect Wood's (1984) account of the elusiveness of sexuality. According to Wood:

> Sexuality has no essence, nor can it be put in a field all of its own. Rather, in our society, it is channelled into many areas, into leisure, consumption and sport. It may be possible to investigate how this channelling contributes to the moral regulation of people if we pay close attention, first to the actual practice of genders.
>
> (Wood 1984: 54)

Sex/gender regimes

As the students moved into the sixth-form and further education colleges, they began to read their secondary schooling in terms of 'learning to be a man'. Now they could see more directly the prescribed boundaries of what constitutes acceptable male and female behaviour in which the teacher–student and student–student relations were embedded. They had become aware of how compulsory heterosexuality pervaded their everyday lives (Rich 1981). The moral order was policed by visible and invisible processes of institutional and self-surveillance that were pervasive throughout their schools and colleges. The sexual and gender imperatives of performing like a man found expression in the official and hidden curriculum – in classrooms, assemblies, counselling, cloakrooms, toilets, playgrounds and leisure activities.

In his study of male youth sub-cultures in an Australian inner-city school, Walker (1988: 5) describes how:

> The specific practices of playing football, drinking, marauding around town, and so on, constituted as it were, almost a quantitative index of manhood: prowess in these culturally exalted forms of masculinity (Carrigan et al, 1985, p. 592) made you more of a man.

Sean's comments provides evidence to support Walker's findings. Sean was an outstanding footballer at secondary school and captain of the first XI team. He came to identify the codes through which male teachers and male students colluded in constructing dominant forms of straight masculinity, which served to devalue, marginalize and threaten femininities and subordinated masculinities. Of specific significance here was the exchange value of the 'straight male body' as a form of high-status physical capital in the competitive school marketplace (Bourdieu 1978; Featherstone *et al.* 1991; Hargreaves 1991).

Sean: I always loved football but there was something about it that I didn't like. I really enjoyed playing the game but it was all the rest of it. You see it wasn't just a game. I came to see that it was about proving yourself as a man. All the boys together, acting tough, bragging about sexual conquests, putting down women and all the macho fooling around in the showers. They had to keep telling each other that they were real men. We had the fit bodies, we had the strength, we had the power. The male teachers and pupils measured everyone against us, though this was usually hidden.

M.M.: What was the main reason you gave it up?

Sean: Schools are incredible on sport. There was more competition there than in the academic stuff. But it just got to me. The teachers were kind of selling our bodies; the school living off them. The sports teachers weren't interested in me, just using my body. And I thought to myself if they only knew, this isn't even a straight body.

M.M.: What do you think would happen?

Sean: They would be completely confused. You see they really fantasize about strength, posture and all that. And gays are supposed to be weak. I don't think it would do much for the school's reputation having a gay sports day, do you?

The students were surprised at the way in which male teachers and male students conflated assumed gay behaviour with femininity in order to traduce the former. They have developed a highly sophisticated understanding of the ambivalent misogyny which is endemic in male straight culture with its internal contradictions. Furthermore, they point to the need to acknowledge that sexuality and gendered identities are not totally separate, as Edwards (1990: 110) argues is usually assumed. There was disagreement concerning the class basis of these sexist and homophobic values and practices. Rajinder pointed to the central role of the state in constructing differential experiences of the sex/gender hierarchical order between and within black and white lesbian and gay groups. He asked me to include the following quotation from Edgar (1981: 218), which he felt represented his political understanding of the interrelationship of different forms of oppression and common strategies of resistance to them:

> Without Black Brotherhood, there would have been no sisterhood: without Black Power and Black Pride there would have been no Gay Power and Gay Pride. The movement against the abuse of powers of the State . . . derived much of its strength and purpose from the exposure of the FBI's surveillance and harassment of the Black Panthers and Black Muslims . . . only the Environmental movement did not have the Black Movement as a central organisational fact or as a defining metaphor and inspiration.

Adrian: It's strange really because heterosexual men are supposed to be attracted to women, so you would think that they would respect them. But the worst thing that they think they can call a gay man is a girl.

Joseph: They see themselves as powerful and superior and then the rest, women and us, are lumped together as inferior but at the same time they are sexually attracted to women!

Gerard: I think that the macho types are mainly from the working class. The middle-class men don't treat women in such a sexist way. I think also that it's easier about coming out and being open about being gay in middle-class areas.

Rajinder: That is not true. When straight men discriminate against women and gays, I don't think it's really about sex at one level. It's mainly about power and the middle classes have the power to control your life. It's the same with me being an Asian gay; I get a lot more problems from whites. If I come out the racism will increase. When I told a teacher I was gay, he came out with all his racist ideas about my parents with their culture not being able to accept it. He meant that he couldn't accept it. Again black lesbians will experience other types of discrimination. Power is used in different ways against people.

M.M.:   Could you expand on that?

Rajinder: I used to think that a lot of discrimination against blacks, gays or women was more at the level of individuals. I mean I always knew about institutional racism and sexism but I have learnt a lot with us talking together about wider structures. My experiences as a black gay are primarily determined by the police and the courts, immigration policy, the control of blacks in the inner-city and the way black and white women are divided up and systematically treated differently by these institutions.

M.M.:   Do you think that many people see this?

Rajinder: No, that's the problem. It's the arguments that we are always having. Like when Gerard says working-class men are more sexist. Yes, I can see what he is saying, but the people who make the policies, make the rules – who are mainly men – are middle-class and they are the real threat because they create the conditions in which the working-class men behave with their tabloids and all the rest of it. It's like we know why black or Irish immigrant men can seem more sexist to the English. Like our marriages, which they always point to, may seem reactionary to them and they may be, but the white liberal does not understand that in a highly racist society marriage can have a different meaning for different social groups. It can be seen to act as a means of solidarity between the community. I understand that, although I still don't agree with it. But if you are really interested in understanding gender and sexual relations, you have to look at the wider power bases don't you? Otherwise you end up divided against each other and not fighting the real enemy. It's like with gays, some of them can't see how badly this society treats women. We have a lot in common.

For the students, the assimilation of non-macho behaviour to feminine behaviour was illustrated in relation to the ubiquity of the term 'poof', which in 'denoting lack of guts, suggests femininity – weakness, softness and inferiority' (Lees 1987: 180). The label has several shifting meanings; sometimes it is used with an explicit sexual connotation, while at other times it is used as a general term of abuse. The notoriety and frequency of use of the label caused much distress to the students throughout their schooling as a major source of derision of their growing awareness of their sexuality.

In the following incident, Adrian describes how official moral codes are covertly transmitted in schools and the resulting differential effects on different students. At his school, a first-year boy was overheard by a member of staff, referring to another male teacher as a 'poof'. The student was reported to the headteacher. The next day at assembly the boy was caned in front of the whole school and given a lecture on respect for teachers without which, they were told, no institution could survive. The headteacher made no reference to what the student had said but claimed that it was the worst thing that he had heard in all his years as a teacher. During the following week, rumours were passed among the students of exaggerated stories with sexual connotations. The unintended effect of the headteacher's response was to highlight the presumed sexual nature of the incident. Adrian asked the first-year student what he had said, and he repeated that he had called one of the teacher's a 'poof'. When Adrian had asked him why he had called him this, the student replied, 'because he had seen the teacher kissing a woman on the bus'.

Adrian: Amazingly, no-one had even asked the kid what he meant. One of the teachers had told us that the staff assumed that he meant homosexual, their definition. But he was going through an "anti-girls phase"! He knew that "poof" meant something bad, so he assumed that kissing girls was what "poofs" did. When things like this happened, it really frightened me. I thought all these teachers are punishing him and he only used the word. What would they do to me because I thought I might be gay? I couldn't sleep for weeks. I couldn't sleep with all the nightmares. I thought they were coming for me and how ashamed my family would be. It was just before my exams that I failed. I had a nervous breakdown. I can still hear the Head saying, "this is the worst thing I've ever heard". There was no-one to talk to, no-one to trust.

For gays and lesbians, as for other oppressed groups in England, including women and the black, Irish and Jewish communities, dominant state discourses play a central role in the maintenance and reproduction of social and sexual hierarchies (Foucault 1979; Walkerdine 1981). Unlike black students of Asian and African Caribbean origin, who use counter-discourses as an effective form of contestation and resistance to institutional incorporation into white cultural identities, young lesbians and gays tend to be more isolated from each other at school, and consequently are unable to develop these particular coping and survival discursive strategies (Mac an Ghaill 1988c; see Giddens 1979).[5]

Being gay: Positive and creative

There is much evidence from the lesbian and gay literature of the physical, psychological and verbal abuse that lesbian and gay people systematically experience in homophobic and heterosexist societies.[6] For example, reporting on a sample of 400 gay teenagers, Trenchard and Warren (1984: 151) state that:

Over half had been verbally abused, a fifth had been beaten up, one in ten had been thrown out of home and many others sent to a doctor or psychiatrist because they were lesbian or gay. One in five had felt under such intolerable pressure that they had attempted suicide.

As has been indicated above, the young men in this study have and continue to experience similar personal and institutional responses. However, it is important for educationalists, in trying to understand young people's social position and how they might respond to it, not to adopt a reductionist approach that sees gays and lesbians as mere victims or problems. Significantly, Trenchard and Warren (1984: 151) add that: 'It is indicative of the strength of these young people that they all survived these crises and are now happy to identify themselves to us as homosexual.' Without wishing to appear patronizing to the young men in this study, I have been surprised at their courage, honesty and emotional strength, living within such a hostile and alienating environment as England at the present time.

These young men provided much evidence to support Peter Aggleton's (1987b: 108) claim that being gay is in many circumstances a positive and creative experience. Here, they indicate their positive self-representations in terms of sexual orientation:

Rajinder: Teachers, especially male teachers, assume your being gay is a problem but there are a lot of plusses. In fact, I think that one of the main reasons that male straights hate us is because they really know that emotionally we are more worked out than them. We can talk about and express our feelings, our emotions in a positive way. They can only express negative feelings like hatred, anger and dominance. Who would like to be like them?

Peter: If you are an outsider in this society, you see things more clearly. You see those who are prejudiced against you but they don't see you. We can't take things for granted. We can stand back, become more observant, more critical. Not all gays do of course, but there is more of a possibility that you will than straights.

Sean: A lot of women like to talk to me and I to them. I am not a threat. They see that I don't treat them as a sex object and we develop real friendships. Gays don't have to keep proving themselves all the time and we don't have the pressures from mates to behave horribly when we don't really want to.

Joseph: I think that as a group gay people can feel very proud.

There is a danger in examining the schooling of young gays that by implicitly adopting a passive concept of subject positioning, the account is over-deterministic (Walkerdine 1990a). As indicated above, the isolation of the students at school from other gays precluded them from adopting collective coping and survival strategies of sub-cultural affirmation and resistance. However, there is evidence from the young men of the development of creative strategies that served to challenge the ascendancy of heterosexism and homophobia.

Colin: I knew this woman. I think that she was a bit lesbian. We used to make up jokes or pass them on. Like what do you call a woman without a brain? A man!

Julian: I went to a teacher and told him that I thought I might be gay. He said, no I mustn't think like that, it was just a phase all boys went through. So I asked him if his own children were going through it, and he went white and mumbled that they're mainly girls. So I asked him, if he or any of the other teachers remembered going through it and he said he hadn't, he went to a mixed school. So I asked him if all the boys in our class were going through it and he was so embarrassed. I felt sorry for him. But I deliberately pushed him because it was important to me not to be lied about how I felt about myself. And I thought I might be helping others if they talked to him.

Matthew: The RE teacher said one day in class that teenage boys go through a homosexual phase just like earlier on they go through an 'anti-girls phase'. All totally sexist of course, no mention about the girls' sexuality. I told him, I didn't think boys did go through phases. I said that if boys go through an 'anti-girls phase', it was a long phase because men were always abusing women all of their lives. I meant straight men, but I didn't want to upset him too much. Then lots of the girls started talking about how horrible men were and why did they act like that. The teacher was mad. It was gays that were supposed to be the problem and I turned it round to show the way it really is. Straight men are dangerous to us all, women and gays.

Summary

Examining student perspectives can provide new insights into the specific dynamics of the interplay of schooling, masculinity and sexuality. The young gay men in this study are especially perceptive in analysing dominant male heterosexual power relations that pervade all young people's coming-of-age in England in the 1990s. They offer evidence that supports feminist analysis that sex/gender regimes are a fundamental organizing principle within schools, which underpins the individual and collective construction of student and teacher identities. The young men also emphasize that in response to these structural conditions, which are further shaped by relations of class, 'race'/ethnicity, age and disability, there are no predetermined outcomes. They describe the rejection of their teachers' presentation of a model of a heterosexist and homophobic society and their own resistance to institutional incorporation into dominant sexual and gender identities. At the same time, they point the way forward to the creation of an emancipatory curriculum for all students and teachers.

Like Gillian Squirrell (1989: 32), in her discussion of issues which surround lesbian and gay teachers, I find it rather inappropriate to try to conclude a chapter on young gays that is so exploratory. I would extend her comment that 'the area [is] a fruitful one for further study', to wider aspects of lesbian and gay experience of schooling, including that of students. Such work, building on feminist scholarship, may offer support to local authorities, such as Haringey and Ealing, who have produced curriculum policy documents that 'help to create an educational atmosphere in which all pupils are able to recognise with confidence, their developing sexuality' (London Borough of Ealing Education Committee 1987). Such policy initiatives have recognized, as Squirrell (1989: 33) suggests, that 'it is clear that there is an urgent need for an awareness of heterosexism and homophobia to be incorporated into initial and in-service training'. Consequently, the development of such understandings may serve to illustrate the range of femininities and masculinities and how these take up the different forms of sexuality which are constructed within state institutions. Here, schools and colleges are of central cultural significance, both in terms of the reproduction and possible transformations of hegemonic sex/gender regimes and the power positions that are contained within them (Connell 1989). The last word lies with Lilley (1985: 8), who claims that: 'Every teacher should be aware that any school where gay [and lesbian] staff and pupils are not made to feel relaxed and wholly open about their sexual orientation, is one that is imposing a daily misery and injustice.'

6

Conclusion: Sociology of schooling, equal opportunities and anti-oppression education

> But it is its nature as a supplement to the centre that the margin is also a place of resistance. The assertion of its existence threatens to deconstruct those forms of knowledge that constitute the subjectivities, discourses and institutions of the dominant hegemonic formations. It is here, where power relations and historical forces have organised meaning in polar opposites that language becomes a site of struggle. Even as difference is pathologised and refused legitimacy, new terms and new identities are produced on the margins. Those early assertions "Black is Beautiful", "Sisterhood is Powerful" and "Gay Pride" break the logic of the otherness of binarism.
>
> (Rutherford 1990: 22)

Central government's systematic demise and exclusion of sociology from the educational map during the last decade has attempted to make invisible the ascendancy of a highly centralized restratified schooling system (Chitty 1989). The institutional pessimism that this has engendered among teachers, students and researchers is pervasive within schools and colleges. We look back nostalgically at the gains, albeit limited, of the 1960s/early 1970s social democratic settlement with its major curriculum focus on equality of opportunity (Centre for Contemporary Cultural Studies 1981). By the 1990s, educational institutions appear to be deterministically shaped by hegemonic forces that have successfully undermined progressive theory and practice. In turn, much critical sociology of education appears defensively to have retreated, preoccupied with its own internal discontents.

A central issue here is the apparent failure of progressive schooling to create a more egalitarian society. Comprehensive reorganization, child-centred pedagogy, anti-racism and anti-sexism are key elements of the modernist project, informed by a belief in collectivism, humanism, rational progression and social justice. In a period that Giddens (1990, 1991) calls 'radicalised modernity', critical theorists are no longer sure what schools are for! Currently, we are a long way from the 'common culture curriculum' suggested by Lawton (1975). Historically, such work has been important in providing radical alternative theoretical and pedagogical frameworks to mainstream conceptions of schooling. We are now more aware of the complex multifaceted nature and historical contextual contingency of the mediation of social oppressions in state institutions, such as schools. Furthermore, such institutions are themselves sites of contradictions, ambiguities and tensions, located within a severe, long-term economic and industrial recession. Weeks (1990: 92) has cogently summarized the current dilemmas involved for progressive theorists:

> Nevertheless there are difficulties for the Left in an all-embracing humanism. As a philosophical position it may be a good starting point, but it really does not tell us how to deal with difference . . . If ever-growing social complexity, cultural diversity and proliferation of identities are indeed a mark of the postmodern world, then all the appeals to our common interest as humans will be as naught unless we can at the same time learn to live with difference. This should be the crux of modern debates about values.

So far, this conclusion has provided a degendered, desexualized and deracialized account. It may be suggested that for many radical sociologists and educationalists, this disciplinary crisis includes a crisis of masculinity, similar to that described by the white heterosexual Old Collectivist males at Parnell School. Further work is required to test such a hypothesis in relation to the academic mode of production. However, what is clear from the above study is that feminist, gay, lesbian and black theories are available, which enable us to understand more adequately what is going on in schools and its relation to wider social contexts. Furthermore, many white male heterosexual social critics continue to marginalize this work by refusing to engage with it.

Against a rather pessimistic political background, a small number of ethnographic studies have recorded student responses to the changing oppressive conditions in schools.[1] This theory-guided empirical work has been significant in exploring the dialectical relationship between class, 'race', gender and sexual mechanisms of control that operate as the fundamental organizing principles of modern schooling systems. Following in this tradition, this book has drawn upon data from a wider research concern with the social and psychic structures of differentiated masculinities and femininities and the power relations contained within them.[2] There is a theoretical shift away from sex-role socialization to deconstructing sex/gender identities – a shift away from simple concepts of power to the complexity of the politics of difference (Parmar 1989; Epstein 1993). Earlier social reproduction models and more specifically resistance theory, have failed to understand this complexity, in tending towards an overly functionalist approach, assuming that teachers and students are unitary subjects occupying predictable power positions. In deconstructing this work, feminist research has shown the romanticism of white male academics' one-dimensional representations of white working-class masculinities. While recording the latter's legitimate resistance to their relative powerlessness in authoritarian school systems, these male academics have underplayed the gendered and sexual relative power of heterosexual male students' social and discursive practices (Skeggs 1993).

Different research areas have their own specific theoretical and political difficulties. I have found the exploration of masculinity and sexuality in schools a very difficult enquiry. Two major interrelated theoretical issues remained with me throughout the study. First, as indicated in the Introduction, was the question of the abstractness of complex theories of sexuality that fail to connect with individuals' lives (see Wood 1984: 81). Presently, this is particularly valid in relation to deconstructionist and psychoanalytic theories. Second, in arguing that male heterosexuality is a highly fragile construct marked by contradictions, ambivalences and contingences, I have found it difficult to locate this within a broader political framework that holds onto the material power relations of domination and subordination. I have identified these power relations in terms of the organizing principles of state schooling; namely, complex interconnecting social divisions around class, gender, sexuality, 'race', ethnicity, disability and age (McCarthy 1990; Morris 1991).

One strategy to counter the abstractness and limits of the politics of deconstructionism and psychoanalysis, is to carry out locally focused studies that hold onto the concrete material conditions of the research participants, in which social and discursive practices are played out. As suggested above, in this study I have found the examination of school microcultures methodologically and theoretically useful in my search for a new way of reading the interplay between schooling, masculinity and sexuality. Like Cohen (1989a: 6), in his study of new vocationalism, I wanted an approach that was sensitive both to 'the first person singular ways' that young people developed in their formation of sex/gender identities and the impact of structural changes.

Methodology: Some reflections

In his ethnographic study of racism in the youth service, Williams (1988: 133) draws on Burton's (1978) work to suggest that participant observation as a sociological method is particularly appropriate to analysing a 'mediated social reality'. Similarly, participant observation was the core methodology of my study in exploring the mediated social reality of the interplay of schooling, sexuality and masculinity. In examining the mediated social reality at Parnell School, I found that participant observation was good for illustrating how the 'fairly subtle aspects of classroom encounters continued to regenerate a sexual hierarchy of worth, in which men emerged as the "naturally" dominant sex' (Stanworth 1981: 23).

Presenting a paper on Willis' (1977) work *Learning to Labour*, Finn (1979) explains that the choice of qualitative methods used in the research was determined by the nature of the interest in the 'cultural'. He claims that:

> The techniques used were particularly suited to record this level and have a sensitivity to subjective meanings and values as well as an ability to represent and interpret symbolic articulations, practices and forms of cultural production. In particular the ethnographic account, without always knowing how, can allow a degree of activity, creativity and human agency within the object of study to come through in the analysis.

I also found that this approach of inferring meanings by understanding the context, through participation in the life of the students and teachers, was very productive. More particularly, participant observation enabled me to explore the specific dynamics of the cultural production of different versions of masculinity.

I have discussed elsewhere that methodology can be of vital importance in the generation of theory (Mac an Ghaill 1991a). Again, I have found that acknowledging the relative autonomy of methodology from interrelated theoretical and substantive issues and the dialectical relationship between these elements, provided me with a major breakthrough in the research. I have undertaken research at Parnell School over a five-year period. My initial research focus was an examination of how students' masculinity influenced their orientation to school, and future occupational and domestic destinies. Participant observation with meaning as its central concern enabled me to develop my theoretical stance. Rajinder and Sean, who were in the sixth form at Parnell School, were aware of my research interest and they suggested that I look at a gay perspective based on their school experiences. I had intended to continue with my original study on the construction of masculinities, but it was postponed for over two years as I explored the gay students' schooling. They highlighted the need for me to make male heterosexuality problematic. In so doing, I developed my research design, examining internal psychic relations as well as external social relations in the making of school masculinities (Epstein, in press).

As I have suggested above, these are specific methodological and ethical issues involved in a study dealing with young people's openness and vulnerability in disclosing to me what were highly personal feelings and memories (Burgess 1989). Throughout the study, they frequently returned to these central issues in their lives. Earlier male ethnographic work on male peer groups has remained silent on the key methodological and ethical question of participants' social relations with them. Some of the male students involved in the study at Parnell School strongly identified with me. At times, they would make comparisons between me and their families. In the following extract, Mark highlights what has emerged as a central issue for these young men, the absence of both a 'safe place' to talk about emotional issues and an emotional language to express their feelings.

> It's funny my dad said to me the other night, how come you're always going round to see that teacher? He's not queer or anything is he? And I thought that's typical of him, because he's so prejudiced. But then thinking about it, I could see why he might feel threatened. I've talked to you in a way that I've never talked to anyone and still don't, can't. At home we never talk like that about how we feel or even show how we care about each other. Not just the boys, mum and my sisters as well. We're not that kind of family. You couldn't do it with your mates. It's really a shame because it really helps you to sort your head out and all the rest of it. But what is funny is that he sees you as a threat to me. I suppose you are a threat in a way but not to me, to them. I feel closer to you than my dad and that's a shame because I know he loves me really.

A critical ethical issue involved the research slipping into forms of therapy. In response, I developed a number of strategies, including discussions with feminist friends involved in similar work and distinguishing between research and counselling sessions, which broke down from time to time as we uneasily muddled our way through the study. I made critical decisions about what could be reported, asking the young people's permission if I intended to publish any of the recorded material, and I tried to ensure that individuals and their families were not identifiable.

A specific strength of qualitative work with its focus on located meanings is that it facilitates the development of substantive areas and research questions in the ongoing development of the research design. This is of particular significance with reference to a male researcher examining female students' schooling experiences. Male ethnographers of young men's schooling have systematically failed to acknowledge the implicit male knowledges, understandings and desires that we share with male research participants' schooling biographies. Although I boarded at a Catholic secondary school, there was much in the male students' accounts at Parnell Comprehensive School with which I had implicit class and gender understanding. Furthermore, this study, with its particular emphases and absences, may be read as a form of male bonding, albeit an ambivalent one, both in terms of the research processes and the selected representations of adult and young masculinities and femininities.

Wolpe (1988: 160) notes in her study of schooling and sexuality that 'the type of information boys would give a female researcher is likely to differ from that given to a male researcher'. I have written elsewhere in work on schooling and racism, that in attempting to go beyond the white male norm, specific methodological and political issues arose concerning a white male researcher in a study with black female research subjects (Mac an Ghaill 1989b). In his study of white girls, Meyenn (1979) found that private areas of their lives were not discussed with him. More importantly, as feminist and black writers argue, in the past researchers have reified the research process with truth claims based on appeals to scientific objectivity and technical expertise, which serve to make invisible the internal complex sets of power relations in operation. (Lawrence 1982; Griffin 1986; Bhavnani 1991; Morris 1991; Holland and Ramazanoglu 1993).

In exploring the ambiguity in students' awareness of school gender divisions, Stanworth (1981: 42) suggests that:

> pupils' experiences of gender differentiation in the classroom, though very real to the pupils themselves, are only partially articulated, in a way that suggests that gender divisions remain, for many of them, a largely unreflected domain. There are many cases where pupils not only report that a teacher reacts differently to the same behaviour when it is manifest by both a girl and a boy, but recognise, furthermore, that the sex of the pupil is the crucial basis of differentiation – yet, despite this, the pupils do not appear to register it as an instance of sexual discrimination.

At earlier stages of my research, most of the working-class young women tended not to be gender-specific in discussions with me about teacher–student interaction. They identified individual teachers who were positive towards them, but gender did not appear to be a consistent salient characteristic. They directed their critique of schooling, informed by an implicit class sensibility, against the social regulatory function of teachers rather than gender differences in pedagogical style. Similarly, black and Irish working-class students emphasized the racial and ethnic structuring in their experience of the school. There were variations in this pattern, but at this stage of the research it was a major barrier to my own focus on the specific dynamics of how female students experienced school masculinities. It also raised important questions about my attempt to operate within a multifaceted theoretical framework, examining the interconnectedness of sex/gender relations with other sets of power relations. An important methodological and political question here was my own status as a white middle-class man. The latter descriptive category is frequently used in a rather clichéd guilt-based way in much of the men's studies literature. In my own study, there did not appear to be any predictable outcomes resulting from my research with white and black female students. Nevertheless, there are complex political questions here if we locate the study within a standpoint epistemology. As Skeggs (1992: 1) explains:

> Feminism operates within a standpoint epistemology: Human activity not only structures but sets limits on understanding. If social activity is structured in fundamentally opposing ways for different groups, one can expect that the vision of each will represent an

inversion of the other, and in systems of domination the vision available to the rulers will be both partial and perverse.

Making visible the power relations operating within the research process and the conditions of the production of situated knowledges helps to keep in focus the limits of a specific enquiry (Harding 1987; Ramazanoglu 1990; Haraway 1991).

Of primary methodological significance, as Whyte (1943: 300) points out, is having the support of key individuals in groups that are studied ethnographically. Nihla, an Asian student, and Niamh, an Irish student, were particularly supportive at the beginning of the research period, in helping me to become familiar with the located meanings embedded in the cultural map that constituted the young women's lives at Parnell School. Contingent biographical variables were unexpectedly significant in my fieldwork. For example, Nihla mediated my access to groups of female students. I had taught her brothers and we had collaborated setting up a local black self-support study group. I also worked with her father on local anti-racist issues. I was known by a number of the Irish students and their families in the local Irish community. However, being Irish was a necessary but not a sufficient condition in order to discuss sensitive issues of sex/gender relations. With Irish parents, I gained acceptance both as a teacher who had supported their children and because of my involvement in anti-Irish racist politics. Irish female students identified strongly with our common ethnic origins and they appeared particularly to enjoy, from within a safe space among insiders, critical discussion of internal sex/ gender relations within the Irish community in England.

I hope that by adopting theoretical frameworks which posit that sexism, homophobia and racism are major material and discursive barriers to the research participants' education at Parnell School, I have become more sensitive to the question of how social location in a stratified society involving complex differential relations informs my perspective and that this, in turn, influences the present study (Bhavnani 1991; Brah 1992; Plummer 1992).

Post-ERA: Post-equal opportunities?

It is important to examine schools at a time of rapid policy change. This serves to uncover how gender and sexual relations are currently being constructed, contested and reconstructed. In recent years, we have witnessed unprecedented, rapid and substantial curriculum policy changes in state schools. This book has explored the impact of these changes on student and teacher masculinities within the context of this wider policy change, which in turn is linked to broader socio-economic and political changes (Johnson R. 1989). One of the key aspects of this study was an examination of the centrality of the curriculum in shaping a range of student masculinities. It has been noted that the New Right cultural restorations have helped create a national curriculum that is hostile to equal opportunities.

The consultative document on the National Curriculum (DES 1988c) sets out its position on equal opportunities in the following terms:

all pupils, *regardless* of sex, ethnic origin and geographical location, have access to broadly the same good and relevant curriculum and programmes of study, which include the key content, skills and processes which they need to learn and which ensure that the content and teaching of the various elements of the national curriculum bring out their *relevance* to and links with pupils' own experiences. [my emphasis]

There have been widespread criticisms raised among academics and teachers concerning the implications of this 'race'- and gender-blind curricular approach. For example, Jones (1989: 96–7) notes critically:

The curriculum, apparently, will be relevant to everyone, even though it will have no regard to where they live, what sex they are, and what their racial background is: it will be the same for all, and yet relevant to all! There is a striking confidence that the learning programme devised by the curriculum planners will be fully congruent with the experience of the students, alongside an equally striking lack of interest in what that experience might be. That students differ in what their society has made of them; that the sexual, class or racial prisms through which they view the world affect their attitudes to learning and their conceptions of relevance are not important matters. Because their lives are seen as empty and cultureless, the national curriculum seems all the more unproblematic.

As Redman (in press) has argued, there are contradictions and gaps in current legislation, although the cultural restorationists (whom he calls the moral traditionalists), have succeeded in establishing the agenda of sexuality teaching within the narrow boundaries of heterosexual familialism. As he points out, liberal stances can be found in the National Curriculum. For example, Curriculum Guidance 5 (Key Stage 3) for Health Education, states that students should: 'Discuss moral values and explore those held by different...groups...[and]...Be aware of the range of sexual attitudes and behaviours in present day society' (National Curriculum Council 1990). Redman also notes that: 'under the Science Order of the national curriculum, teaching about human reproduction and HIV infection has become a legal requirement for eleven to fourteen year olds (Department of Education and Science, 1991)'. I would agree with his assessment of the pedagogical limits of these more liberal approaches, particularly with reference to the failure to 'genuinely seek to integrate the reality of gay and lesbian sexuality into the taken for granted life of the school as just one more aspect of social diversity' (Redman, in press). More recently the situation has altered again. Chitty (1994), in a critical examination of the Sex Education Amendment to the 1993 Education Act, points out that:

In April 1993 the DFE published the draft of a proposed revision of Circular 11/87 in which Section 19 appeared in a truncated version which no longer allowed for the recognition of lesbian and gay sexualities. But the ensuing process of consultation was overtaken by the Government's own shattering amendment to the new Education Bill passing through Parliament. As a result of this amendment (which now forms Section 241 of the 1993 Education Act), the provision of effective sex education is to be seriously impaired by the removal of everything but the biology of reproduction from National Curriculum Science and the granting to parents of the right to withdraw their children from 'compulsory' sex education lessons. Teachers must, it seems, be 'punished' for refusing to provide sex education in the context of moral values and family life.

This is an important arena in which progressive views need to be represented. Hopefully, my study may make a contribution to such debates, in providing information and understandings about a highly sensitive area, in which there are no 'quick fix' solutions. Further studies are needed in an under-researched area that is of critical significance to young people (Davies *et al*. 1990; *Sex Education Forum* 1992).

This study suggests the need to conceptualize a comprehensive and inclusive theoretical framework in which to locate anti-oppressive schooling. The mainstream Left's additive model, with its hierarchy of oppressions, is a theoretical, political and educational cul-de-sac with limited explanatory power, which has contributed indirectly to the maintenance of the New Right moral hegemony. It serves to reinforce, albeit unintendedly, a 'commonsense' binary social logic of an 'us' (gender, sexual, racial, ethnic, able-bodied 'majorities') and a 'them' (women, gay, lesbian, black, Irish, disabled 'minorities')(see Mama 1992: 80; Hevey 1992). State schools are offered disparate policy documents that fail to address the complex and contradictory articulation of different forms of oppression. We have not yet addressed some of the important findings of the MacDonald Report (1989). It pointed to such a complexity, suggesting that white parents and students should not be excluded from taking responsibility for anti-racism. Similarly, in my study it is suggested that gender and sexual majorities need to be included in the development of anti-oppressive educational policies. As Tutchell (1990: 13) has argued, stressing a non-essentialist understanding of gender categories:

> I have long been convinced of the need to develop anti-sexist strategies with boys as well as girls. Despite the undoubted and completely unjustifiable greater power wielded by men in our society (and therefore perceived even by the youngest boys as an indicator for their future roles) no one is born an oppressor and I am reluctant to lay the blame for patriarchal attitudes totally with conspiracy theorists. The reality is far more complicated. Masculinity and femininity are constantly being constructed and reconstructed by all of us.

The MacDonald Report (1989) also made an appeal that in contesting social oppressions in school, we should not adopt a reductive pedagogical approach that is premised on the guilt of social majorities. As my study has shown, there is a real tension here for the gender and/or sexual majority between not feeling guilty, and not taking responsibility both for the cultural investments one has in oppression and the privileges that are ascribed to you and that you take up as part of a dominant group (Jones and Moore 1992).

'Really useful sex/sexuality knowledge': Students as active makers of sex/gender identities

In researching teacher and student cultures in relation to curriculum changes, one of the most consistent themes I have found in secondary schools is the divisive culture of pedagogic relations. The epistemological premise shared by policy makers, school managers and many teachers, informs their failure to acknowledge, as Riseborough (1985) argues, that students are active overt and hidden curriculum makers. He suggests that:

> Thus the lesson does not belong to the teacher, children can and do make it their own. They put so much on the agenda of a lesson, to a point where, they are the curriculum decision-makers. They make a major contribution to the social construction of classroom knowledge. Children actively select, organise and evaluate knowledge in schools.
>
> (Riseborough 1985: 209)

Despite an overly prescriptive National Curriculum and testing regime, Riseborough's claim remains valid. Furthermore, as the young people in this study show, they have diverse values, understandings and feelings as well as local cultural knowledges that they bring with them into the classroom. Young people are active makers of sex/gender identities. A major flaw in much equal opportunities work, exemplified in the 'positive images' approach, has been a failure to conceptualize the complexity of student identity formation. In this process, schools can be seen as crucial cultural sites in which material, ideological and discursive resources serve to affirm hegemonic masculinity, while producing a range of masculine subject positions that young men come to inhabit. Most importantly, the students illustrate above that misogyny, homophobia, heterosexism and racism are not passively inherited in a unitary or total way. Located within local gender and sexual peer group cultures, they actively select from a range of socially oppressive contructs and in this process make their own individual and collective meanings (Gramsci 1971). Male heterosexuality can be seen as a highly fragile and fractured construction, hence the contradictory social and discursive pratices within which the male students are positioned and in turn position others.

Examining student perspectives of schooling can provide teachers, researchers and policy makers with fresh insights into how the curriculum is differentially experienced by different social groups. Furthermore, oppressed groups are in specific material and social locations within schools and colleges from which they can highlight the hidden dynamics that are of central significance to the wider concerns of state schooling. What is clear from the previous chapters is that what is happening at the microcultural level is ahead of our educational theorization of what is going on in schools. This is made particularly clear in relation to the group of gay students' responses to current school arrangements.

As I have reported in an earlier paper (Mac an Ghaill 1992: 230) on Parnell School, institutional authoritarianism prevented the development of formal mechanisms, which would operate to democratize teacher–student relations and provide student representation and emancipation (Freire and Shor 1987). For example, there was no formal acknowledgement of the students' perspective of how to manage curriculum innovation as a legitimate view. Through the framework of existing power relations, teacher responses were ideologically presented and represented as legitimate educational strategies, with students' responses juxtaposed as illegitimate. Much of the dated sociological representations of working-class males has reinforced this dominant perception, with its over-emphasis on the negative elements of their contestation of schooling. In such accounts, there is little acknowledgement of the participants' creative construction of 'really useful knowledge', which combines rigour and relevance, academic success and personal and collective empowerment (Johnson 1979; Cohen 1989a). More specifically here, there is a concern with a search for 'really useful sex/sexuality knowledge'.

In the study of the gay students' schooling experiences, they provided a broad agenda for sex/sexuality education that would be of value to all young people in the development of their sexual and gender identities. They outlined an approach that included a student-centred pedagogy with a focus on the development of adolescent sexuality, an understanding of the power relations that exist between and within social groups, and a discussion-based programme that would include such issues as feelings and emotional growth (Allen 1987). As Fine (1988) points out, a discourse of desire traditionally has been excluded from the curriculum (Lee 1983; Lanskyi 1990).

This finds congruence with Redman's (in press) suggestion for a new agenda for sexuality education. He concludes his paper by noting that:

> Put together these four factors – the need to address sexual diversity, relations of power, the construction of sexuality in schooling processes, and pupil sexual cultures – offer the bases for a fundamental reevaluation of sexuality education. As is surely obvious they do not in themselves provide any easy answers or a blueprint for "how to do it". However, what they do suggest is a new sense of direction; markers on the way to developing alternatives to the current

sub-moral Right hegemony that holds sway over sex education in schools.

(Redman, in press)

Conclusion

Like *Education Limited* (Cultural Studies 1991: 267), in this book I am arguing for:

> a transformed educational and professional practice more appropriate to a socially and culturally divided society. The personal implications of attempting to teach in new ways are related to the wider questions of politics and power . . . a search for alternatives to the political tendencies of the day are based on the practical realities of [a school].

Further theory-guided empirical work may help the search for alternatives to current central government educational policy, which is informed by market-led principles of intensified stratification, differentiation, hierarchy and social closure.

Finally, Aggleton (1990: 99–100) concludes his citical review of Walker's (1988) study of young males suggesting that:

> This is not good enough. Those who are so systematically oppressed on the grounds of "race" and sexuality, and who so willingly give of their time and energy to educational and social researchers, deserve more than to have their status as second class citizens confirmed.

I fully agree. I hope that this book is good enough!

Notes

Introduction Schooling as a masculinizing agency

1. See Beynon (1989).
2. The Centre for Contemporary Cultural Studies (1981: 25) makes the following distinctions between gender and sexuality: 'By "gender" we mean the socially constructed forms of masculinity and femininity. By "sexuality" we mean the bodily capacities of males and females for sexual pleasure and for procreation as these too are shaped by social relations and by culture.' See also Griffin (1993).
3. See also Weeks (1986), Cockburn (1987), Wolpe (1988), Hollway (1989), Watney (1987) and Epstein (1993).
4. One of the main theoretical influences on this study is the work of past and present members of the Department of Cultural Studies, University of Birmingham (formerly the Centre for Contemporary Cultural Studies). I am particularly indebted to the scholarship of Richard Johnson. See Connell *et al.* (1982: 162–6) for a critique of the Department's early ethnographic approach. The collective work of Bob Connell and co-workers has also been a major influence on this study.
5. See Griffin (1986), Roberts (1990), Westwood (1992a) and Holland and Ramazanoglu (1993). See also Plummer (1983), Pearson (1984) and Morgan (1990).
6. See McCarthy (1990: 14–15) who brings together two meanings of contradiction in his study of 'race' and education: first, that associated with a deconstructionist project, focusing on moments of rupture, discontinuity and structural silence in existing school practices; second, a more positive application, in the Hegelian use of the concept, suggesting that discontinuities in minority/majority experiences in schooling can help to shape qualitative change in social relations between blacks and whites. I use the concept in a similar manner throughout the study with reference to sex/gender relations in schools.

7. See Gaine (1987) for a discussion of this dichotomy in relation to schooling and racism.
8. Bhavnani and Coulson (1986) discuss studying racism based on the concept of racially structured capitalist patriarchies.
9. Like Rattansi (1992: 42), I am using the term 'black' to signify British communities of African-Caribbean, African and Asian descent. For a discussion of the changing use of this category, see Donald and Rattansi 1992).

Chapter 1   Teacher ideologies, representations and practices

1. See Barrett (1991) and Eagleton (1991). Sharp and Green (1975) provide a definition of teaching ideology.
2. See Riseborough (1981: 376–7) for a distinction between cliques and cabals. Riseborough's (1981) work offers particularly rich accounts of the changing nature of teachers' working lives (see also Poppleton and Riseborough 1990).
3. See Joyce (1987), de Lyon and Widdowson (1989), Squirrell (1989) and Mac an Ghaill and Dunne (1991) for a history of the relationship between teaching and the organizing principles of schooling – namely, class, 'race'/ethnicity, gender/ sexuality and disability.
4. In Chapter 4, I examine the 'making of young women'.
5. Churchill's speech has been critically discussed in the media with reference to the Asian community. In fact, his comments were more specifically focused upon Muslims.

Chapter 2   Local student cultures of masculinity and sexuality

1. Gillborn's (1990) rich, sophisticated ethnography of an inner-city comprehensive is particularly recommended. He vividly illustrates the complexity of the intersection of 'race', ethnicity, class and masculinity.
2. See Redman (1993).
3. See Aggleton (1987a: 14–15) on choosing groups and purposive sampling.
4. See Giroux (1983) for a critical discussion of resistance in education.
5. This section draws heavily on the work of Phil Cohen and Bob Hollands.
6. Writing of the fragmentation of post-war English working-class communities, Cohen (1972) focused on the interrelated elements of economic, occupational and domestic changes. Twenty years on, there has been much change. Weis (1990) carried out a study in which she focused on youth cultural formation in a period of intense de-industrialization in the US economy. She found that for many working-class males, they were unlikely to be doing the heavy industrial manual jobs that were available to their fathers. Rather, they were more likely to be unemployed or to be engaged in low-paid service sector work.
7. Similar contradictory masculine narratives of survival are to be found in Northern Irish working-class republican popular songs, which in response to long-term structural male unemployment tell stories of 'men doing women's jobs'.
8. See David (1993) on the New Right moral entrepreneurs identified in the 1980s. The Centre for Contemporary Cultural Studies (1981: 27) decribes the 'modern school . . . [as] . . . facing two ways: towards wage labour and the task

of housewife and mother on the one side, and towards the child's family of origin on the other'. More recently, Carlen *et al.* (1992: 48) have discussed state regulation of family, education and work relations.
 9. Gaine's (1987) work is a notable exception.
10. See the MacDonald Report (MacDonald *et al.* 1989) on the killing of a an Asian student by a white peer in a Manchester school.
11. Carlton was a heterosexual African Caribbean student. Rajinder, a gay Asian student, is one of the main research participants in Chapter 5.

Chapter 3   Sexuality: learning to become a heterosexual man at school

1. Aggleton (1990: 99–100), in his citical review of Walker's (1988) study of young males, notes that: '*Louts and Legends* identifies some of the more sexist, racist and heterosexist aspects of modern-day Australian urban culture. It does so in a way which runs the risk of celebrating these divisive and oppressive structures, since it describes them graphically and with relatively few critical comments.' In order to avoid this political error, I have limited the use of misogynist, heterosexist, homophobic and racist comments. A more detailed discussion of male students' misogyny takes place in Chapter 4.
2. See Walkerdine (1984). This is, of course, a reference to the title of her paper: 'Some day my prince will come'.
3. See Parker's (1992) excellent study of masculine representation in school sport.

Chapter 4   Young women's experiences of teacher and student masculinities

1. See, for example, Griffin (1985b, 1993), Riley (1985), Holland (1988), Skeggs (1988), Wolpe (1988) and Mirza (1992).
2. In Chapter 6, I discuss the politics of male researcher and female research participants. Griffin's (1986: 95–111) paper, 'It's different for girls: The use of qualitative methods in the study of young women's lives', provides a discussion of the male norm in academic research.
3. For a discussion of patriarchy, feminine representation and schooling, see Gilbert and Taylor (1991) and Walby (1990).
4. In earlier work, at one end of the continuum one finds McRobbie's (1978) description of the solidarity between girls and the importance of the concept of 'best friend', and at the other is Llewellyn's (1980) account of the isolation of the non-examination girls. See Bryan *et al.* (1985) and Brah and Minhas (1985).

Chapter 5   Schooling, sexuality and male power: Towards an emancipatory curriculum

1. This chapter is an amended version of an article 'Schooling, sexuality and power: Towards an emancipatory curriculum', *Gender and Education*, 3(3), 291–309.
2. See Wolfenden (1957), DES (1988b) and Stop the Clause Education Group (1989). As Gillian Squirrell (1989: 20) informs us: 'From what has been said so far it will be obvious that there has been very little research on which I can draw

. . . The existing literature offers three main foci: curriculum development largely within English, PSE and RE (Patrick, 1982; Slayton and Vogel, 1986); growing up gay and the role of the school (Trenchard and Warren, 1984; Plummer, 1986); and finally some work on gay and lesbian teachers (London Gay Teachers' Group, 1987; Leicester City NUT, 1987).' See also Campbell (1991).

3. Phil Cohen (1987) provides a similar argument concerning anti-racist teaching.
4. See also McIntosh (1968), Oakley (1972), Brake (1976), Tolson (1977), Plummer (1981, 1992), Tsang (1981), Weeks (1981), Watney (1987) and Connell (1992).
5. Giddens (1979) makes a useful distinction between practical and discursive consciousness.
6. See, in particular, Burbage and Walters (1981), where young gays speak for themselves. More recently, I have completed a study with African Caribbean and Asian young gay men (Mac an Ghaill, in press).

Chapter 6   Conclusion

1. See Griffin (1985b), Skeggs (1988), Avis (1990), Gillborn (1990) and Harris *et al.* (1993).
2. See, in particular, Wood (1984), Carrigan *et al.* (1985), Connell (1987) and Segal (1990).

References

Aggleton, P. (1987a) *Rebels Without a Cause? Middle Class Youth and the Transition from School to Work*. Lewes, Falmer Press.

Aggleton, P. (1987b) *Deviance*. London, Tavistock.

Aggleton, P. (1990) Review of 'Louts and Legends', *British Journal of Sociology of Education*, 11(1), 97–100.

Aggleton, P., Homans, H. and Warwick, I. (1989) Health education, sexuality and aids. In S. Walker and L. Walker (eds) *Politics and the Processes of Schooling*. Milton Keynes, Open University Press.

Allen, M. (1987) *Education in Sex and Personal Relations*. London, Policy Studies Institute.

Anderson, B. (1986) *Imagined Communities*. London, Verso.

Anyon, J. (1983) Intersections of gender and class: Accommodation and resistance by working-class and affluent females to contradictory sex-role ideologies. In S. Walker and L. Barton (eds) *Gender, Class and Education*. Lewes, Falmer Press.

Arnot, M. (1984) How shall we educate our sons? In R. Deem (ed.) *Co-education Reconsidered*. Milton Keynes, Open University Press.

Arnot, M. (1991) Equality and democracy: A decade of struggle over education, *British Journal of Sociology of Education*, 12(4), 447–66.

Arnot, M. (1992) Feminism, education and the New Right. In M. Arnot and L. Barton (eds) *Voicing Concerns: Sociological Perspectives on Contemporary Education Reforms*. Oxford, Triangle Books.

Arnot, M. and Weiner, G. (eds) (1987) *Gender and the Politics of Schooling*. London, Hutchinson/Open University.

Askew, S. and Ross, C. (1988) *Boys Don't Cry: Boys and Sexism in Education*. Milton Keynes, Open University Press.

Avis, J. (1990) Student responses to the curriculum: Towards an alternative practice. In D. Gleeson (ed.) *Training and Its Alternatives*. Milton Keynes, Open University Press.

Avis, J. (1991) The strange fate of progressive education. In Cultural Studies Birmingham, *Education Limited: Schooling, Training and the New Right Since 1979*. London, Unwin.

Ball, S. (1990) *Politics & Policy Making in Education: Explorations in Policy Sociology*. London, Routledge.

Barker, M. (1981) *The New Racism*. London, Junction Books.

Barrat, D. (1986) *Media Sociology*. London, Tavistock.

Barrett, M. (1980) *Women's Oppression Today*. London, Verso.

Barrett, M. (1991) *The Politics of Truth: From Marx to Foucault*. London, Polity Press.

Bates, I. and Riseborough, G. (eds) (1993) *Youth and Inequality*. Milton Keynes, Open University Press.

Bates, I., Baxter, G., Woods, A., Robeson, M. and Sullivan, C. (1989) '*I Really Think You've Got an Attitude Problem': Women Teachers Writing and Talking About Their Experience – Education*. Sheffield, USDE Papers in Education, Division of Education, Sheffield University.

Becker, H.S. (1952) Social class variations in the teacher–pupil relationship, *Journal of Educational Psychology*, April, 137–50.

Beechey, V. (1985) Familial ideology. In V. Beechey and J. Donald (eds) *Subjectivity and Social Relations*. Milton Keynes, Open University Press.

Bernstein, B. (1975) *Class, Codes and Control: Towards a Theory of Educational Transmission*. London, Routledge and Kegan Paul.

Bernstein, B. (1982) *Codes, Modalities and the Process of Cultural and Economic Reproduction in Education*. London, Routledge and Kegan Paul.

Bernstein, B. (1990) Structuring of Pedagogic Discourse, *Class, Codes and Control* Vol. 4. London, Routledge.

Beynon, J. (1989) A school for men: An ethnographic case study of routine violence in schooling. In S. Walker and L. Barton (eds) *Politics and the Processes of Schooling*. Milton Keynes, Open University Press.

Bhavnani, K.K. (1991) *Talking Politics: A Psychological Framing for Views from Youth in Britain*. Cambridge, Cambridge University Press.

Bhavnani, K.K. and Coulson, M. (1986) Transforming socialist feminism: the challenge of racism. *Feminist Review*, 23, 81–92.

Billig, M. (1978) *Fascists: A Social Psychological View of the National Front*. London, Harcourt Brace Jovanovich.

Bourdieu, P. (1978) Sport and social class, *Social Science Information*, 17, 819–40.

Bourdieu, P. (1986) *Distinction: A Social Critique of Judgement and Taste*. London, Routledge and Kegan Paul.

Brah, A. (1992) Difference, diversity and differentiation. In J. Donald and A. Rattansi (eds) '*Race', Culture and Difference*. Milton Keynes, Open University Press/Sage.

Brah, A. and Minhas, R. (1985) Structural racism or cultural differences: Schooling for Asian girls. In G. Weiner (ed.) *Just a Bunch of Girls*. Milton Keynes, Open University Press.

Brake, M. (1976) I may be queer but at least I'm a man: Male hegemony and ascribed achieved gender. In D. Barker and S. Allen (eds) *Dependence and Exploitation in Work and Marriage*. London, Longman.

Brindle, D. (1993) One in 6 live on safety net benefit, *Guardian*, 17 April, p. 8.

Brittan, A. and Maynard, M. (1984) *Sexism, Racism and Oppression*. London, Basil Blackwell.

Brown, C. (1992) Same difference: The persistence of racial disadvantage in the British employment market. In P. Braham, A. Rattansi and R.S. Kellington (eds) *Racism and Antiracism: Inequalities, Opportunities and Policies*. London, Sage/Open University.

Brown, P. (1989) Schooling for inequality? Ordinary kids in school and the labour market. In B. Cosin, M. Flude and M. Hales (eds) *School, Work and Equality*. London, Hodder and Stoughton.

Bryan, B., Dadzie, S. and Scafe, S. (1985) *The Heart of the Race: Black Women's Lives in Britain*. London, Virago.

Burbage, M. and Walters, J. (eds) (1981) *Breaking the Silence: Gay Teenagers Speak for Themselves*. London, Joint Council for Gay Teenagers.

Burgess, R. (1989) Grey areas: Ethical dilemmas in educational ethnography. In R. Burgess (ed.) *The Ethics of Educational Research*. Lewes, Falmer Press.

Burton, F. (1978) *The Politics of Legitimacy*. London, Routledge and Kegan Paul.

Burton, L. and Weiner, G. (1993) From rhetoric to reality: Strategies for developing a social justice approach to educational decision-making. In I. Singh-Blatchford (ed.) *'Race', Gender and the Education of Teachers*. Buckingham, Open University Press.

Butler, J. (1990) *Gender Trouble, Feminism and the Subversion of Identity*. London, Routledge.

Campbell, D. (1991) Whatever became of Goopy?, *Guardian*, 16 March, pp. 14–15.

Canaan, J. E. (1991) Is 'doing nothing nothing' just boys' play? Integrating feminist and cultural studies perspectives on working–class young men's masculinity. In S. Fran Klin, C. Lury and J. Stacey (eds) *Off-Centre: Feminism and Cultural Studies*. London, Harper Collins.

Canaan, J.E. and Griffin, C. (1990) The new men's studies: Part of the problem or part of the solution? In J. Hearn and D. Morgan (eds) *Men, Masculinities and Social Theory*. London, Hyman Unwin.

Caplan, P. (1987) *Cultural Construction of Sexuality*. London, Tavistock.

Carby, H.V.(1980) *Multicultural Fictions*. Occasional Stencilled Paper. Race Series: SP No. 58. Birmingham, Centre for Contemporary Cultural Studies, University of Birmingham.

Carlen, P., Gleeson, D. and Wardhaugh, J. (1992) *Truancy: The Politics of Compulsory Schooling*. Milton Keynes, Open University Press.

Carr, W. (1989) Introduction. In W. Carr. (ed.) *Quality in Teaching: Arguments for a Reflective Profession*. Lewes, Falmer Press.

Carrigan, T., Connell, R.W. and Lee, J. (1985) Hard and heavy phenomena: The sociology of masculinity, *Theory and Society*, 14, 551–604.

Carrigan, T., Connell, B. and Lee. J. (1987) The 'sex role' framework and the sociology of masculinity. In G. Weiner and M. Arnot (eds) *Gender Under Scrutiny: New Enquiries in Education*. London, Hutchinson.

Centre for Contemporary Cultural Studies (1981) *Unpopular Education: Schooling and Social Democracy since 1944*. London, Hutchinson/CCCS, University of Birmingham.

Chigwada, R. (1987) Not victims – not superwoman, *Spare Rib*, 183, 14–18.

Chitty, C. (1987) *Redefining the Comprehensive Experience*. London, Institute of Education.

Chitty, C. (1989) *Towards a New Education System: The Victory of the New Right?* Lewes, Falmer Press.

Chitty, C. (1994) Sex, lies and indoctrination, *Forum*, 36(1), 15–18.

Chodorow, N. (1978) *The Reproduction of Mothering: Psychoanalysis and the Sociology of Gender*. Berkeley, CA, University of California Press.

Clarke, J., Hall, S., Jefferson, T. and Roberts, B. (1975) Subcultures, culture and subcultures. In S. Hall and T. Jefferson (ed.) *Resistance through Rituals: Youth Subcultures in Post-war Britain*. London, Hutchinson.

Cockburn, C.K. (1983) *Brothers: Male Dominance and Technological Change*. London, Pluto Press.

Cockburn, C. (1985) *The Machinery of Dominance*. London, Pluto Press.

Cockburn, C.K. (1987) *Two-track Training: Sex Inequalities and the YTS*. London, Macmillan.

Cohen, P. (1972) Subcultural conflict and working class community, *Working Papers in Cultural Studies*, 2.

Cohen, P. (1983) Losing the generation game, *New Socialist*, 14, 5.

Cohen, P. (1986a) *Rethinking the Youth Question*. Working Paper No. 3. Post-16 Education Centre, January, London, Institute of Education.

Cohen, P. (1986b) *Anti-racist Cultural Studies*. Curriculum Development Project in Schools and Community Education, June.

Cohen, P. (1987) *Racism and Popular Culture: A Cultural Studies Approach*. Working Papers No. 9. Centre for Multicultural Education, Institute of Education.

Cohen, P. (1988) The perversions of inheritance: Studies in the making of multi-racist Britain. In P. Cohen and H. Bains (eds) *Multi-racist Britain*. London, Macmillan.

Cohen, P. (1989a) *Really Useful Knowledge: Photography and Cultural Studies in the Transition from School*. London, Trentham.

Cohen, P. (1989b) *The Cultural Geography of Adolescent Racism*. London, University of London.

Connell, R.W. (1982) *Making the Difference: School, Families and Social Division*. Sydney, George Allen and Unwin.

Connell, R.W. (1985) *Teachers' Work*. London, Allen and Unwin.

Connell, R.W. (1987) *Gender and Power*. Cambridge, Polity Press.

Connell, R.W. (1989) Cool guys, swots and wimps: The inter-play of masculinity and education, *Oxford Review of Education*, 15(3), 291–303.

Connell, R.W. (1992) A very straight gay: Masculinity, homosexual experience, and the dynamics of gender, *American Sociological Review*, 57(6), 735–51.

Connell, R.W., Ashenden, D.J., Kessler, S. and Dowsett, G.W. (1982) *Making the Difference: Schools, Families and Social Division*. London, Allen and Unwin.

Conner, S. (1993) Gay gene located by researchers, *The Independent*, 16 July, p. 1.

Conner, T. (1985) *Irish Youth in London Research Report*. London, Action Group for Irish Youth.

Corrigan, P. (1979) *Schooling the Smash Street Kids*. London, Macmillan.

Corrigan, P. and Frith, S. (1976) The politics of youth culture. In S. Hall and T. Jefferson (eds) *Resistance Through Rituals*. London, Hutchinson.

Cowie, C. and Lees, S. (1981) Slags or drags, *Feminist Review*, 9, 17–31.

Cultural Studies (ed.) (1991) *Education Limited: Schooling, Training and the New Right Since 1979*. London, Unwin Hyman/University of Birmingham.

Curtis, L. (1985) *Nothing but the Same Old Story: The Roots of Anti-Irish Racism*. London, Information on Ireland.

Daily Mirror (1992) One million kids jobless, 11 December, p. 19.

David, M. (1993) *Parents, Gender and Education Reform*. London, Polity Press.

Davidson, H. (1985) Unfriendly myths about women teachers. In J. Whyte *et al.* (eds) *Girl Friendly Schooling*. London, Routledge and Kegan Paul.

Davies, A.M., Holland, J. and Minhas, R. (1990) *Equal Opportunities in The New Era*. Hillcole Group Paper No. 2. London, Tufnell Press.

Davies, L. (1975) The contribution of the secondary school to the sex typing of girls. Unpublished MEd dissertation, University of Birmingham.

Davies, L. (1984) *Pupil Power: Deviance and Gender in Education*. Lewes, Falmer Press.

Davies, L. (1992) School power cultures under economic constraint, *Educational Review*, 43(2), 127–36.

Dean, M. (1993) Core problems on the periphery, *Guardian*, 9 January, p. 22.

Deem, R. (ed.) (1984) *Co-education Reconsidered*. Milton Keynes, Open University Press.

De Lyon, H. and Widdowson, F. (1989) *Women Teachers: Issues and Experiences*. Milton Keynes, Open University Press.

Department of Education and Science (1985) *Better Schools*. Cmnd 9469. London, HMSO.

Department of Education and Science (1988a) *Sex Education at School*. Circular 11/87. London, HMSO.

Department of Education and Science (1988b) *Local Government Act 1988: Section 28*. Circular 88/90. London, HMSO.

Department of Education and Science (1988c) *Education Reform Act*. London, HMSO.

Department of Education and Science (1989) *National Curriculum: From Policy to Practice*. London, HMSO.

Diamond, A. (1991) Gender and education: Public policy and pedagogic practice, *British Journal of Sociology of Education*, 12(2), 141–61.

Dollimore, J. (1991) *Sexual Dissidence: Augustine to Wilde, Freud to Foucault*. Oxford, Clarendon Press.

Donald, J. and Rattansi, A. (eds) (1992) *'Race', Culture and Difference*. London, Sage/The Open University.

Eagleton, T. (1991) *Ideology: An Introduction*. London, Verso.

Edgar, D. (1981) Reagan's hidden agenda, *Race and Class*, 22(3), 207–223.

Edwards, T. (1990) Beyond sex and gender: Masculinity, homosexuality and social theory. In J. Hearn and D. Morgan (eds) *Men: Masculinities and Social Theory*. London, Hyman and Unwin.

Egerton, J. (1986) *Danger: Heterosexism at Work*. London, Greater London Council.

Epstein, D. (1993) *Changing Classroom Cultures: Anti-racism, Politics and Schools*. Stoke-on-Trent, Trentham Books.

Epstein, D. (in press) *Challenging Gay and Lesbian Inequalities in Education*. Buckingham, Open University Press.

Evans, J. (1992) A short paper about people, power and educational reform. Authority and representation in ethnographic research. Subjectivity, ideology and educational reform: The case of physical education. In A.C. Sparkes (ed.) *Research in Physical Education and Sport*. London, Falmer Press.

Evening Mail (1993) Ethnic jobs famine shock, 9 March, p. 7.

Fanon, F. (1967) *Black Skins, White Masks*. London, Paladin.

Featherstone, M., Hepworth, M. and Turner, B. S. (1991) *The Body: Social Process and Cultural Theory*. London, Sage.

Ferguson, R. (1988) *Looking at Teaching*. Unit CI, Block C, Working in Classrooms. Milton Keynes, Open University.

Fine, M. (1988) Sexuality, schooling and adolescent females: The missing discourse, *Harvard Educational Review*, 5(1), 29–53.

Finn, D. (1987) *Training Without Jobs*. London, Macmillan.

Finn, D. (1979) Learning to labour: How working-class kids get working-class jobs. Unpublished paper presented to the fourth Dutch conference in sociology of education, 11/12 June, Utrecht.

Finn, D., Grant, M. and Johnson, R. (1977) *Social Democracy, Education and the Crisis*. Working Papers in Cultural Studies No. 10: Ideology. London, Hutchinson/Centre for Contemporary Cultural Studies, University of Birmingham.

Foucault, M. (1979) *The History of Sexuality,* Vol. 1. Harmondsworth, Penguin.

Foucault, M. (1982) *Discipline and Punish*. London, Peregrine Books.

Franklin, S., Lury, C. and Stacey, J. (1991) *Off-centre: Feminism and Cultural Studies*. London, Harper Collins/Cultural Studies, University of Birmingham.

Fraser, N. (1989) *Unruly Practices: Power, Discourse and Gender in Contemporary Social Theory*. Cambridge, Polity Press.

Freire, P. and Shor, I. (1987) *A Pedagogy for Liberation*, London, Macmillan.

Freud, S. (1975) *Three Essays on the Theory of Sexuality*. Harmondsworth, Pelican Freud Library.

Freud, S. (1933) *Standard Edition of the Complete Psychological Works of Sigmund Freud*, Vol. XII. London, Hogarth Press/Institute of Psychoanalysis.

Frith, S. (1992) The cultural study of popular music. In L. Grossberg, G. Nelson and P. Treichler (eds) *Cultural Studies*. London, Routledge.

Fullan, M. (1982) *The Meaning of Educational Change*. Ontario, OISE.

Fuller, M. (1980) Black girls in a London comprehensive school. In R. Deem (ed.) *School for Women's Work*. London, Routledge and Kegan Paul.

Furlong, V.J. (1991) Disaffected pupils: The sociological perspective, *British Journal of Sociology of Education*, 12(3), 293–307.

Gaine, C. (1987) *No Problem Here: A Practical Approach to Education and 'Race' in White Schools*. London, Hutchinson.

Gamble, A. (1988) *The Free Economy and the Strong State: The Politics of Thatcherism*. London, Macmillan.

Giddens, A. (1979) *Central Problems in Social Theory*. London, Macmillan.

Giddens, A. (1990) *The Consequences of Modernity*. Cambridge, Polity Press.

Giddens, A. (1991) *Modernity and Self-identity*. Cambridge, Polity Press.

Gilbert, P. and Taylor, S. (1991) *Fashioning the Feminine: Girls, Popular Culture and Schooling*. Sydney, George Allen and Unwin.

Gillborn, D. (1989) Talking heads: Reflections on secondary headship at a time of rapid educational change, *School Organisation*, 9(1), 65–84.

Gillborn, D. (1990) *'Race', Ethnicity and Education: Teaching and Learning in Multi-ethnic Schools*. London, Unwin Hyman.

Gillborn, D. (1993) Racial violence and harassment. In D. Tattam (ed.) *Understanding and Managing Bullying*. London, Heinemann.

Gillespie, N., Lovett, T. and Garner, W. (1992) *Youth Work and Working Class Youth Cultural: Rules and Resistance in West Belfast*. Milton Keynes, Open University Press.

Gilroy, P. (1987) *There Ain't No Black in the Union Jack*. London, Hutchinson.

Giroux, H.A. (1983) *Theory and Resistance in Education: A Pedagogy for the Opposition*. London, Heinemann.

Gleeson, D. (ed.) (1983) *Youth Training and the Search for Work*. London, Routledge and Kegan Paul.

Gleeson, D. (1984) Someone else's children: The new vocationalism in FE and training. In L. Barton and S. Walker (eds) *Social Crisis and Educational Research*. London, Croom Helm.

Gramsci, A. (1971) *Selections from the Prison Notebooks*. London, Lawrence and Wishart.

Gribben, P. (1993) A community haemorrhage: Number of Irish people working in Britain dropped by nearly 100,000, *Irish Post*. 26 June, p. 1.

Griffin, C. (1982) *Cultures of Femininity: Romance Revisited*. Stencilled Paper. Birmingham, Centre for Contemporary Cultural Studies, University of Birmingham.

Griffin, C. (1985a) Qualitative methods and cultural analysis: Young women and the transition from school to unemployment. In R. Burgess (ed.) *Field Methods in the Study of Education*. Lewes, Falmer Press.

Griffin, C. (1985b) *Typical Girls? Young Women From School to the Job Market*. London, Routledge and Kegan Paul.

Griffin, C. (1986) It's different for girls: The use of qualitative methods in the study of young women's lives. In H. Beloff (ed.) *Getting into Life*. London, Methuen.

Griffin, C. (1988) Youth research: Young women and the 'gang of lads' model. In J. Hazekamp, W. Mees and Y. te Peol (eds) *European Contributions to Youth Research*. Amsterdam, Free University Press.

Griffin, C. (1993) *Representations of Youth: The Study of Youth and Adolescence in Britain and America*. Cambridge, Polity Press.

Hall, L. (1991) *Hidden Anxieties: Male Sexuality, 1950–1990*. London, Polity Press.

Hall, S. (1983) The great moving right show. In S. Hall and M. Jacques (eds) *The Politics of Thatcherism*. London, Lawrence and Wishart.

Hall, S. (1988) The toad in the garden: Thatcherism among the theorists. In C. Nelson and L. Grosberg (eds) *Marxism and the Interpretation of Culture*. London, Macmillan.

Hall, S. (1990) Cultural identity and the diaspora. In J. Rutherford (ed.) *Identity: Community, Culture, Difference*. London, Lawrence and Wishart.

Hall, S. (1992) New ethnicities. In J. Donald and A. Rattansi (eds) *'Race', Culture and Difference*. London, Sage/Open University.

Halston, J. (1989) The sexual harassment of young women. In L. Holly (ed.) *Girls and Sexuality: Teaching and Learning*. Milton Keynes, Open University Press.

Hamilton, P. (1986) Forward. In J. Weeks, *Sexuality*. London, Tavistock.

Haraway, D.J. (1991). *Simians, Cyborgs and Women: The Reinvention of Nature*. London, Free Association Books.

Harding, S. (ed.) (1987) *Feminism and Methodology*. Milton Keynes, Open University Press.

Hargreaves, J. (1991) *Sport, Power and Culture: A Social and Historical Analysis of Popular Sports in Britain*. Cambridge, Polity Press.

Harris, S. (1990) *Lesbian and Gay Issues in the English Classroom: The Importance of Being Honest*. Milton Keynes, Open University Press.

Harris (1992) *From Class Struggle to the Politics of Pleasure: The Effects of Gramscianism on Cultural Studies*. London, Routledge.

Harris, S., Nixon, J. and Rudduck, J. (1993) School work, homework and gender, *Gender and Education*, 5(1), 3–15.

Harrison, K. (1993) Don't hold your breadth, *Sunday Mercury*, 2 May, p. 10.

Haywood, C. P. (1993) Using sexuality: an exploration into the fixing of sexuality to make male identities in a mixed sex sixth form. Unpublished MA dissertation, University of Warwick.

Hazelkorn, E. (1990) *Irish Immigrants Today: A Socio-economic Profile of Contemporary Irish Emigrants and Immigrants in the U.K.* Irish Studies Centre Occasional Paper Series No.1, London, Polytechnic of North London Press.

Hearn, J. (1988) *The Critique of Men: Current Lessons for the Theory and Practice of Men*. Hallsworth Research Fellowship Working Papers No. 1, University of Manchester.

Hearn, J. and Morgan, D. (eds) (1990) *Men: Masculinities and Social Theory*. London, Hyman and Unwin.

Hearn, J. and Parkin, W. (1987) *Sex at Work: The Power and Paradox of Organisation Sexuality*. London, Wheatsheaf Books.

Henriques, J., Hollway, W., Urwin, C., Venn, C. and Walkerdine, V. (1984) *Changing the Subject: Psychology, Social Regulation and Subjectivity*. London, Methuen.

Her Majesty's Inspectorate (1985) *Education Observed 3: Good Teachers*. London, HMSO.

Her Majesty's Inspectorate (1989) *Standards in Education, 1987–88*. London, HMSO.

Hevey, D. (1992) *The Creatures Time Forgot: Photography and Disability Imagery*. London, Routledge.

Heward, C. (1988) *Making a Man of Him*. London, Routledge.

Heward, C. (1991) Public school masculinities: an essay in gender and power. In G. Walford (ed.) *Private Schooling: Tradition, Change and Diversity*. London, Paul Chapman Publishing.

Hickman, M. J. (ed.) (1986) *The History of the Irish in Britain: A Bibliography*. London, Irish in Britain History Centre.

Hill, L. and Collins, P. (1990) *Black Feminist Thought, Knowledge, Consciousness and the Politics of Empowerment*. London, Unwin Hyman.

Hillgate Group (1986) *The Reform of British Education: From Principles to Practice*. London, The Hillgate Group.

Holland, J. (1993) *Sexuality and Ethnicity: Sexual Knowledge and Practice*. Women Risk Aids Project Paper No. 8, London, Tufnell Press.

Holland, J. and Ramazanoglu, C. (1993) Accounting for sexuality, living sexual politics: Can feminist research be valid? Paper presented to the *British Sociological Association Conference*, April.

Holland, J., Ramazanoglu, C. and Scott, S. (1990) From panic stations to power relations: Sociological perspectives and problems, *Sociology*, 24, 499–518.

Holland, J., Ramazanoglu, C. and Sharpe, S. (1993) *Wimp or Gladiator: Contradictions in Acquiring Masculine Sexuality*. London, Tufnell Press.

Hollands, R. G. (1990) *The Long Transition: Class, Culture and Youth Training*. London, Macmillan.

Hollway, W. (1984a) Gender difference and the production of subjectivity. In J.

Henriques, W. Hollway, C. Urwin, C. Venn and V. Walkerdine, *Changing the Subject: Psychology, Social Relations and Subjectivity*. London, Methuen.

Hollway, W. (1984b) Women's power in heterosexual sex, *Women's Studies International Forum*, 7(1), 63–8.

Hollway, W. (1989) *Subjectivity and Method in Psychology: Gender, Meaning and Science*. London, Sage.

Holly, L. (1989a) Introduction: The sexual agenda of schools. In L. Holly (ed.) *Girls and Sexuality: Teaching and Learning*. Milton Keynes, Open University Press.

Holly, L. (ed.) (1989b) *Girls and Sexuality: Teaching and Learning*. Milton Keynes, Open University Press.

Hooks, B. (1991) *Yearning: Race, Gender and Cultural Politics*. London, Turnaround.

Hooks, B. (1992) Representing blackness in white imagination. In L. Grossberg, G. Nelson and P. Treichler (eds) *Cultural Studies*. London, Routledge.

Hornby, N. (1992) Agony, ecstasy and the nil–nil draw, *Weekend Guardian*, 5–6 September, pp. 4–7.

Hudson, B. (1984) Femininity and adolescence. In A. McRobbie and M. Nava (eds) *Gender and Generation*. London, Macmillan.

Hugill, B. (1991) Fury greets the Tory flagship's plan to mark teachers, *Observer*, 9 June, p. 9.

Hutton, W. (1993) A country of casuals, *Guardian*, 30 March, p. 20.

Hutton, W. (1991) Pendulum is ready to swing back, *Guardian*, 30 December, p. 11.

Inglis, F. (1989) Managerialism and morality. In W. Carr (ed.) *Quality in Teaching: Arguments for a Reflective Profession*. Lewes, Falmer Press.

Jackson, P.W. (1968) *Life in Classrooms*. New York, Holt, Rinehart and Winson.

Jenkins, R. (1983) *Lads, Citizens and Ordinary Kids: Working-class Youth Life Styles in Belfast*. London, Routledge and Kegan Paul.

Johnson, A. (1989) Lesbians and gays in the schools: Teachers, students and courses of study. In *Off Our Backs*. New York, Women's World.

Johnson, R. (1979) Really useful knowledge: Radical education and working-class culture, 1790–1848. In J. Clarke, C. Critcher and R. Johnson, *Working Class Culture: Studies in History and Theory*. London, Hutchinson.

Johnson, R. (1989) Thatcherism and English education: Breaking the mould, or confirming the pattern, *History of Education*, 18(2), 91–121.

Johnson, R. (1991a) My New Right education. In Cultural Studies (ed.) *Education Limited: Schooling, Training and the New Right Since 1979*. London, Unwin Hyman/University of Birmingham.

Johnson, R. (1991b) Ten theses on a Monday morning. In Cultural Studies (ed.) *Education Limited: Schooling, Training and the New Right Since 1979*. London, Unwin Hyman/University of Birmingham.

Johnson, R. (1992) Radical education and the New Right. In A. Rattansi and D. Reeder (eds) *Rethinking Radical Education: Essays in Honour of Brian Simon*. London, Lawrence and Wishart.

Jones, C. (1985) Sexual tyranny in mixed-set schools: An in-depth study of male violence. In G. Weiner (ed.) *Just a Bunch of Girls*. Milton Keynes, Open University Press.

Jones, C. and Mahony, P. (eds) (1989) *Learning Our Lines: Sexuality and Social Control in Education*. London, Women's Press.

Jones, K. (1989) *Right Turn: The Conservative Revolution in Education*. London, Hutchinson.

Jones, L. and Moore, R. (1992) Equal opportunities: The curriculum and the subject, *Cambridge Journal of Education*, 1(22), 243–53.

Jones, S. (1988) *Black Culture, White Youth: The Reggae Tradition from JA to UK*. London, Macmillan.

Joyce, M. (1987) Being a feminist teacher. In M. Lawn and G. Grace (eds) *Teachers: The Culture and Politics of Work*. Lewes, Falmer Press.

Jung, C.G. (1936) *Modern Man in Search of a Soul*. New York, Harcourt.

Keddie, N. (1971) Classroom knowledge. In M.F.D. Young (ed.) *Knowledge and Control*. London, Collier/Macmillan.

Kelly, A. (1985) The construction of masculine science, *British Journal of Sociology of Education*, 6(2), 133–54.

Kelly, L. (1992) Not in front of the children: Responding to right wing agendas on sexuality and education. In M. Arnot and L. Barton (eds) *Voicing Concerns: Sociological Perspectives on Contemporary Education Reforms*. London, Triangle Books.

Kessler, S., Ashenden, D.J., Connell, R.W. and Dowsett, G.W. (1985) Gender relations in secondary schooling, *Sociology of Education*, 58, 34–48.

Kitzinger, C. (1990) *The Social Construction of Lesbianism*. London, Sage.

Lacan, J. (1977) *Ecrits: A Selection*. London, Tavistock.

Lacey, C. (1970) *Hightown Grammar*. Manchester, Manchester University Press.

Lanskyi, H. (1990) Beyond plumbing and prevention: Feminist approaches to sex education, *Gender and Education*, 2, 217–30.

Lather, P. (1986) Research as praxis, *Harvard Educational Review*, 56(3), 257–77.

Lawn, M. and Grace, G. (1987) *Teachers: The Cultural and Politics of Work*. Lewes, Falmer Press.

Lawrence, E. (1982) In the abundance of water the fool is thirsty: sociology and black 'pathology'. In Centre for Contemporary Cultural Studies (Race and Politics Group), *Resistance through Rituals: Youth Subcultures in Post-war Britain*. London, Hutchinson/CCCS University of Birmingham.

Lawton, D. (1975) *Class, Culture and the Curriculum*. London, Routledge and Kegan Paul.

Lee, C. (1983) *The Ostrich Position*. London, Readers and Writers.

Lee, C. (1993) *Talking Tough: The Fight for Masculinity*. London, Arrow.

Lees, S. (1986) *Losing Out: Sexuality and Adolescent Girls*. London, Hutchinson.

Lees, S. (1987) The structure of sexual relations in school. In M. Arnot and G. Weiner (eds) *Gender and the Politics of Schooling*. Milton Keynes, Open University Press.

Lees, S. (1993) *Sugar and Spice: Sexuality and Adolescence*. Harmondsworth, Penguin.

Leicester City National Union of Teachers Association (1987) *Outlaws in the Classroom*. Leicester, Leicester NUT Association.

Lilley, M. (1985) Gay pupils, *Times Educational Supplement*, 5 April, p. 18.

Litewka, J. (1977) The socialised penis. In J. Snodgrass (ed.) *For Men against Sexism*. California, Times Change Press.

Llewellyn, M. (1980) Studying girls at school: The implications of confusion. In R. Deem (ed.) *Schooling for Women's Work*. London, Routledge and Kegan Paul.

Loftman, P. and Nevin, B. (1992) Urban regeneration and social equity: A case study of Birmingham 1986–1992, *Research Papers 8*. Birmingham, University of Central England.

London Borough of Ealing Education Committee (1987) *Policy Statement on Sexual Equality*. London, London Borough of Ealing.

London Feminist History Group (1983) *The Sexual Dynamics of History: Men's Power, Women's Resistance*. London, Pluto Press.

London Gay Teachers' Group (1987) *School's Out*. London, Gay Teachers' Group.

Mac an Ghaill, M. (1980) Teachers, professionalism and teachers. Unpublished MSc Thesis, University of Aston, Birmingham.

Mac an Ghaill, M. (1988a) Review of 'Rebels Without a Cause', *British Journal of Sociology of Education*, 9(2), 226–31.

Mac an Ghaill, M. (1988b) The new vocationalism: The response of a sixth form college. In A. Pollard, J. Purvis and G. Walford (eds) *Education, Training and the New Vocationalism*. Milton Keynes, Open University Press.

Mac an Ghaill, M. (1988c) *Young, Gifted and Black: Student–Teacher Relations in the Schooling of Black Youth*. Milton Keynes, Open University Press.

Mac an Ghaill, M. (1989a) Beyond the white norm: The use of qualitative research in the study of black youths' schooling in England, *Qualitative Studies in Education*, 2(3), 175–89.

Mac an Ghaill, M. (1989b) Coming of age in 1980s England: Reconceptualising black students' schooling experiences, *British Journal of Sociology of Education*, 10(3), 273–85.

Mac an Ghaill, M. (1991a) Methodology, masculinity and praxis: An 'alternative curriculum' case-study. Paper presented at York University, 15 June.

Mac an Ghaill, M. (1991b) Schooling, sexuality and male power: Towards an emancipatory curriculum, *Gender and Education*, 3(3), 291–309.

Mac an Ghaill, M. (1992) Student perspectives on curriculum innovation and change in an English secondary school: An empirical study, *British Educational Research Journal*, 18(3), 221–34.

Mac an Ghaill, M. (in press) The making of black English masculinities. In H. Brod and M. Kaufman (eds) *Theorizing Masculinities*. London, Sage.

Mac an Ghaill, M. and Dunne, M. (1991) Whose account counts? Epistemology, power and skill within the research process. Paper presented at the *British Educational Research Association Conference*, Nottingham, August.

MacDonald, I., Bhavnani, R., Khan, L. and John, G. (1989) *Murder in the Playground: Report of the MacDonald Inquiry into Racism and Racial Violence in Manchester Schools*. London, Longsight Press.

MacDonald, M. (1981) Schooling and the reproduction of class and gender relations. In R. Dale (ed.) *Politics, Patriarchy and Practice*. Lewes, Falmer Press/Open University Press.

Mahony, P. (1985) *Schools for Boys? Co-education Reconsidered*. London, Hutchinson.

Mama, A. (1992) Black women and the British state: Race, class and gender analysis for the 1990s. In P. Braham, A. Rattansi and R. Skellington (eds) *Racism and Antiracism: Inequalities, Opportunities and Policies*. London, Sage/The Open University.

Marland, M. (1992) When words can kill, *Guardian*, 2 June, p. 20.

Marx, K. (1954) *Capital*, Vol. 1. London, Lawrence and Wishart.

Matthews, J.J. (1989) *Good and Mad Women: The Historical Construction of Feminism in Twentieth Century Australia*. London, Allen and Unwin.

Mayes, P. (1986) *Gender*. London, Longman.

McCarthy, C. (1990) *Race and Curriculum*. Lewes, Falmer Press.

McIntosh, M. (1968) The homosexual role, *Social Problems*, 16(2), 65–73.

McKie, R. (1993) The myth of the gay gene, *Observer*, 18 July, p. 21.

McRobbie, A. (1978) Working class girls and the culture of femininity. In

Women's Study Group, CCCS (eds) *Women Take Issue: Aspects of Women's Subordination*, London, Hutchinson.

McRobbie, A. (1980) Setting accounts with subcultures: A feminist critique, *Screen Education*, 34, 37–49.

McRobbie, A. (1984) Dance and social fantasy. In A. McRobbie and M. Nava (eds) *Gender and Generation*. London, Macmillan.

McRobbie, A. (1991) *Feminism and Youth Culture: From 'Jackie' to 'Just Seventeen'*. London, Macmillan.

McRobbie, A. and McCabe, T. (eds) (1981) *Feminism for Girls*. London, Routledge and Kegan Paul.

Measor, L. (1989) Are you coming to see any dirty films today? Sex education and adolescent sexuality. In L. Holly (ed.) *Girls and Sexuality: Teaching and Learning* Milton Keynes, Open University Press.

Mercer, K. (1990) Welcome to the jungle: Identity and diversity in postmodern politics. In J. Rutherford (ed.) *Identity: Community, Culture and Difference*. London, Lawrence and Wishart.

Mercer, K. and Julien, I. (1988) Race, sexual politics and black masculinity: A dossier. In R. Chapman and J. Rutherford (eds) *Male Order: Unwrapping Masculinities*. London, Lawrence and Wishart.

Metcalf, A. (1985) Introduction. In A. Metcalf and M. Humphries (eds) *The Sexuality of Men*. London, Pluto Press.

Metcalf, A. and Humphries, M. (eds) (1985) *The Sexuality of Men*. London, Pluto Press.

Meyenn, R.J. (1979) Peer networks and school performance. Unpublished PhD, University of Aston in Birmingham.

Middleton, P. (1992) *The Inward Gaze: Masculinity and Subjectivity in Modern Culture*. London, Routledge.

Mirza, H.S. (1992) *Young, Female and Black*. London, Routledge.

Mitchell, J. (1975) *Psychoanalysis and Feminism*. Harmondsworth, Penguin.

Moore, R. (1984) Schooling and the world of work. In J. Bates, J. Clarke, P. Cohen, D. Finn, R. Moore and P. Willis, *Schooling for the Dole? The New Vocationalism*. London, Macmillan.

Morgan, D.H.J. (1990) Men, masculinity and sociological enquiry. In H. Roberts (ed.) *Doing Feminist Research*. London, Routledge.

Morgan, D.H.J. (1992) *Discovering Men: Critical Studies on Men and Masculinities*, Vol. 3. London, Routledge.

Morris, J. (1991) *Pride against Prejudice: Transforming Attitudes to Disability*. London, Women's Press.

National Curriculum Council (1990) *Curriculum Guidance 5: Health Education*. York, National Curriculum Council.

Nava, M. (1984) Youth service provision, social order and the question of girls. In A. McRobbie and M. Nava (eds) *Gender and Generation*. London, Macmillan.

Nava, M. (1992) *Changing Cultures: Feminism, Youth and Consumerism*. London, Sage.

Norman, P. (1993) Sex and masculinity in the nineties, *Guardian Weekend*, 24–25 July, pp. 7–9.

Oakley, A. (1972) *Sex, Gender and Society*. London, Temple Smith.

Oakley, A. (1991) *The Men's Room*. London, Flamingo.

Ozga, J. (ed.) (1988) *School Work: Approaches to the Labour Processes of Teaching*. Milton Keynes, Open University Press.

Pajaczkowska, C. and Young, L. (1992) Racism, representation and psycho-analysis. In J. Donald and A. Rattansi (eds) *'Race', Culture and Difference*. Milton Keynes, Sage/Open University Press.

Parker, A. (1992) One of the boys? Images of masculinity within boys' physical education. Unpublished MA dissertation, University of Warwick.

Parker, A., Russo, M., Sommer, D. and Yaeger, P. (1992) *Nationalisms and Sexualities*. London, Routledge.

Parmar, P. (1989) Other kinds of dreams, *Feminist Review*, 31, pp. 55–65.

Patrick, P. (1982) Trying hard to hear you, *Teaching London Kids*, 23, 7–11.

Pearson, C. (1984) Male sexual politics and men's gender practice, *Women's Studies International Forum*, 7(1), 29–32.

Perkins, T.E. (1979) Rethinking stereotypes. In M. Barrett, P. Corrigan, A. Khun and J. Wolfe (eds) *Ideology and Cultural Production*. London, Croom Helm.

Phizaklea, A. (1990) *Unpacking the Fashion Industry: Gender, Racism and Class*. London, Routledge.

Plummer, K. (1981) *The Making of the Modern Homosexual*. London, Hutchinson.

Plummer, K. (1983) *Documents of Life*. London, Allen and Unwin.

Plummer, K. (1986) *Growing up Gay in England*, Mimeograph.

Plummer, K. (1989) Being gay: The social construction of homosexuality, *Gay Times*, March, pp. 26–8.

Plummer, K. (ed.) (1992) *Modern Homosexualities*. London, Routledge.

Poppleton, P. and Riseborough, G.F. (1990) Teaching in the mid-1980s: the centrality of work in secondary teachers' lives, *British Educational Research Journal*, 16(2), 105–124.

Poppleton, P. and Riseborough, G.F. (1991) Ch1.

Poulantzas, N. (1975) *Classes in Contemporary Capitalism*. London, New Left Books.

Race Today (1975) Who's afraid of ghetto schools?, *Race Today*, 1 January, pp. 8–10.

Ramazanoglu, C. (1989) *Feminism and the Contradictions of Oppression*. London, Routledge.

Rance, S. (1982) Going all the way. In M. Rowe (ed.) *Spare Rib Reader*. Harmondsworth, Penguin.

Rattansi, A. (1992) Changing the subject? Racism, culture and education. In J. Donald and A. Rattansi (eds) *'Race', Culture and Difference*. London, Sage/Open University.

Redman, P. (in press) Shifting ground: Rethinking sexuality education. In D. Epstein (ed.) *Challenging Lesbian and Gay Inequalities in Education*. Buckingham, Open University Press.

Rees, T. (1992) *Women and the Labour Market*. London, Routledge.

Rich, A. (1981) Compulsory heterosexuality and lesbian existence, *Signs*, 5(4), 631–60.

Riley, K. (1985) Black girls speak for themselves. In G. Weiner (ed.) *Just a Bunch of Girls*. Milton Keynes, Open University Press.

Riseborough, G.F. (1981) Teacher careers and comprehensive schooling: An empirical study, *Sociology*, 15(3), 352–80.

Riseborough, G. (1985) Pupils, teachers' careers and schooling: An empirical study. In S.J. Ball and I.F. Goodson (eds) *Teachers' Lives and Careers*, London, Falmer Press.

Riseborough, G.F. and Poppleton, P. (1991) Veterans versus beginners: A study of teachers at a time of fundamental change in secondary schooling. *Educational Review*, 43(3), 307–34.

Roberts, H. (ed.) (1990) *Doing Feminist Research*. London, Routledge.

Robinson, P. (1988) *Do Schools Make A Difference?* Block I, Unit 12. Milton Keynes, Open University Press.

Roman, L. and Christian-Smith, L. (eds) (1988) *Becoming Feminine: The Politics of Popular Culture*. Lewes, Falmer Press.

Rudduck, J. (1991) *Innovation and Change*. Milton Keynes, Open University Press.

Rutherford, J. (1990) A place called home: Identity and the cultural politics of difference. In J. Rutherford (ed.) *Identity: Community, Culture and Difference*. London, Lawrence and Wishart.

Segal, L. (1990) *Slow Motion: Changing Masculinities, Changing Men*. London, Virago.

Seidler, V.J. (1988) Fathering, authority and masculinity. In R. Chapman and J. Rutherford (eds) *Male Order: Unwrapping Masculinity*. London, Lawrence and Wishart.

Seidler, V.J. (1990) Men, feminism and power. In J. Hearn and D. Morgan (eds) *Men, Masculinities and Social Theory*. London, Hyman Unwin.

Sex Education Forum (1992) *A Framework for School Sex Education*. London, National Children's Bureau

Sharp, R. and Green, A. (1975) *Education and the Social Control*. London, Routledge and Kegan Paul.

Simon, B. (1992) *What Future for Education?* London, Lawrence and Wishart.

Skeggs, B. (1988) Gender reproduction and further education, *British Journal of Sociology of Education*, 9(2), 131–49.

Skeggs, B. (1989) Review, *British Journal of Sociology of Education*, 16(4), 484–90.

Skeggs, B. (1991) Challenging masculinity and using sexuality, *British Journal of Sociology of Education*, 12(1), 127–40.

Skeggs, B. (1992) The constraints of neutrality. Paper presented at *ESRC Seminar Series*, University of Warwick, November.

Skeggs, B. (1993) The cultural production of 'Learning to Labour'. In M. Barker and A. Breezer (eds) *Readings in Culture*. London, Routledge.

Slayton, P. and Vogel, B. (1986) People without faces, *English in Education*, 20(1), 5–13.

Smart, B. (1985) *Michel Foucault*. London, Tavistock.

Smart, C. (1988) Review of 'Rebels Without A Cause', *British Journal of Sociology of Education*, 9(2), 231–3.

Smart, C. (ed.) (1992) *Regulating Motherhood: Historical Essays on Marriage, Motherhood and Sexuality*. London, Routledge.

Smetherham, D. (1988) Hot management!, *School Organization*, 8, 1–4.

Squirrell, G. (1989) Teachers and issues of sexual orientation, *Gender and Education*, 10(1), 5–34.

Stacey, J. (1991) Promoting normality: Section 28 and the regulation of sexuality. In S. Franklin, C. Lury and J. Stacey (eds) *Off-Centre: Feminism and Cultural Studies*. London, Harper Collins.

Stafford, A. (1981) Learning not to labour, *Capital and Labour*, 51, 55–77.

Stanley, L. and Wise, S. (1983) *Breaking Out: Feminist Consciousness and Feminist Research*. London, Routledge and Kegan Paul.

Stanworth, M. (1981) *Gender and Schooling*. London, Women's Research and Resources Centre.

Stanworth, M. (1983) *Gender and Schooling: Study of Social Divisions in the Classroom*. London, Hutchinson/Explorations in Feminism Collective.

Stop the Clause Education Group (1989) *Section 28: A Guide for Schools, Teachers and*

Governors. London, Stop the Clause Group in association with All London Teachers against Racism and Fascism.

Sullivan, C. (1993) Dog days and nights, *Guardian*, 9 April, pp. 4–5.

Thomson, R. (1993) Unholy alliances: the recent politics of sex education. In J. Bristow and A. Wilson (eds) *Activating Theory*. London, Lawrence and Wishart.

Tiefer, L. (1987) In pursuit of the perfect penis: The medicalisation of male sexuality. In M.S. Kimmel (ed.) *Changing Men: New Directions in Research on Men and Masculinity*. Beverly Hills, CA, Sage.

Tolson, A. (1977) *The Limits of Masculinity*. London, Tavistock.

Trenchard, L. and Warren, H. (1984) *Something to Tell You*. London, Gay Teenagers' Project.

Troupe, Q. (1989) *James Baldwin: The Legacy*. New York, Simon and Schuster/ Touchstone.

Tsang, D. (1981) *The Age Taboo: Gay Male Homosexuality*. London, Gay Men's Press.

Tutchell, E. (1990) Contradictory identities: theory into practice. In E. Tutchell (ed.) *Dolls and Dungarees: Gender Issues in the Primary School Curriculum*. Milton Keynes, Open University Press.

Walby, S. (1990) *Theorizing Patriarchy*. London, Basil Blackwell.

Walford, G. and Miller, H. (1991) *City Technology College*. Milton Keynes, Open University Press.

Walker, J. (1988) *Louts and Legends: Male Youth Cultures in an Inner-city School*. London, Allen and Unwin.

Walkerdine, V. (1981) Sex, power and pedagogies, *Screen Education*, 38, 14–26.

Walkerdine, V. (1984) Developmental psychology and the child-centred pedagogy: The insertion of Piaget into early education. In J. Henriques, W. Hollway, C. Urwin, C. Venn and V. Walkerdine, *Changing the Subject: Psychology, Social Regulation and Subjectivity*. London, Methuen.

Walkerdine, V. (1990a) *Schoolgirl Fictions*. London, Verso.

Walkerdine, V. (1990b) *The Mastery of Reason: Cognitive Development and the Production of Rationality*. London, Routledge.

Walkerdine, V. (1991) *Feminism and Youth Culture: From 'Jackie' to 'Just Seventeen'*. London, Macmillan.

Warren, H. (1984) *Talking about School*. London, Gay Teachers' Project.

Watney, S. (1987) *Policing Desire: Pornography, Aids and the Media*. London, Methuen.

Watney, S. (1993) Simon Watney column: Sex education, *Gay Times*, 2 February.

Weeks, J. (1981) *Sex, Politics and Desire*. London, Longman.

Weeks, J. (1986) *Sexuality*. London, Tavistock.

Weeks, J. (1989) *Sexuality and its Discontents: Meanings, Myths and Modern Sexualities*. London, Routledge.

Weeks, J. (1990) The value of difference. In J. Rutherford (ed.) *Identity: Community, Culture and Difference*. London, Lawrence and Wishart.

Weis, L. (1991) *Working-class without Work*. London, Routledge.

Westwood, S. (1990) Racism, black masculinity and the politics of space. In J. Headen and D. Morgan (eds) *Men, Masculinities and Social Theory*. London, Unwin Hyman.

Westwood, S. (1992a) Power/knowledge: The politics of transformative research, *Studies in the Education of Adults*, 24(2), 191–8.

Westwood, S. (1992b) When class became community: Radicalism in adult education. In A. Rattansi and D. Reeder (eds) *Rethinking Radical Education: Essays in Honour of Brian Simon*. London, Lawrence and Wishart.

White, E. (1983) *A Boy's Own Story*. London, Picador.

Whyte, W.F. (1943) *Street Corner Society: The Social Structure of an Italian Slum*. Chicago, University of Chicago Press.

Williams, L. (1988) *Partial Surrender: Race and Resistance in the Youth Service*. Lewes, Falmer Press.

Williams, R. (1961) *The Long Revolution*. Harmondsworth, Penguin.

Williams, R. (1977) *Marxism and Literature*. Oxford, Oxford University Press.

Willis, P. (1977) *Learning to Labour: How Working Class Kids Get Working Class Jobs*. Aldershot, Saxon House.

Willis, P. (1985) *Youth Unemployment and the New Poverty: A Summary of Local Authority Review and Framework for Policy Department on Youth and Youth Unemployment*. Wolverhampton, Wolverhampton Local Authority.

Willis, P. (1990) *Common Culture*. Milton Keynes, Open University Press.

Willis, P., Jones, S., Canaan, J. and Hurd, G. (1990) *Common Culture: Symbolic Work in Everyday Cultures of the Young*. Milton Keynes, Open University Press.

Wolfenden, J. (1957) *The Wolfenden Report: Report of the Committee on Homosexual Offences and Prostitution*. Cmnd 247. London, HMSO.

Wolpe, A.M. (1977) Sex education, *Feminist Review*, 27, 30–4.

Wolpe, A.M. (1988) *Within School Walls: The Role of Discipline, Sexuality and the Curriculum*. London, Routledge.

Wood, J. (1984) Groping towards sexism: Boys' sex talk. In A. McRobbie and M. Nava (eds) *Gender and Generation*. London, Macmillan.

Woods, P. (1990a) *Teacher Skills and Strategies*. Lewes, Falmer Press.

Woods, P. (1990b) *The Happiest Days: How Pupils Cope with Schools*. London, Falmer Press.

Wragg, T. (1992) And for our top scorers a gilt-edged P45, *Times Educational Supplement*, 1 May, p. 60.

Author index

Subject index

BOYS DON'T CRY
BOYS AND SEXISM IN EDUCATION

Sue Askew and Carol Ross

Boys Don't Cry looks at the factors in schools that affect the socialization of boys; at pressures on them to conform to damaging male stereotypes; at relationships between boys and at bullying and aggressive behaviour in general.

The book provides an analysis of the ways in which schools may unintentionally reinforce and perpetuate certain aspects of 'masculinity' which operate against the boys' best interests. It also considers some constraints put on boys and looks at how these may affect both their social development and their approach to various learning activities. Women teachers might also be adversely affected by these pressures. The book explores ways in which this is particularly apparent in the 'masculine' atmosphere of boys' schools.

The authors have been involved in the area of anti-sexist education for boys during the last five years. In the book they draw on their experience of developing specific anti-sexist initiatives and materials for work with boys. This includes classroom observation; extensive interviews with teachers; and advisory and support work for anti-sexist education for boys throughout an inner-city education authority.

Contents
The construction of masculinity – Classroom dynamics – Sexism in the school structure and organization – Women teachers' experience – Strategies for working with boys – In-service work with teachers – Conclusions – Bibliography – Index.

128pp   0 335 10296 4 (Paperback)

DEVELOPING A GENDER POLICY IN SECONDARY SCHOOLS

Jean Rudduck

Jean Rudduck explores how secondary schools have tried to build concern for gender equality into whole-school structures and practices. Taking such a step requires strength of commitment and purpose. Gender equality, when raised as a whole-school issue, often proves to be controversial and divisive. The book reflects the experience of a number of comprehensive schools which were moving towards a whole-school policy for gender. The schools all serve urban communities of moderate to more severe social and economic disadvantage.

The book opens with extracts from conversations with individuals, both women and men, who talk about the origin of their commitment to working for equality. This is followed by the stories of a number of 'gender leaders' – the people whose vision and commitment helped to launch work on gender in their schools. The stories recall the periods of frustration, the critical incidents, the excitement of progress. The next section of the book examines different approaches to starting work on gender; and it concludes with a substantial case study reflecting the experience of one comprehensive school over a period of three years.

Contents
Introduction – Individuals and their commitment to gender equality – Gender leaders in action – Points of departure – Developing a whole-school policy – Policy and progress: guidelines for action – Individuals and institutions: the dilemmas of change – References – Index.

160pp   0 335 19152 5 (Paperback)   0 335 19153 3 (Hardback)

CHALLENGING LESBIAN AND GAY INEQUALITIES IN EDUCATION

Debbie Epstein (ed.)

Challenging Lesbian and Gay Inequalities in Education is an essential addition to the library of anyone concerned about developing education for social justice and about challenging inequalities in society. Through a series of historically-located articles ranging from personal stories, through examples of 'good practice', to theoretical analyses of the interweaving of heterosexism, sexism and racism, the book traces the ways in which these oppressions are constructed and played out within and through the system of schooling and through education policies. The majority of contributors to the book are lesbian or gay activists and educators. The book will be of interest to all those involved, in the education system and in studying education, and to those interested in cultural studies, gender and the study of masculinity, lesbian and gay studies, sociology and women's studies.

Contents

Contributors

Akanke, Alistair, Dave, Rachel and Teresa, Roy Bartell, Helena Burke, Debbie Epstein, Richard Johnson, KOLA, Máirtín Mac an Ghaill, Paul Patrick, Peter Redman, Marigold Rogers, Susan A.L. Sanders, Gillian Spraggs.

c208pp   0 335 19130 4 (Paperback)